S0-AHZ-710

# The Romantic Tradition in American Literature

# The Romantic Tradition in American Literature

*Advisory Editor*

HAROLD BLOOM
Professor of English, Yale University

# WAR POETRY

OF

# THE SOUTH

EDITED BY

WILLIAM GILMORE SIMMS, LL. D.

ARNO PRESS
A NEW YORK TIMES COMPANY
New York • 1972

Reprint Edition 1972 by Arno Press Inc.

Reprinted from a copy in The University of Illinois Library

The Romantic Tradition in American Literature
ISBN for complete set: 0-405-04620-0
See last pages of this volume for titles.

Manufactured in the United States of America

**Library of Congress Cataloging in Publication Data**

Simms, William Gilmore, 1806-1870, ed.
War poetry of the South.

(The Romantic tradition in American literature)
1. United States--History--Civil War--Poetry--Confederate States. 2. American poetry--Southern States.
I. Title. II. Series.
E647.S6 1972 811'.4'0803 72-4974
ISBN 0-405-04644-8

# WAR POETRY

OF

# THE SOUTH

EDITED BY

WILLIAM GILMORE SIMMS, LL. D.

NEW YORK:
RICHARDSON & COMPANY,
540 BROADWAY.
1866.

Press of Geo. C. Rand & Avery,

540 Broadway.

TO

# THE WOMEN OF THE SOUTH,

## I Inscribe This Volume.

They have lost a cause, but they have made a triumph! They have shown themselves worthy of any manhood; and will leave a record which shall survive all the caprices of time. They have proved themselves worthy of the best womanhood, and, in their posterity, will leave no race which shall be unworthy of the cause which is lost, or of the mothers, sisters and wives, who have taught such noble lessons of virtuous effort, and womanly endurance.

W. G. S.

# PREFACE.

SEVERAL considerations have prompted the editor of this volume in the compilation of its pages. It constitutes a contribution to the national literature which is assumed to be not unworthy of it, and which is otherwise valuable as illustrating the degree of mental and art development which has been made, in a large section of the country, under circumstances greatly calculated to stimulate talent and provoke expression, through the higher utterances of passion and imagination. Though sectional in its character, and indicative of a temper and a feeling which were in conflict with nationality, yet, now that the States of the Union have been resolved into one nation, this collection is essentially as much the property of the whole as are the captured cannon which were employed against it during the progress of the late war. It belongs to the national literature, and will hereafter be regarded as constituting a proper part of it, just as legitimately to be recognized by the nation as are the rival ballads of the cavaliers and roundheads, by the English, in the great civil conflict of their country.

The emotional literature of a people is as necessary to the philosophical historian as the mere details of events in the progress of a nation. This is essential to the reputation of the Southern people, as illustrating their feelings, sentiments, ideas, and opinions—the motives which influenced their actions, and the objects which they had in contemplation, and which seemed to them to justify the struggle in which they were engaged. It shows with what spirit the popular mind regarded the course of events, whether favorable or adverse; and, in this aspect, it is even of more importance to the writer of history than any mere chronicle of facts. The mere facts in a history do not always, or often, indicate the true *animus* of the action. But, in poetry and song, the emotional nature is apt to declare itself without reserve—speaking out with a passion which disdains subterfuge, and through media of imagination and fancy, which are not only without reserve, but which are too coercive in their own nature, too arbitrary in their influence, to acknowledge any restraints upon that expression, which glows or weeps with emotions that gush freely and freshly from the heart. With this persuasion, we can also forgive the muse who, in her fervor, is sometimes forgetful of her art.

And yet, it is believed that the numerous pieces of this volume will be found creditable to the genius and culture of the Southern people, and honorable, as in accordance with their convictions. They are derived from all the States of the late Southern Confederacy, and will be found truthfully to exhibit the sentiment and opinion prevailing more or less generally throughout the whole. The editor has had special advantages in making the compilation. Having a large correspondence in most of the Southern States, he has found no difficulty in procuring his material. Contributions have poured in upon him from all portions of the South; the original publications having been, in a large number of cases, subjected to the careful revision of the several authors. It is a matter of great regret with him that the limits of the present volume have not suffered him to do justice to, and find a place for, many of the pieces which fully deserve to be put on record. Some of the poems were quite too long for his purpose; a large number, delayed by the mails and other causes, were received too late for publication. Several collections, from Louisiana, North Carolina, and Texas, especially, are omitted for this reason. Many of these pieces are distinguished by fire, force, passion, and a free play of fancy. Briefly, his material would enable him to prepare another volume, similar to the present, which would not be unworthy of its companionship. He is authorized by his publisher to say that, in the event of the popular success of the present volume, he will cheerfully follow up its publication by a second, of like style, character, and dimensions.

The editor has seen with pleasure the volume of "Rebel Rhymes" edited by Mr. Moore, and of "South Songs," by Mr. De Leon. He has seen, besides, a single number of a periodical pamphlet called "The Southern Monthly," published at Memphis, Tenn. This has been supplied him by a contributor. He has seen no other publications of this nature, though he has heard of others, and has sought for them in vain. There may be others still forthcoming; for, in so large a field, with a population so greatly scattered as that of the South, it is a physical impossibility adequately to do justice to the whole by any one editor; and each of the sections must make its own contributions, in its own time, and according to its several opportunities. There will be room enough for all; and each, I doubt not, will possess its special claims to recognition and reward.

His own collections, made during the progress of the war, from the newspapers, chiefly, of South Carolina, Virginia, and Georgia, were copious. Of these, many have been omitted from this collection, which, he trusts, will some day find another medium of publication. He has been able to ascertain the authorship, in many cases, of these writings; but must regret still that so many others, under a too fastidious delicacy, deny that their names should be made known. It is to be hoped that they will hereafter be supplied. To the numerous ladies who have so frankly and generously contributed to this collection, by sending originals and making copies, he begs to offer his most grateful acknowledgments.

A large proportion of the pieces omitted are of elegiac character. Of this class, he could find a place for such pieces only as were dedicated to the most distinguished of the persons falling in battle, or such as are marked by the higher characteristics of poetry—freshness, thought, and imagination. But many of the omitted pieces are quite worthy of preservation. Much space has not been given to that class of songs, camp catches, or marching ballads, which are so numerous in the "Rebel Rhymes" of Mr. Moore. The songs which are most popular are rarely such as may claim poetical rank. They depend upon lively music and certain spirit-stirring catchwords, and are rarely worked up with much regard to art or even propriety. Still, many of these should have found a place in this volume, had adequate space been allowed the editor. It is his desire, as well as that of the publisher, to collect and bind together these fugitives in yet another publication. He will preserve the manuscripts and copies of all unpublished pieces, with the view to this object—keeping them always subject to the wishes of their several writers.

At the close, he must express the hope that these poems will be recognized, not only as highly creditable to the Southern mind, but as truly illustrative, if not justificatory of, that sentiment and opinion with which they have been written; which sentiment and opinion have sustained their people through a war unexampled in its horrors in modern times, and which has fully tested their powers of endurance, as well as their ability in creating their own resources, under all reverses, and amidst every form of privation.

W. G. S.

BROOKLYN, September 8, 1866.

# CONTENTS.



1*

# WAR POETRY OF THE SOUTH.

---

## ETHNOGENESIS.

BY HENRY TIMROD, OF S. C.

WRITTEN DURING THE MEETING OF THE FIRST SOUTHERN CONGRESS, AT MONTGOMERY, FEBRUARY, 1861.

I.

HATH not the morning dawned with added light?
And shall not evening call another star
Out of the infinite regions of the night,
To mark this day in Heaven? At last, we are
A nation among nations; and the world
Shall soon behold in many a distant port
        Another flag unfurled!
Now, come what may, whose favor need we court?
And, under God, whose thunder need we fear?
        Thank Him who placed us here
Beneath so kind a sky—the very sun
Takes part with us; and on our errands run
All breezes of the ocean; dew and rain
Do noiseless battle for us; and the Year,

And all the gentle daughters in her train,
March in our ranks, and in our service wield
Long spears of golden grain !
A yellow blossom as her fairy shield,
June flings her azure banner to the wind,
While in the order of their birth
Her sisters pass; and many an ample field
Grows white beneath their steps, till now, behold
Its endless sheets unfold
THE SNOW OF SOUTHERN SUMMERS ! Let the earth
Rejoice ! beneath those fleeces soft and warm
Our happy land shall sleep
In a repose as deep
As if we lay intrenched behind
Whole leagues of Russian ice and Arctic storm !

II.

And what if, mad with wrongs themselves have wrought,
In their own treachery caught,
By their own fears made bold,
And leagued with him of old,
Who long since, in the limits of the North,
Set up his evil throne, and warred with God—
What if, both mad and blinded in their rage,
Our foes should fling us down their mortal gage,
And with a hostile step profane our sod !
We shall not shrink, my brothers, but go forth
To meet them, marshalled by the Lord of Hosts,

And overshadowed by the mighty ghosts
Of Moultrie and of Eutaw—who shall foil
Auxiliars such as these? Nor these alone,
    But every stock and stone
    Shall help us; but the very soil,
And all the generous wealth it gives to toil,
And all for which we love our noble land,
Shall fight beside, and through us, sea and strand,
    The heart of woman, and her hand,
Tree, fruit, and flower, and every influence,
    Gentle, or grave, or grand;
    The winds in our defence
Shall seem to blow; to us the hills shall lend
    Their firmness and their calm;
And in our stiffened sinews we shall blend
    The strength of pine and palm!

III.

Nor would we shun the battle-ground,
    Though weak as we are strong;
Call up the clashing elements around,
    And test the right and wrong!
On one side, creeds that dare to teach
What Christ and Paul refrained to preach;
Codes built upon a broken pledge,
And charity that whets a poniard's edge;
Fair schemes that leave the neighboring poor
To starve and shiver at the schemer's door,

While in the world's most liberal ranks enrolled,
He turns some vast philanthropy to gold ;
Religion taking every mortal form
But that a pure and Christian faith makes warm,
Where not to vile fanatic passion urged,
Or not in vague philosophies submerged,
Repulsive with all Pharisaic leaven,
And making laws to stay the laws of Heaven !
And on the other, scorn of sordid gain,
Unblemished honor, truth without a stain,
Faith, justice, reverence, charitable wealth,
And, for the poor and humble, laws which give,
Not the mean right to buy the right to live,
        But life, and home, and health !
To doubt the end were want of trust in God,
        Who, if he has decreed
That we must pass a redder sea
Than that which rang to Miriam's holy glee,
        Will surely raise at need
        A Moses with his rod !

IV.

But let our fears—if fears we have—be still,
And turn us to the future ! Could we climb
Some mighty Alp, and view the coming time,
The rapturous sight would fill
        Our eyes with happy tears !
Not only for the glories which the years
Shall bring us ; not for lands from sea to sea,

And wealth, and power, and peace, though these shall be ;
But for the distant peoples we shall bless,
And the hushed murmurs of a world's distress :
For, to give labor to the poor,
The whole sad planet o'er,
And save from want and crime the humblest door,
Is one among the many ends for which
God makes us great and rich !
The hour perchance is not yet wholly ripe
When all shall own it, but the type
Whereby we shall be known in every land
Is that vast gulf which laves our Southern strand,
And through the cold, untempered ocean pours
Its genial streams, that far-off Arctic shores
May sometimes catch upon the softened breeze
Strange tropic warmth and hints of summer seas.

---

## GOD SAVE THE SOUTH.

GEORGE H. MILES, OF BALTIMORE.

God save the South !
God save the South !
Her altars and firesides—
God save the South !
Now that the war is nigh—
Now that we arm to die—
Chanting our battle-cry,
Freedom or Death !

God be our shield !
At home or a-field,
Stretch Thine arm over us,
  Strengthen and save !
What though they're five to one,
Forward each sire and son,
Strike till the war is done,
  Strike to the grave.

God make the right
Stronger than might !
Millions would trample us
  Down in their pride.
Lay, thou, their legions low ;
Roll back the ruthless foe ;
Let the proud spoiler know
  God's on our side !

Hark ! honor's call,
Summoning all—
Summoning all of us
  Up to the strife.
Sons of the South, awake !
Strike till the brand shall break !
Strike for dear honor's sake,
  Freedom and Life !

Rebels before
Were our fathers of yore;
Rebel, the glorious name
  Washington bore.
Why, then, be ours the same
Title he snatched from shame;
Making it first in fame,
  Odious no more.

War to the hilt!
Theirs be the guilt,
Who fetter the freeman
  To ransom the slave.
Up, then, and undismayed,
Sheathe not the battle-blade,
Till the last foe is laid
  Low in the grave.

God save the South!
God save the South!
Dry the dim eyes that now
  Follow our path.
Still let the light feet rove
Safe through the orange grove;
Still keep the land we love
  Safe from all wrath.

God save the South !
God save the South !
Her altars and firesides—
God save the South !
For the rude war is nigh,
And we must win or die ;
Chanting our battle-cry
Freedom or Death !

---

## YOU CAN NEVER WIN THEM BACK.

BY CATHERINE M. WARFIELD.

You can never win them back,
never ! never !
Though they perish on the track
of your endeavor ;
Though their corses strew the earth
That smiled upon their birth,
And blood pollutes each hearth-
stone forever !

They have risen, to a man
stern and fearless ;
Of your curses and your ban
they are careless.

Every hand is on its knife ;
Every gun is primed for strife ;
Every palm contains a life
high and peerless !

You have no such blood as theirs
for the shedding,
In the veins of Cavaliers
was its heading.
You have no such stately men
In your abolition den,
To march through foe and fen,
nothing dreading.

They may fall before the fire
of your legions,
Paid in gold for murd'rous hire—
bought allegiance !
But for every drop you shed
You shall leave a mound of dead ;
And the vultures shall be fed
in our regions.

But the battle to the strong
is not given,
While the Judge of right and wrong
sits in heaven !

And the God of David still
Guides each pebble by His will ;
There are giants yet to kill—
wrongs unshriven.

---

## THE SOUTHERN CROSS.

BY E. K. BLUNT.

In the name of God ! Amen !
Stand for our Southern rights ;
On our side, Southern men,
The God of battles fights !
Fling the invaders far—
Hurl back their work of woe—
The voice is the voice of a brother,
But the hands are the hands of a foe.
They come with a trampling army,
Invading our native sod—
Stand, Southrons ! fight and conquer,
In the name of the mighty God !

They are singing *our* song of triumph,*
Which proclaimed *us* proud and free—
While breaking away the heartstrings
Of our nation's harmony.

* The Star Spangled Banner. Written by F. S. Key, of Baltimore ; all whose descendants are Confederates.

Sadly it floateth from us,
  Sighing o'er land and wave ;
Till, mute on the lips of the poet,
  It sleeps in his Southern grave.
Spirit and song departed !
  Minstrel and minstrelsy !
We mourn ye, heavy hearted,—
  But we will—we will be free !

They are waving *our* flag above us,
  With the despot's tyrant will ;
With our blood they have stained its colors,
  And they call it holy still.
With tearful eyes, but steady hand,
  We'll tear its stripes apart,
And fling them, like broken fetters,
  That may not bind the heart.
But we'll save our stars of glory,
  In the might of the sacred sign
Of Him who has fixed forever
  One "Southern Cross" to shine.

Stand, Southrons ! fight and conquer !
  Solemn, and strong, and sure !
The fight shall not be longer
  Than God shall bid endure.
By the life that but yesterday
  Waked with the infant's breath !

By the feet which, ere morning, may
  Tread to the soldier's death !
By the blood which cries to heaven—
  Crimson upon our sod !
Stand, Southrons ! fight and conquer,
  In the name of the mighty God !

---

## SOUTH CAROLINA.

December 20, 1860.

S. HENRY DICKSON.

The deed is done ! the die is cast ;
The glorious Rubicon is passed :
Hail, Carolina ! free at last !

Strong in the right, I see her stand
Where ocean laves the shelving sand ;
Her own Palmetto decks the strand.

She turns aloft her flashing eye ;
Radiant, her lonely star* on high
Shines clear amidst the darkening sky.

---

* The flag showed a star within a crescent or new moon.

Silent, along those azure deeps
Its course her silver crescent keeps,
And in soft light the landscape steeps.

Fling forth her banner to the gale!
Let all the hosts of earth assail,—
Their fury and their force shall fail.

Echoes the wide resounding shore,
With voice above th' Atlantic roar,
Her sons proclaim her free once more!

Oh, land of heroes! Spartan State!
In numbers few, in daring great,
Thus to affront the frowns of fate!

And while mad triumph rules the hour,
And thickening clouds of menace lower,
Bear back the tide of tyrant power.

With steadfast courage, faltering never,
Sternly resolved, her bonds we sever:
Hail, Carolina! free forever!

## THE NEW STAR.

BY B. M. ANDERSON.

ANOTHER star arisen ; another flag unfurled ;
Another name inscribed among the nations of the world ;
Another mighty struggle 'gainst a tyrant's fell decree,
And again a burdened people have uprisen, and are free.

The spirit of the fathers in the children liveth yet ;
Liveth still the olden blood which dimmed the foreign bayonet ;
And the fathers fought for freedom, and the sons for freedom fight ;
Their God was with the fathers—and is still the God of right !

Behold ! the skies are darkened ! A gloomy cloud hath lowered !
Shall it break before the sun of peace, or spread in rage impowered ?
Shall we have the smile of friendship, or shall it be the blow ?
Shall it be the right hand to the friend, or the red hand to the foe ?

In peacefulness we wish to live, but not in slavish fear ;
In peacefulness we dare not die, dishonored on our bier.
To our allies of the Northern land we offer heart and hand,
But if they scorn our friendship—then the banner and the
brand !

Honor to the new-born nation ! and honor to the brave !
A country freed from thraldom, or a soldier's honored grave.
Every step shall be contested ; every rivulet run red,
And the invader, should he conquer, find the conquered in
the dead.

But victory shall follow where the sons of freedom go,
And the signal for the onset be the death-knell of the foe ;
And hallowed shall the spot be where he was so bravely
met,
And the star which yonder rises, rises never more to set.

---

## THE IRREPRESSIBLE CONFLICT.

TYRTÆUS.—*Charleston Mercury.*

THEN welcome be it, if indeed it be
The Irrepressible Conflict ! Let it come ;
There will be mitigation of the doom,
If, battling to the last, our sires shall see
Their sons contending for the homes made free
In ancient conflict with the foreign foe !

If those who call us brethren strike the blow,
No common conflict shall the invader know!
War to the knife, and to the last, until
The sacred land we keep shall overflow
With blood as sacred—valley, wave, and hill,
Or the last enemy finds his bloody grave!
Aye, welcome to your graves—or ours! The brave
May perish, but ye shall not bind one slave.

---

## THE SOUTHERN REPUBLIC.

BY OLIVIA TULLY THOMAS, OF MISSISSIPPI.

In the galaxy of nations,
A nation's flag's unfurled,
Transcending in its martial pride
The nations of the world.
Though born of war, baptized in blood,
Yet mighty from the time,
Like fabled phœnix, forth she stood—
Dismembered, yet sublime.

And braver heart, and bolder hand,
Ne'er formed a fabric fair
As Southern wisdom can command,
And Southern valor rear.

Though kingdoms scorn to own her sway,
  Or recognize her birth,
The land blood-bought for Liberty
  Will reign supreme on earth.

Clime of the Sun ! Home of the Brave !
  Thy sons are bold and free,
And pour life's crimson tide to save
  Their birthright, Liberty !
Their fertile fields and sunny plains
  That yield the wealth alone,
That's coveted for greedy gains
  By despots—and a throne !

Proud country ! battling, bleeding, torn,
  Thy altars desolate ;
Thy lovely dark-eyed daughters mourn
  At war's relentless fate ;
And widow's prayers, and orphan's tears,
  Her homes will consecrate,
While more than brass or marble rears
  The trophy of her great.

Oh ! land that boasts each gallant name
  Of JACKSON, JOHNSON, LEE,
And hosts of valiant sons, whose fame
  Extends beyond the sea ;

Far rather let thy plains become,
  From gulf to mountain cave,
One honored sepulchre and tomb,
  Than we the tyrant's slave!

Fair, favored land! thou mayst be free,
  Redeemed by blood and war;
Through agony and gloom we see
  Thy hope—a glimmering star;
Thy banner, too, may proudly float,
  A herald on the seas—
Thy deeds of daring worlds remote
  Will emulate and praise!

But who can paint the impulse pure,
  That thrills and nerves thy brave
To deeds of valor, that secure
  The rights their fathers gave?
Oh! grieve not, hearts; her matchless slain,
  Crowned with the warrior's wreath,
From beds of fame their proud refrain
  Was "Liberty or Death!"

## "IS THERE, THEN, NO HOPE FOR THE NATIONS?"

CHARLESTON COURIER.

Is there, then, no hope for the nations?
  Must the record of Time be the same?
And shall History, in all her narrations,
  Still close each last chapter in shame?
Shall the valor which grew to be glorious,
  Prove the shame, as the pride of a race:
And a people, for ages victorious,
  Through the arts of the chapman, grow base?

Greek, Hebrew, Assyrian, and Roman,
  Each strides o'er the scene and departs!
How valiant their deeds 'gainst the foeman,
  How wondrous their virtues and arts!
Rude valor, at first, when beginning,
  The nation through blood took its name;
Then the wisdom, which hourly winning
  New heights in its march, rose to Fame!

How noble the tale for long ages,
  Blending Beauty with courage and might!
What Heroes, what Poets, and Sages,
  Made eminent stars for each height!

While their people, with reverence ample,
  Brought tribute of praise to the Great,
Whose wisdom and virtuous example,
  Made virtue the pride of the State!

Ours, too, was as noble a dawning,
  With hopes of the Future as high:
Great men, each a star of the morning,
  Taught us bravely to live and to die!
We fought the long fight with our foeman,
  And through trial—well-borne—won a name,
Not less glorious than Grecian or Roman,
  And worthy as lasting a fame!

* * * * *

Shut the Book! We must open another!
  O Southron! if taught by the Past,
Beware, when thou choosest a brother,
  With what ally thy fortunes are cast!
Beware of all foreign alliance,
  Of their pleadings and pleasings beware,
Better meet the old snake with defiance,
  Than find in his charming a snare!

## THE FATE OF THE REPUBLICS.

CHARLESTON MERCURY.

Thus, the grand fabric of a thousand years—
Rear'd with such art and wisdom—by a race
Of giant sires, in virtue all compact,
Self-sacrificing; having grand ideals
Of public strength, and peoples capable
Of great conceptions for the common good,
And of enduring liberties, kept strong
Through purity;—tumbles and falls apart,
Lacking cement in virtue; and assail'd
Within, without, by greed of avarice,
And vain ambition for supremacy.

So fell the old Republics—Gentile and Jew,
Roman and Greek—such evermore the record;
Mix'd glory and shame, still lapsing into greed,
From conquest and from triumph, into fall!
The glory that we see exchanged for guilt
Might yet be glory. There were pride enough,
And emulous ambition to achieve,—
Both generous powers, when coupled with endowment,
To do the work of States—and there were courage
And sense of public need, and public welfare,—
And duty—in a brave but scattered few,
Throughout the States—had these been credited

To combat 'gainst the popular appetites.
But these were scorn'd and set aside for naught,
As lacking favor with the popular lusts!
They found reward in exile or in death!
And he alone who could debase his spirit,
And file his mind down to the basest nature
Grew capp'd with rule!—

So, with the lapse
From virtue, the great nation forfeits all
The pride with the security—the liberty,
With that prime modesty which keeps the heart
Upright, in meek subjection, to the doubts
That wait upon Humanity, and teach
Humility, as best check and guaranty,
Against the wolfish greed of appetite!
Worst of all signs, assuring coming doom,
When peoples loathe to listen to the praise
Of their great men; and, jealous of just claims,
Eagerly set upon them to revile,
And banish from their councils! Worse than all
When the great man, succumbing to the mass,
Yields up his mind as a low instrument
To vulgar fingers, to be played upon :—
Yields to the vulgar lure, the cunning bribe
Of place or profit, and makes sale of States
To Party!

Thus and then are States subdued—
'Till one vast central tyranny upstarts,
With front of glittering brass, but legs of clay;
Insolent, reckless of account as right,—
While lust grows license, and tears off the robes
From justice; and makes right a thing of mock;
And puts a foolscap on the head of law,
And plucks the baton of authority
From his right hand, and breaks it o'er his head.

So rages still the irresponsible power,
Using the madden'd populace as hounds,
To hunt down freedom where she seeks retreat.
The ancient history becomes the new—
The ages move in circles, and the snake
Ends ever with his tail in his own mouth.
Thus still in all the past!—and man the same
In all the ages—a poor thing of passion,
Hot greed, and miserable vanity,
And all infirmities of lust and error,
Makes of himself the wretched instrument
To murder his own hope.

So empires fall,—
Past, present, and to come!—
There is no hope
For nations or peoples, once they lapse from virtue

And fail in modest sense of what they are—
Creatures of weakness, whose security
Lies in meek resting on the law of God,
And in that wise humility which pleads
Ever for his guardian watch and Government,
Though men may bear the open signs of rule.
Humility is safety! could men learn
The law, "*ne sutor ultra crepidam*,"
And the sagacious cobbler, at his last,
Content himself with paring leather down
To heel and instep, nicely fitting parts,
In proper adaptation, to the foot,
We might have safety.

Rightly to conceive
What's right, and limit the o'erreaching will
To this one measure only, is the whole
Of that grand rule, and wise necessity,
Which only gives us safety.

Where a State,
Or blended States, or peoples, pass the bounds
Set for their progress, they must topple and fall
Into that gulf of ruin which has swallowed
All ancient Empires, States, Republics; all
Perishing, in like manner, from the selfsame cause!
The terrible conjunction of the event,

Close with the provocation, stands apart,
A social beacon in all histories;
And yet we take no heed, but still rush on,
Under mixed sway of greed and vanity,
And like the silly boy with his card-castle,
Precipitate to ruin as we build.

---

## THE VOICE OF THE SOUTH.

TYRTÆUS.—*Charleston Mercury.*

'TWAS a goodly boon that our fathers gave,
And fits but ill to be held by the slave;
And sad were the thought, if one of our band
Should give up the hope of so fair a land.

But the hour has come, and the times that tried
The souls of men in our days of pride,
Return once more, and now for the brave,
To merit the boon which our fathers gave.

And if there be one base spirit who stands
Now, in our peril, with folded hands,
Let his grave at once in the soil be wrought,
With the sword with which his old father fought.

An oath sublime should the freeman take,
Still braving the fight and the felon stake,—
The oath that his sires brought over the sea,
When they pledged their swords to Liberty!

'Twas a goodly oath, and in Heaven's own sight,
They battled and bled in behalf of the right;
'Twas hallowed by God with the holiest sign,
And seal'd with the blood of your sires and mine.

We cannot forget, and we dare not forego,
The holy duty to them that we owe,
The duty that pledges the soul of the son
To keep the freedom his sire hath won.

To suffer no proud transgressor to spoil
One right of our homes, or one foot of our soil,
One privilege pluck from our keeping, or dare
Usurp one blessing 'tis fit that we share!

Art ready for this, dear brother, who still
Keep'st Washington's bones upon Vernon's hill?
Art ready for this, dear brother, whose ear,
Should ever the voices of Mecklenberg hear?

Thou art ready, I know, brother nearest my heart,
Son of Eutaw and Ashley, to do thy part;
The sword and the rifle are bright in thy hands,
And waits but the word for the flashing of brands!

And thou, by Savannah's broad valleys,—and thou
Where the Black Warrior murmurs in echoes the vow;
And thou, youngest son of our sires, who roves
Where Apala-chicola* glides through her groves.

Nor shall Tennessee pause, when like voice from the steep,
The great South shall summon her sons from their sleep;
Nor Kentucky be slow, when our trumpet shall call,
To tear down the rifle that hangs on her wall!

Oh, sound, to awaken the dead from their graves,
The will that would thrust us from place for our slaves,
That, by fraud which lacks courage, and plea that lacks truth,
Would rob us of right without reason or ruth.

Dost thou hearken, brave Creole, as fearless as strong,
Nor rouse thee to combat the infamous wrong?
Ye hear it, I know, in the depth of your souls,
Valiant race, through whose valley the great river rolls.

---

* The reader will place the accent on the *ante-penultimate*, which affords not only the most musical, but the correct pronunciation.

At last ye are wakened, all rising at length,
In the passion of pride, in the fulness of strength;
And now let the struggle begin which shall see,
If the son, like the sire, is fit to be free.

We are sworn to the State, from our fathers that came,
To welcome the ruin, but never the shame;
To yield not a foot of our soil, nor a right,
While the soul and the sword are still fit for the fight.

Then, brothers, your hands and your hearts, while we draw
The bright sword of right, on the charter of law;—
Here the record was writ by our fathers, and here,
To keep, with the sword, that old record, we swear.

Let those who defile and deface it, be sure,
No longer their wrong or their fraud we endure;
We will scatter in scorn every link of the chain,
With which they would fetter our free souls in vain.

How goodly and bright were its links at the first!
How loathly and foul, in their usage accurst!
We had worn it in pride while it honor'd the brave,
But we rend it, when only grown fit for the slave.

## THE OATH OF FREEDOM.

BY JAMES BARRON HOPE.

"*Liberty is always won where there exists the unconquerable will to be free.*"

Born free, thus we resolve to live :
By Heaven we will be free !
By all the stars which burn on high—
By the green earth—the mighty sea—
By God's unshaken majesty,
We will be free or die !
Then let the drums all roll !
Let all the trumpets blow !
Mind, heart, and soul,
We spurn control
Attempted by a foe !

Born free, thus we resolve to live :
By Heaven we will be free !
And, vainly now the Northmen try
To beat us down—in arms we stand
To strike for this our native land !
We will be free or die !
Then let the drums all roll ! etc., etc.

Born free, we thus resolve to live :
  By Heaven we will be free !
Our wives and children look on high,
Pray God to smile upon the right !
And bid us in the deadly fight
  As freemen live or die !
    Then let the drums all roll ! etc., etc.

Born free, thus we resolve to live :
  By Heaven we will be free !
And ere we cease this battle-cry,
Be all our blood, our kindred's spilt,
On bayonet or sabre hilt !
  We will be free or die !
    Then let the drums all roll ! etc., etc.

Born free, thus we resolve to live :
  By Heaven we will be free !
Defiant let the banners fly,
Shake out their glories to the air,
And, kneeling, brothers, let us swear
  We will be free or die !
    Then let the drums all roll ! etc., etc.

Born free, thus we resolve to live :
  By Heaven we will be free !

And to this oath the dead reply—
Our valiant fathers' sacred ghosts—
These with us, and the God of hosts,
We will be free or die!
Then let the drums all roll! etc., **etc.**

---

## THE BATTLE-CRY OF THE SOUTH.

BY JAMES R. RANDALL.

**Arm yourselves and be valiant men, and see that ye be in readiness against the morning, that ye may fight with these nations that are assembled against us, to destroy us and our sanctuary.**

**For it is better for us to die in battle than to behold the calamities of our people and our sanctuary.—*Maccabees I.***

BROTHERS! the thunder-cloud is black,
And the wail of the South wings forth;
Will ye cringe to the hot tornado's rack,
And the vampires of the North?
Strike! ye can win a martyr's goal,
Strike! with a ruthless hand—
Strike! with the vengeance of the soul,
For your bright, beleaguered land!
To arms! to arms! for the South needs help,
And a craven is he who flees—
For ye have the sword of the Lion's Whelp,*
And the God of the Maccabees!

---

* The surname of the great Maccabeus.

Arise ! though the stars have a rugged glare,
  And the moon has a wrath-blurred crown—
Brothers ! a blessing is ambushed there
  In the cliffs of the Father's frown :
Arise ! ye are worthy the wondrous light
  Which the Sun of Justice gives—
In the caves and sepulchres of night
  Jehovah the Lord King lives !
    To arms ! to arms ! for the South needs help,
      And a craven is he who flees—
    For ye have the sword of the Lion's Whelp,
      And the God of the Maccabees !

Think of the dead by the Tennessee,
  In their frozen shrouds of gore—
Think of the mothers who shall see
  Those darling eyes no more !
But better are they in a hero grave
  Than the serfs of time and breath,
For they are the children of the brave,
  And the cherubim of death !
    To arms ! to arms ! for the South needs help,
      And a craven is he who flees—
    For ye have the sword of the Lion's Whelp,
      And the God of the Maccabees !

Better the charnels of the West,
  And a hecatomb of lives,

Than the foul invader as a guest
'Mid your sisters and your wives—
But a spirit lurketh in every maid,
Though, brothers, ye should quail,
To sharpen a Judith's lurid blade,
And the livid spike of Jael!
To arms! to arms! for the South needs help,
And a craven is he who flees—
For ye have the sword of the Lion's Whelp,
And the God of the Maccabees!

Brothers! I see you tramping by,
With the gladiator gaze,
And your shout is the Macedonian cry
Of the old, heroic days!
March on! with trumpet and with drum,
With rifle, pike, and dart,
And die—if even death must come—
Upon your country's heart!
To arms! to arms! for the South needs help,
And a craven is he who flees—
For ye have the sword of the Lion's Whelp,
And the God of the Maccabees!

Brothers! the thunder-cloud is black,
And the wail of the South wings forth;
Will ye cringe to the hot tornado's rack,
And the vampires of the North?

Strike! ye can win a martyr's goal,
Strike! with a ruthless hand—
Strike! with the vengeance of the soul
For your bright, beleaguered land!
To arms! to arms! for the South needs help,
And a craven is he who flees—
For ye have the sword of the Lion's Whelp,
And the God of the Maccabees!

---

## SONNET.

### CHARLESTON MERCURY.

DEMOCRACY hath done its work of ill,
And, seeming freemen, never to be free,
While the poor people shout in vanity,
The Demagogue triumphs o'er the popular will.
How swift the abasement follows! But few years,
And we stood eminent. Great men were ours,
Of virtue stern, and armed with mightiest powers!
How have we sunk below our proper spheres!
No Heroes, Virtues, Men! But in their place,
The nimble marmozet and magpie men;
Creatures that only mock and mimic, when
They run astride the shoulders of the race;
Democracy, in vanity elate,
Clothing but sycophants in robes of state.

## SEVENTY-SIX AND SIXTY-ONE.

BY JOHN W. OVERALL, OF LOUISIANA.

Ye spirits of the glorious dead!
Ye watchers in the sky!
Who sought the patriot's crimson bed,
With holy trust and high—
Come, lend your inspiration now,
Come, fire each Southern son,
Who nobly fights for freemen's rights,
And shouts for sixty-one.

Come, teach them how, on hill on glade,
Quick leaping from your side,
The lightning flash of sabres made
A red and flowing tide—
How well ye fought, how bravely fell,
Beneath our burning sun;
And let the lyre, in strains of fire,
So speak of sixty-one.

There's many a grave in all the land,
And many a crucifix,
Which tells how that heroic band
Stood firm in seventy-six—

Ye heroes of the deathless past,
Your glorious race is run,
But from your dust springs freemen's trust,
And blows for sixty-one.

We build our altars where you lie,
On many a verdant sod,
With sabres pointing to the sky,
And sanctified of God;
The smoke shall rise from every pile,
Till freedom's cause is wòn,
And every mouth throughout the South,
Shall shout for sixty-one!

---

## "REDDATO GLADIUM."

### VIRGINIA TO WINFIELD SCOTT.

A VOICE is heard in Ramah!
High sounds are on the gale!
Notes to wake buried patriots!
Notes to strike traitors pale!
Wild notes of outraged feeling
Cry aloud and spare him not!
'Tis Virginia's strong appealing,
And she calls to Winfield Scott!

Oh! chief among ten thousand!
  Thou whom I loved so well,
Star that has set, as never yet
  Since son of morning fell!
I call not in reviling,
  Nor to speak thee what thou art;
I leave thee to thy death-bed,
  And I leave thee to thy heart!

But by every mortal hope,
  And by every mortal fear;
By all that man deems sacred,
  And that woman holds most dear;
Yea! by thy mother's honor,
  And by thy father's grave,
By hell beneath, and heaven above,
  Give back the sword I gave!

Not since God's sword was planted
  To guard life's heavenly tree,
Has ever blade been granted,
  Like that bestowed on thee!
To pierce me with the steel I gave
  To guard mine honor's shrine,
Not since Iscariot lived and died,
  Was treason like to thine!

Give back the sword! and sever
Our strong and mighty tie!
We part, and part forever,
To conquer or to die!
In sorrow, not in anger,
I speak the word, "We part!"
For I leave thee to thy death-bed,
And I leave thee to thy heart!

RICHMOND WHIG.

---

## NAY, KEEP THE SWORD.

BY CARRIE CLIFFORD.

NAY, keep the sword which once we gave,
A token of our trust in thee;
The steel is true, the blade is keen—
False as thou art it cannot be.

We hailed thee as our glorious chief,
With laurel-wreaths we bound thy brow;
Thy name then thrilled from tongue to tongue:
In whispers hushed we breathe it now.

Yes, keep it till thy dying day;
Momentous ever let it be,
Of a great treasure once possessed—
A people's love now lost to thee.

Thy mother will not bow her head;
  She bares her bosom to thee now;
But may the bright steel fail to wound—
  It is more merciful than thou.

And ere thou strik'st the fatal blow,
  Thousands of sons of this fair land
Will rise, and, in their anger just,
  Will stay the rash act of thy hand.

And when in terror thou shalt hear
  Thy murderous deeds of vengeance cry
And feel the weight of thy great crime,
  Then fall upon thy sword and die.

Those aged locks I'll not reproach,
  Although upon a traitor's brow;
We've looked with reverence on them once,
  We'll try and not revile them now.

But her true sons and daughters pray,
  That ere thy day of reckoning be,
Thy ingrate heart may feel the pain
  To know thy mother once more free.

## COERCION: A POEM FOR THEN AND NOW.

BY JOHN R. THOMPSON, OF VIRGINIA.

WHO talks of coercion? who dares to deny
  A resolute people the right to be free?
Let him blot out forever one star from the sky,
  Or curb with his fetter the wave of the sea!

Who prates of coercion? Can love be restored
  To bosoms where only resentment may dwell?
Can peace upon earth be proclaimed by the sword,
  Or good-will among men be established by shell?

Shame! shame!—that the statesman and trickster, forsooth,
  Should have for a crisis no other recourse,
Beneath the fair day-spring of light and of truth,
  Than the old *brutum fulmen* of tyranny—force!

From the holes where fraud, falsehood, and hate slink away—
  From the crypt in which error lies buried in chains—
This foul apparition stalks forth to the day,
  And would ravage the land which his presence profanes.

Could you conquer us, men of the North—could you bring
  Desolation and death on our homes as a flood—
Can you hope the pure lily, affection, will spring
  From ashes all reeking and sodden with blood?

Could you brand us as villains and serfs, know ye not
  What fierce, sullen hatred lurks under the scar?
How loyal to Hapsburg is Venice, I wot!
  How dearly the Pole loves his father, the Czar!

But 'twere well to remember this land of the sun
  Is a *nutrix leonum*, and suckles a race
Strong-armed, lion-hearted, and banded as one,
  Who brook not oppression and know not disgrace.

And well may the schemers in office beware
  The swift retribution that waits upon crime,
When the lion, RESISTANCE, shall leap from his lair,
  With a fury that renders his vengeance sublime.

Once, men of the North, we were brothers, and still,
  Though brothers no more, we would gladly be friends;
Nor join in a conflict accursed, that must fill
  With ruin the country on which it descends.

But, if smitten with blindness, and mad with the rage
  The gods gave to all whom they wished to destroy,

You would act a new Iliad, to darken the age
  With horrors beyond what is told us of Troy—

If, deaf as the adder itself to the cries,
  When wisdom, humanity, justice implore,
You would have our proud eagle to feed on the eyes
  Of those who have taught him so grandly to soar—

If there be to your malice no limit imposed,
  And you purpose hereafter to rule with the rod
The men upon whom you already have closed
  Our goodly domain and the temples of God :

To the breeze then your banner dishonored unfold,
  And, at once, let the tocsin be sounded afar;
We greet you, as greeted the Swiss, Charles the Bold—
  With a farewell to peace and a welcome to war!

For the courage that clings to our soil, ever bright,
  Shall catch inspiration from turf and from tide;
Our sons unappalled shall go forth to the fight,
  With the smile of the fair, the pure kiss of the bride;

And the bugle its echoes shall send through the past,
  In the trenches of Yorktown to waken the slain;
While the sod of King's Mountain shall heave at the blast,
  And give up its heroes to glory again.

## A CRY TO ARMS.

BY HENRY TIMROD.

Ho! woodsmen of the mountain-side!
  Ho! dwellers in the vales!
Ho! ye who by the chafing tide
  Have roughened in the gales!
Leave barn and byre, leave kin and cot,
  Lay by the bloodless spade;
Let desk, and case, and counter rot,
  And burn your books of trade.

The despot roves your fairest lands;
  And till he flies or fears,
Your fields must grow but armed bands,
  Your sheaves be sheaves of spears!
Give up to mildew and to rust
  The useless tools of gain;
And feed your country's sacred dust
  With floods of crimson rain!

Come, with the weapons at your call—
  With musket, pike, or knife;
He wields the deadliest blade of all
  Who lightest holds his life.

The arm that drives its unbought blows
With all a patriot's scorn,
Might brain a tyrant with a rose,
Or stab him with a thorn.

Does any falter? let him turn
To some brave maiden's eyes,
And catch the holy fires that burn
In those sublunar skies.
Oh! could you like your women feel,
And in their spirit march,
A day might see your lines of steel
Beneath the victor's arch.

What hope, O God! would not grow warm
When thoughts like these give cheer?
The lily calmly braves the storm,
And shall the palm-tree fear?
No! rather let its branches court
The rack that sweeps the plain;
And from the lily's regal port
Learn how to breast the strain!

Ho! woodsmen of the mountain-side!
Ho! dwellers in the vales!
Ho! ye who by the roaring tide
Have roughened in the gales!

Come! flocking gayly to the fight
  From forest, hill, and lake ;
We battle for our country's right,
  And for the lily's sake!

---

## JACKSON, THE ALEXANDRIA MARTYR.

BY WM. H. HOLCOMBE, M. D., OF VIRGINIA.

'Twas not the private insult galled him most,
But public outrage of his country's flag,
To which his patriotic heart had pledged
Its faith as to a bride. The bold, proud chief,
Th' avenging host, and the swift-coming death
Appalled him not. Nor life with all its charms,
Nor home, nor wife, nor children could weigh down
The fierce, heroic instincts to destroy
The insolent invader. Ellsworth fell,
And Jackson perished 'mid the pack of wolves,
Befriended only by his own great heart
And God approving. More than Roman soul!
O type of our impetuous chivalry!
May this young nation ever boast her sons
A vast, and inconceivable multitude,
Standing like thee in her extremest van,
Self-poised and ready, in defence of rights
Or in revenge of wrongs, to dare and die!

## THE MARTYR OF ALEXANDRIA.

BY JAMES W. SIMMONS, OF TEXAS.

Revealed, as in a lightning flash,
A hero stood !
The invading foe, the trumpet's crash,
Set up his blood.

High o'er the sacred pile that bends
Those forms above,
Thy star, O Freedom ! brightly blends
Its rays with love.

The banner of a mighty race,
Serenely there,
Unfurls the genius of the place,
In haunted air.

A vow is registered in Heaven !
Patriot ! 'tis thine !
To guard those matchless colors, given
By hands divine.

Jackson ! thy spirit may not hear
Our wail ascend :
A nation gathers round thy bier,
And mourns its friend.

The example is thy monument,
And organ tones
Thy name resound, with glory blent,
Prouder than thrones!

And they whose loss hath been our gain,
A people's cares
Shall win their wounded hearts from pain,
And wipe their tears.

When time shall set the captives free,
Now scathed by wrath,
Heirs of his immortality,
Bright be their path.

---

## THE BLESSED UNION—EPIGRAM.

Doubtless to some, with length of ears,
To gratify an ape's desire,
The blessed Union still endears;—
The stripes, if not the stars, be theirs!
"Greek faith" they gave us eighty years,
And then—"Greek fire!"
But, better all their fires of scath
Than one hour's trust in Yankee faith!

## THE FIRE OF FREEDOM.

THE holy fire that nerved the Greek
  To make his stand at Marathon,
Until the last red foeman's shriek
  Proclaimed that freedom's fight was won,
Still lives unquenched—unquenchable :
  Through every age its fires will burn—
Lives in the hermit's lonely cell,
  And springs from every storied urn.

The hearthstone embers hold the spark
  Where fell oppression's foot hath trod ;
Through superstition's shadow dark
  It flashes to the living God !
From Moscow's ashes springs the Russ ;
  In Warsaw, Poland lives again :
Schamyl, on frosty Caucasus,
  Strikes liberty's electric chain !

Tell's freedom-beacon lights the Swiss ;
  Vainly the invader ever strives ;
He finds *Sic Semper Tyrannis*
  In San Jacinto's bowie-knives!

Than these—than all—a holier fire
  Now burns thy soul, Virginia's son!
Strike then for wife, babe, gray-haired sire,
  Strike for the grave of Washington!

The Northern rabble arms for greed;
  The hireling parson goads the train—
In that foul crop from bigot seed,
  Old "Praise God Barebones" howls again!
We welcome them to "Southern lands,"
  We welcome them to "Southern slaves,"
We welcome them "with bloody hands
  To hospitable Southern graves!"

---

## HYMN TO THE NATIONAL FLAG.

BY MRS. M. J. PRESTON.

FLOAT aloft, thou stainless banner!
  Azure cross and field of light;
Be thy brilliant stars the symbol
  Of the pure and true and right.
Shelter freedom's holy cause—
Liberty and sacred laws;
Guard the youngest of the nations—
  Keep her virgin honor bright.

From Virginia's storied border,
  Down to Tampa's furthest shore—
From the blue Atlantic's clashings
  To the Rio Grande's roar—
Over many a crimson plain,
Where our martyred ones lie slain—
Fling abroad thy blessed shelter,
  Stream and mount and valley o'er.

In thy cross of heavenly azure
  Has our faith its emblem high;
In thy field of white, the hallow'd
  Truth for which we'll dare and die;
In thy red, the patriot blood—
Ah! the consecrated flood.
Lift thyself, resistless banner!
  Ever fill our Southern sky!

Flash with living, lightning motion
  In the sight of all the brave!
Tell the price at which we purchased
  Room and right for thee to wave
Freely in our God's free air,
Pure and proud and stainless fair,
Banner of the youngest nation—
  Banner we would die to save!

Strike Thou for us! King of armies!
  Grant us room in Thy broad world!
Loosen all the despot's fetters,
  Back be all his legions hurled!
Give us peace and liberty,
Let the land we love be free—
Then, oh! bright and stainless banner!
  Never shall thy folds be furled!

---

## SONNET—MORAL OF PARTY

CHARLESTON MERCURY.

The moral of a party—if it be
  That healthy States need parties, lies in this,
  That we consider well what race it is,
And what the germ that first has made it free.
That germ must constitute the living tie
  That binds its generations to the end,
Change measures if it need, or policy,
  But neither break the principle, nor bend.
Each race hath its own nature—fixed, defined,
  By Heaven, and if its principle be won,
  Kept changeless as the progress of the sun,
It mocks at storm and rage, at sea and wind,
And grows to consummation, as the tree,
Matured, that ever grew in culture free.

## OUR FAITH IN '61.

BY A. J. REQUIER.

"That governments are instituted among men, deriving their just powers from the consent of the governed: that whenever any form of government becomes destructive of these ends, it is the right of the people to alter or abolish it, and to institute a new government, laying its foundation on such principles, and organizing its powers in such form, as TO THEM SHALL SEEM most likely to effect their safety and happiness."—[Declaration of Independence, July 4, '76.]

Not yet one hundred years have flown
Since on this very spot,
The subjects of a sovereign throne—
Liege-master of their lot—
This high degree sped o'er the sea,
From council-board and tent,
"No earthly power can rule the free
But by their own consent!"

For this, they fought as Saxons fight,
On bloody fields and long—
Themselves the champions of the right,
And judges of the wrong;
For this their stainless knighthood wore
The branded rebel's name,
Until the starry cross they bore
Set all the skies aflame!

And States co-equal and distinct
  Outshone the western sun,
By one great charter interlinked—
  Not blended into one ;
Whose graven key that high decree
  The grand inscription lent,
"No earthly power can rule the free
  But by their own consent !"

Oh ! sordid age ! Oh ! ruthless rage !
  Oh ! sacrilegious wrong !
A deed to blast the record page,
  And snap the strings of song ;
In that great charter's name, a band
  By grovelling greed enticed,
Whose warrant is the grasping hand
  Of creeds without a Christ—

States that have trampled every pledge
  Its crystal code contains,
Now give their swords a keener edge
  To harness it with chains—
To make a bond of brotherhood
  The sanction and the seal,
By which to arm a rabble brood
  With fratricidal steel.

Who, conscious that their cause is black,
In puling prose and rhyme,
Talk hatefully of love, and tack
Hypocrisy to crime;
Who smile and smite, engross the gorge
Or impotently frown;
And call us "rebels" with King George,
As if they wore his crown!

Most venal of a venal race,
Who think you cheat the sky
With every pharisaic face
And simulated lie;
Round Freedom's lair, with weapons bare,
We greet the light divine
Of those who throned the goddess there,
And yet inspire the shrine!

Our loved ones' graves are at our feet,
Their homesteads at our back—
No belted Southron can retreat
With women on his track;
Peal, bannered host, the proud decree
Which from your fathers went,
"No earthly power can rule the free
But by their own consent!"

## WOULDST THOU HAVE ME LOVE THEE.

BY ALEX. B. MEEK.

Wouldst thou have me love thee, dearest,
  With a woman's proudest heart,
Which shall ever hold thee nearest,
  Shrined in its inmost heart?
Listen, then! My country's calling
  On her sons to meet the foe!
Leave these groves of rose and myrtle;
  Drop thy dreamy harp of love!
Like young Korner—scorn the turtle,
  When the eagle screams above!

Dost thou pause?—Let dastards dally—
  Do thou for thy country fight!
'Neath her noble emblem rally—
  "God, our country, and our right!"
Listen! now her trumpet's calling
  On her sons to meet the foe!
Woman's heart is soft and tender,
  But 'tis proud and faithful too:
Shall she be her land's defender?
  Lover! Soldier! up and do!

Seize thy father's ancient falchion,
  Which once flashed as freedom's star!
Till sweet peace—the bow and halcyon,
  Stilled the stormy strife of war.
Listen! now thy country's calling
  On her sons to meet her foe!
Sweet is love in moonlight bowers!
  Sweet the altar and the flame!
Sweet the spring-time with her flowers!
  Sweeter far the patriot's name!

Should the God who smiles above thee,
  Doom thee to a soldier's grave,
Hearts will break, but fame will love thee,
  Canonized among the brave!
Listen, then! thy country's calling
  On her sons to meet the foe!
Rather would I view thee lying
  On the last red field of strife,
'Mid thy country's heroes dying,
  Than become a dastard's wife!

## ENLISTED TO-DAY.

I KNOW the sun shines, and the lilacs are blowing,
And summer sends kisses by beautiful May—
Oh! to see all the treasures the spring is bestowing,
And think—my boy Willie enlisted to-day.

It seems but a day since at twilight, low humming,
I rocked him to sleep with his cheek upon mine,
While Robby, the four-year old, watched for the coming
Of father, adown the street's indistinct line.

It is many a year since my Harry departed,
To come back no more in the twilight or dawn;
And Robby grew weary of watching, and started
Alone on the journey his father had gone.

It is many a year—and this afternoon sitting
At Robby's old window, I heard the band play,
And suddenly ceased dreaming over my knitting,
To recollect Willie is twenty to-day.

And that, standing beside him this soft May-day morning,
The sun making gold of his wreathed cigar smoke,
I saw in his sweet eyes and lips a faint warning,
And choked down the tears when he eagerly spoke:

"Dear mother, you know how these Northmen are crowing,
They would trample the rights of the South in the dust;
The boys are all fire ; and they wish I were going—"
He stopped, but his eyes said, " Oh, say if I must !"

I smiled on the boy, though my heart it seemed breaking,
My eyes filled with tears, so I turned them away,
And answered him, " Willie, 'tis well you are waking—
Go, act as your father would bid you, to-day !"

I sit in the window, and see the flags flying,
And drearily list to the roll of the drum,
And smother the pain in my heart that is lying,
And bid all the fears in my bosom be dumb.

I shall sit in the window when summer is lying
Out over the fields, and the honey-bee's hum
Lulls the rose at the porch from her tremulous sighing,
And watch for the face of my darling to come.

And if he should fall—his young life he has given
For freedom's sweet sake ; and for me, I will pray
Once more with my Harry and Robby in Heaven
To meet the dear boy that enlisted to-day.

## MY MARYLAND.

WRITTEN AT POINTE COUPEE, LA., APRIL 26, 1861. FIRST PUBLISHED IN THE NEW ORLEANS DELTA.

THE despot's heel is on thy shore,
Maryland!
His torch is at thy temple door,
Maryland!
Avenge the patriotic gore
That flecked the streets of Baltimore,
And be the battle-queen of yore,
Maryland! My Maryland!

Hark to an exiled son's appeal,
Maryland!
My Mother-State, to thee I kneel,
Maryland!
For life and death, for woe and weal,
Thy peerless chivalry reveal,
And gird thy beauteous limbs with steel,
Maryland! My Maryland!

Thou wilt not cower in the dust,
Maryland!
Thy beaming sword shall never rust,
Maryland!

Remember Carroll's sacred trust,
Remember Howard's warlike thrust,
And all thy slumberers with the just,
Maryland! My Maryland!

Come! 'tis the red dawn of the day,
Maryland!
Come! with thy panoplied array,
Maryland!
With Ringgold's spirit for the fray,
With Watson's blood at Monterey,
With fearless Lowe and dashing May,
Maryland! My Maryland!

Come! for thy shield is bright and strong,
Maryland!
Come! for thy dalliance does thee wrong,
Maryland!
Come! to thine own heroic throng,
That stalks with Liberty along,
And ring thy dauntless Slogan-song,
Maryland! My Maryland!

Dear Mother! burst the tyrant's chain,
Maryland!
Virginia should not call in vain,
Maryland!

*She* meets her sisters on the plain—
"*Sic semper*," 'tis the proud refrain
That baffles minions back amain,
Maryland!
Arise, in majesty again,
Maryland! My Maryland!

I see the blush upon thy cheek,
Maryland!
For thou wast ever bravely meek,
Maryland!
But lo! there surges forth a shriek
From hill to hill, from creek to creek—
Potomac calls to Chesapeake,
Maryland! My Maryland!

Thou wilt not yield the Vandal toll,
Maryland!
Thou wilt not crook to his control,
Maryland!
Better the fire upon thee roll,
Better the shot, the blade, the bowl,
Than crucifixion of the soul,
Maryland! My Maryland!

I hear the distant thunder hum,
Maryland!
The Old Line bugle, fife, and drum,
Maryland!

She is not dead, nor deaf, nor dumb—
Huzza! she spurns the Northern scum!
She breathes—she burns! she'll come! she'll come!
Maryland! My Maryland!

---

## THE BOY-SOLDIER.

BY A LADY OF SAVANNAH.

He is acting o'er the battle,
With his cap and feather gay,
Singing out his soldier-prattle,
In a mockish manly way—
With the boldest, bravest footstep,
Treading firmly up and down,
And his banner waving softly,
O'er his boyish locks of brown.

And I sit beside him sewing,
With a busy heart and hand,
For the gallant soldiers going
To the far-off battle land—
And I gaze upon my jewel,
In his baby spirit bold,
My little blue-eyed soldier,
Just a second summer old.

Still a deep, deep well of feeling,
  In my mother's heart is stirred,
And the tears come softly stealing
  At each imitative word!
There's a struggle in my bosom,
  For I love my darling boy—
He's the gladness of my spirit,
  He's the sunlight of my joy!
Yet I think upon my country,
  And my spirit groweth bold—
Oh! I wish my blue-eyed soldier
  Were but twenty summers old!

I would speed him to the battle—
  I would arm him for the fight;
I would give him to his country,
  For his country's wrong and right!
I would nerve his hand with blessing
  From the "God of battles" won—
With His helmet and His armor,
  I would cover o'er my son.

Oh! I know there'd be a struggle,
  For I love my darling boy;
He's the gladness of my spirit,
  He's the sunlight of my joy!

Yet in thinking of my country,
  Oh! my spirit groweth bold,
And I with my blue-eyed soldier
  Were but twenty summers old!

---

## THE GOOD OLD CAUSE.

BY JOHN D. PHELAN, OF MONTGOMERY, ALA.

I.

Huzza! huzza! for the *Good Old Cause,*
  'Tis a stirring sound to hear,
For it tells of rights and liberties,
  Our fathers bought so dear;
It brings up the *Jersey prison-ship,*
  The spot where *Warren* fell,
And the scaffold which echoes the dying words
  Of *murdered Hayne's* farewell.

II.

The *Good Old Cause!* it is still the same
  Though age upon age may roll;
'Tis the cause of *the right* against *the wrong,*
  Burning bright in each generous soul;
'Tis the cause of all who claim to live
  As freemen on Freedom's sod;
Of the widow, who wails her husband and sons,
  By Tyranny's heel down-trod.

III.

And whoever burns with a holy zeal,
  To behold his country free,
And would sooner see her *baptized in blood,*
  Than to bend the suppliant knee ;
Must agree to follow her *White-Cross flag,*
  Where the storms of battle roll,
*A soldier*—A SOLDIER !—with *arms in his hands,*
  And the *love of the South in his soul!*

IV.

Come one, come all, at your country's call,
  Let none remain behind,
But those too young, and those too old,
  The feeble, the halt, the blind ;
Let *every man,* whether rich or poor,
  Who can carry a knapsack and gun,
Repair to the ranks of our Southern host,
  'Till the cause of the South is won.

V.

But the son of the South, if such there be,
  Who will shrink from the contest now,
From a love of ease, or the lust of gain,
  Or through fear of the Yankee foe ;
May his neighbors shrink from his proffered hand,
  As though it was soiled for aye,

And may every woman turn her cheek
From his craven lips away ;
May his country's curse be on his head,
And may no man ever see,
A gentle bride by the traitor's side,
Or children about his knee.

VI.

Huzza ! huzza ! for the Good Old Cause,
'Tis a stirring sound to hear ;
For it tells of rights and liberties,
Our fathers bought so dear ;
It summons our braves from their bloody graves,
To receive our fond applause,
And bids us tread in the steps of those
Who *died* for the *Good Old Cause.*

---

## MANASSAS.

BY CATHERINE M. WARFIELD.

They have met at last—as storm-clouds
meet in heaven ;
And the Northmen, back and bleeding,
have been driven :
And their thunders have been stilled,
And their leaders crushed or killed,
And their ranks, with terror thrilled,
rent and riven !

Like the leaves of Vallambrosa
they are lying ;
In the moonlight, in the midnight,
dead and dying :
Like those leaves before the gale,
Swept their legions, wild and pale ;
While the host that made them quail
stood, defying.

When aloft in morning sunlight
flags were flaunted,
And "swift vengeance on the rebel"
proudly vaunted :
Little did they think that night
Should close upon their shameful flight,
And rebels, victors in the fight,
stand undaunted.

But peace to those who perished
in our passes !
Light be the earth above them !
green the grasses !
Long shall Northmen rue the day,
When they met our stern array,
And shrunk from battle's wild affray
at Manassas !

## VIRGINIA.

BY CATHERINE M. WARFIELD.

Glorious Virginia! Freedom sprang
Light to her feet at thy trumpet's clang:
At the first sound of that clarion blast,
Foes like the chaff from the whirlwind passed—
Passed to their doom: from that hour no more
Triumphs their cause by sea or shore.

Glorious Virginia! noble the blood
That hath bathed thy fields in a crimson flood;
On many a wide-spread and sunny plain,
Like leaves of autumn thy dead have lain:
The Southron heart is their funeral urn!
The Southern slogan their requiem stern!

Glorious Virginia! to thee, to thee
We lean, as the shoots to the parent tree;
Bending in awe at thy glance of might;—
First in the council, first in the fight!
While our flag is fanned by the breath of fame,
Glorious Virginia! we'll bless thy name.

## THE WAR-CHRISTIAN'S THANKSGIVING.

RESPECTFULLY DEDICATED TO THE WAR-CLERGY OF THE UNITED STATES.

BY S. TEACKLE WALLIS.

Oh, God of battles ! once again,
With banner, trump, and drum,
And garments in thy wine-press dyed,
To give Thee thanks we come.

No goats or bullocks garlanded,
Unto thine altars go ;
With brothers' blood, by brothers shed,
Our glad libations flow,

From pest-house and from dungeon foul,
Where, maimed and torn, they die,
From gory trench and charnel-house,
Where, heap on heap, they lie.

In every groan that yields a soul,
Each shriek a heart that rends,
With every breath of tainted air,
Our homage, Lord, ascends.

We thank Thee for the sabre's gash,
The cannon's havoc wild ;
We bless Thee for the widow's tears,
The want that starves her child !

We give Thee praise that Thou hast lit
  The torch, and fanned the flame ;
That lust and rapine hunt their prey,
  Kind Father, in Thy name !

That, for the songs of idle joy
  False angels sang of yore,
Thou sendest War on earth—ill-will
  To men for evermore !

We know that wisdom, truth, and right
  To us and ours are given ;
That Thou hast clothed us with the wrath,
  To do the work of heaven.

We know that plains and cities waste
  Are pleasant in Thine eyes—
Thou lov'st a hearthstone desolate,
  Thou lov'st a mourner's cries.

Let not our weakness fall below
  The measure of Thy will,
And while the press hath wine to bleed,
  Oh, tread it with us still !

Teach us to hate—as Jesus taught
  Fond fools, of yore, to love ;

Give us Thy vengeance as our own—
  Thy pity, hide above!

Teach us to turn, with reeking hands,
  The pages of Thy word,
And learn the blessed curses there,
  On them that sheathe the sword.

Where'er we tread may deserts spring,
  'Till none are left to slay;
And when the last red drop is shed,
  We'll kneel again—and pray!

---

## SONNET.

CHARLESTON MERCURY.

MAN makes his own dread fates, and these in turn
Create his tyrants. In our lust and passion,
Our appetite and ignorance, he springs.
The creature of our need as our desert,
The scourge that whips us for decaying virtue,
He chastens to reform us! Never yet,
In mortal life, did tyrant rise to power,
But in the people's worst infirmities
Of crime and greed. The creature of our vices,
The loathsome ulcer of our vicious moods,
He is decreed their proper punishment.

## MARCHING TO DEATH.

BY J. HERBERT SASS, OF SOUTH CAROLINA.

1862.

"The National Quarterly depicts a remarkable scene, which occurred some years since on one of the British transport ships. The commander of the troops on board, seeing that the vessel must soon sink, and that there was no hope of saving his men, drew them up in order of battle, and, as in the presence of a human enemy, bravely faced the doom that was before them. We know of no more impressive illustration of the power of military discipline in the presence of death."

I.

The last farewells are breathed by loving lips,
The last fond prayer for darling ones is said,
And o'er each heart stern sorrow's dark eclipse
Her sable pall hath spread.

II.

Far, far beyond each anxious watcher's sight,
Baring her bosom to the wanton sea,
The lordly ship sweeps onward in her might,
Her tameless majesty.

III.

Forth from his fortress in the western sky,
Flashing defiance on each crested wave,
Out glares the sun, with red and lowering eye,
Grand, even in his grave.

IV.

Till, waxing bolder as his rays decline,
The clustering billows o'er his ramparts sweep,
Slow droops his banner—fades his light divine,
And darkness rules the deep.

V.

Look once again!—Night's sombre shades have fled:
But the pale rays that glimmer from their sheath,
Serve but to show the blackness overhead,
And the wild void beneath.

VI.

Mastless and helmless drifts the helpless bark;
Her pride, her majesty, her glory gone;
While o'er the waters broods the tempest dark,
And the wild winds howl on.

VII.

But hark! amid the madness of the storm
There comes an echo o'er the surging wave;
Firm at its call the dauntless legions form,
The resolute and brave.

VIII.

Eight hundred men, the pride of England's host,
In stern array stand marshall'd on her deck,

Calmly as though they knew not they were lost—
    Lost in that shattered wreck.

IX.

Eight hundred men,—old England's tried and true,
Their hopes, their fears, their tasks of glory done,
Steadfast, till the last foe be conquered too,
    And the last fight be won.

X.

Free floats their banner o'er them as they stand;
No mournful dirge may o'er the waters ring;
Out peals the anthem, glorious and grand,
    "The king! God save the king!"

XI.

Lower and lower sinks the fated bark,
Closer and closer creeps the ruthless wave,
But loud outswells, across the waters dark,
    The death-song of the brave.

XII.

Over their heads the gurgling billows sweep;
Still o'er the waves the last fond echoes ring,
Out-thrilling from the caverns of the deep,
    "The king! God save the king!"

XIII.

Oh thou ! whoe'er thou art that reads this page,
Learn here a lesson of high, holy faith,
For all throughout our earthly pilgrimage,
We hold a tryst with death.

XIV.

Not in the battle-field's tumultuous strife,
Not in the hour when vanquished foemen fly,
Not in the midst of bright and happy life,
Is it most hard to die.

XV.

Greater the guerdon, holier the prize,
Of him who trusts, and waits in lowly mood ;
Oh ! learn how high, how holy courage lies
In patient fortitude.

---

## CHARLESTON.

BY HENRY TIMROD.

CALM as that second summer which precedes
The first fall of the snow,
In the broad sunlight of heroic deeds,
The city bides the foe.

As yet, behind their ramparts, stern and proud,
  Her bolted thunders sleep—
Dark Sumter, like a battlemented cloud,
  Looms o'er the solemn deep.

No Calpe frowns from lofty cliff or scaur
  To guard the holy strand ;
But Moultrie holds in leash her dogs of war,
  Above the level sand.

And down the dunes a thousand guns lie couched,
  Unseen, beside the flood—
Like tigers in some Orient jungle crouched,
  That wait and watch for blood.

Meanwhile, through streets still echoing with trade,
  Walk grave and thoughtful men,
Whose hands may one day wield the patriot's blade
  As lightly as the pen.

And maidens, with such eyes as would grow dim
  Over a bleeding hound,
Seem each one to have caught the strength of him
  Whose sword she sadly bound.

Thus girt without and garrisoned at home,
  Day patient following day,
Old Charleston looks from roof, and spire, and dome,
  Across her tranquil bay.

Ships, through a hundred foes, from Saxon lands
  And spicy Indian ports,
Bring Saxon steel and iron to her hands,
  And summer to her courts.

But still, along yon dim Atlantic line,
  The only hostile smoke
Creeps like a harmless mist above the brine,
  From some frail, floating oak.

Shall the spring dawn, and she still clad in smiles,
  And with an unscathed brow,
Rest in the strong arms of her palm-crowned isles,
  As fair and free as now?

We know not; in the temple of the Fates
  God has inscribed her doom;
And, all untroubled in her faith, she waits
  The triumph or the tomb.

## CHARLESTON.

BY PAUL H. HAYNE.

I.

WHAT ! still does the Mother of Treason uprear
Her crest 'gainst the Furies that darken her sea ?
Unquelled by mistrust, and unblanched by a Fear,
Unbowed her proud head, and unbending her knee,
Calm, steadfast, and free ?

II.

Aye ! launch your red lightnings, blaspheme in your wrath,
Shock earth, wave, and heaven with the blasts of your ire ;—
But she seizes your death-bolts, yet hot from their path,
And hurls back your lightnings, and mocks at the fire
Of your fruitless desire.

III.

Ringed round by her Brave, a fierce circlet of flame,
Flashes up from the sword-points that cover her breast ;
She is guarded by Love, and enhaloed by Fame,
And never, we swear, shall *your* footsteps be pressed
Where her dead heroes rest !

IV.

Her voice shook the Tyrant !—sublime from her tongue
  Fell the accents of warning,—a Prophetess grand,—
On her soil the first life-notes of Liberty rung,
  *And the first stalwart blow of her gauntleted hand*
    Broke the sleep of her land !

V.

What more ! she hath grasped with her iron-bound will
  The Fate that would trample her honor to earth,—
The light in those deep eyes is luminous still
  With the warmth of her valor, the glow of her worth,
    Which illumine the Earth !

VI.

And beside her a Knight the great Bayard had loved,
  "Without fear or reproach," lifts her Banner on high ;
He stands in the vanguard, majestic, unmoved,
  And a thousand firm souls, when that Chieftain is nigh,
    Vow, "'tis easy to die !"

VII.

Their swords have gone forth on the fetterless air !
  The world's breath is hushed at the conflict ! before
Gleams the bright form of Freedom with wreaths in her hair—
  And what though the chaplet be crimsoned with gore,
    We shall prize her the more !

VIII.

And while Freedom lures on with her passionate eyes
To the height of her promise, the voices of yore,
From the storied Profound of past ages arise,
And the pomps of their magical music outpour
O'er the war-beaten shore.

IX.

Then gird your brave Empress, O! Heroes, with flame
Flashed up from the sword-points that cover her breast,
She is guarded by Love, and enhaloed by Fame,
And never, base Foe! shall your footsteps be pressed
Where her dead Martyrs rest!

---

## "YE MEN OF ALABAMA!"

BY JOHN D. PHELAN, OF MONTGOMERY, ALA.

Air—"Ye Mariners of England."

I.

Ye men of Alabama,
Awake, arise, awake!
And rend the coils asunder
Of this Abolition snake.
If another fold he fastens—
If this final coil he plies—

In the cold clasp of hate and power
  Fair Alabama dies.

II.

Though round your lower limbs and waist
  His deadly coils I see,
Yet, yet, thank Heaven! your head and arms,
  And good right hand, are free;
And in that hand there glistens—
  O God! what joy to feel!—
A polished blade, full sharp and keen,
  Of tempered State Rights steel.

III.

Now, by the free-born sires
  From whose brave loins ye sprung!
And by the noble mothers
  At whose fond breasts ye hung!
And by your wives and daughters,
  And by the ills they dread,
Drive deep that good Secession steel
  Right through the Monster's head.

IV.

This serpent Abolition
  Has been coiling on for years;
We have reasoned, we have threatened,
  We have begged almost with tears:

Now, away, away with Union,
  Since on our Southern soil
The only *union* left us
  Is an anaconda's coil.

V.

Brave little South Carolina
  Will strike the self-same blow,
And Florida, and Georgia,
  And Mississippi too;
And Arkansas, and Texas;
  And at the death, I ween,
The head will fall beneath the blows
  Of all the brave Fifteen.

VI.

In this our day of trial,
  Let feuds and factions cease,
Until above this howling storm
  We see the sign of Peace.
Let Southern men, like brothers,
  In solid phalanx stand,
And poise their spears, and lock their shields,
  To guard their native land.

VII.

The love that for the Union
  Once in our bosoms beat,

From insult and from injury
  Has turned to scorn and hate ;
And the banner of Secession
  To-day we lift on high,
Resolved, beneath that sacred flag,
  To conquer, or TO DIE !

MONTGOMERY ADVERTISER, October, 1860.

---

## NEC TEMERE, NEC TIMIDE.

BY ANNIE CHAMBERS KETCHUM.

GENTLEMEN OF THE SOUTH,
  Gird on your glittering swords !
Darkly along our borders fair
  Gather the Northern hordes.
Ruthless and fierce they come
  At the fiery cannon's mouth,
To blast the glory of our land,
  Gentlemen of the South !

Ride forth in your stately pride,
  Each bearing on his shield
Ensigns our fathers won of yore
  On many a well-fought field !
Let this be your battle-cry,
  Even to the cannon's mouth,

*Cor unum via una!* Onward,
Gentlemen of the South!

Brave knights of a knightly race,
Gordon, and Chambers, and Gray,
Show to the minions of the North
How Valor dares the fray!
Let them read on each stainless crest
At the belching cannon's mouth,
*Decori decus addit avito,*
Gentlemen of the South!

Morrison, Douglas, Stuart,
Erskine, and Bradford, and West,
Your gauntlets on many a bloody field
Have stood the battle's test!
*Animo non astutia!*
March to the cannon's mouth,
Heirs of the brave dead centuries! Onward,
Gentlemen of the South!

Call forth your stalwart men,
Workers in brass and steel!
Bid the swart artisans come forth
At sound of the trumpet's peal!
Give them your war-cry, Erskine!
*Fight!* to the cannon's mouth!
Bid the men *Forward!* Douglas, *Forward!*
Yeomanry of the South!

Brave hunters! Ye have met
  The fierce black bear in the fray;
Ye have trailed the panther night by night,
  Ye have chased the fox by day!
Your prancing chargers pant
  To dash at the gray wolf's mouth,
Your arms are sure of their quarry! Onward!
  Gentlemen of the South!

Fight! that the lowly serf
  And the high-born lady still
May bide in their proud dependency,
  Free subjects of your will!
Teach the base North how ill,
  At the fiery cannon's mouth,
He fares who touches your household gods,
  Gentlemen of the South!

From mother, and wife, and child,
  From faithful and happy slave,
Prayers for your sakes ascend to Him
  Whose arm is strong to save!
We check the gathering tears,
  Though ye go to the cannon's mouth;
*Dominus providebit!* Onward,
  Gentlemen of the South!

MEMPHIS APPEAL.

## DIXIE.

BY ALBERT PIKE.

I.

SOUTHRONS, hear your Country call you !
Up ! lest worse than death befall you !
    To arms ! to arms ! to arms ! in Dixie !
Lo ! all the beacon-fires are lighted,
Let all hearts be now united !
    To arms ! to arms ! to arms ! in Dixie !
        Advance the flag of Dixie !
          Hurrah ! hurrah !
    For Dixie's land we'll take our stand,
        To live or die for Dixie !
      To arms ! to arms !
        And conquer peace for Dixie !
      To arms ! to arms !
        And conquer peace for Dixie !

II.

Hear the Northern thunders mutter !
Northern flags in South winds flutter !
    To arms ! etc.
Send them back your fierce defiance !
Stamp upon the accursed alliance !
    To arms ! etc.
      Advance the flag of Dixie ! etc.

III.

Fear no danger ! shun no labor !
Lift up rifle, pike, and sabre !
To arms ! etc.
Shoulder pressing close to shoulder,
Let the odds make each heart bolder !
To arms ! etc.
Advance the flag of Dixie, etc.

IV.

How the South's great heart rejoices
At your cannon's ringing voices ;
To arms ! etc.
For faith betrayed and pledges broken,
Wrong inflicted, insults spoken.
To arms ! etc.
Advance the flag of Dixie, etc.

V.

Strong as lions, swift as eagles,
Back to their kennels hunt these beagles !
To arms ! etc.
Cut the unequal bonds asunder !
Let them hence each other plunder !
To arms ! etc.
Advance the flag of Dixie ! etc.

VI.

Swear upon your Country's altar,
Never to submit or falter;
    To arms! etc.
Till the spoilers are defeated,
Till the Lord's work is completed.
    To arms! etc.
        Advance the flag of Dixie! etc.

VII.

Halt not till our Federation
Secures among earth's Powers its station!
    To arms! etc.
Then at peace, and crowned with glory,
Hear your children tell the story!
    To arms! etc.
        Advance the flag of Dixie! etc.

VIII.

If the loved ones weep in sadness,
Victory soon shall bring them gladness;
    To arms! etc.
Exultant pride soon banish sorrow;
Smiles chase tears away to-morrow.
    To arms! etc.
        Advance the flag of Dixie! etc.

## THE OLD RIFLEMAN.

BY FRANK TICKNOR, OF GEORGIA.

Now bring me out my buckskin suit!
  My pouch and powder, too!
We'll see if seventy-six can shoot
  As sixteen used to do.

Old Bess! we've kept our barrels bright!
  Our trigger quick and true!
As far, if not as *fine* a sight,
  As long ago we drew!

And pick me out a trusty flint!
  A real white and blue,
Perhaps 'twill win the *other* tint
  Before the hunt is through!

Give boys your brass percussion caps!
  Old "shut-pan" suits as well!
There's something in the *sparks:* perhaps
  There's something in the smell!

We've seen the red-coat Briton bleed!
  The red-skin Indian, too!

We've never thought to draw a bead
  On Yanke-doodle-doo !

But, Bessie ! bless your dear old heart !
  Those days are mostly done ;
And now we must revive the art
  Of shooting on the run !

If Doodle must be meddling, why,
  There's only this to do—
Select the black spot in his eye,
  And let the daylight through !

And if he doesn't like the way
  That Bess presents the view,
He'll maybe change his mind, and stay
  Where the good Doodles do !

Where Lincoln lives. The man, you know,
  Who kissed the Testament ;
To keep the Constitution ? No !
  *To keep the Government !*

We'll hunt for Lincoln, Bess ! old tool,
  And take him half and half ;
We'll aim to *hit* him, if a fool,
  And *miss* him, if a calf !

We'll teach these shot-gun boys the tricks
By which a war is won ;
Especially how Seventy-six
Took Tories on the run.

---

## BATTLE HYMN.

CHARLESTON MERCURY.

Lord of Hosts, that beholds us in battle, defending
The homes of our sires 'gainst the hosts of the foe,
Send us help on the wings of thy angels descending,
And shield from his terrors, and baffle his blow.
Warm the faith of our sons, till they flame as the iron,
Red-glowing from the fire-forge, kindled by zeal ;
Make them forward to grapple the hordes that environ,
In the storm-rush of battle, through forests of steel !

Teach them, Lord, that the cause of their country makes glorious
The martyr who falls in the front of the fight ;—
That the faith which is steadfast makes ever victorious
The arm which strikes boldly defending the right ;—
That the zeal, which is roused by the wrongs of a nation,
Is a war-horse that sweeps o'er the field as his own ;
And the Faith, which is winged by the soul's approbation,
Is a warrior, in proof, that can ne'er be o'erthrown.

## KENTUCKY, SHE IS SOLD

BY J. R. BARRICK, OF KENTUCKY.

A TEAR for "the dark and bloody ground,"
For the land of hills and caves;
Her Kentons, Boones, and her Shelbys sleep
Where the vandals tread their graves;
A sigh for the loss of her honored fame,
Dear won in the days of old;
Her ship is manned by a foreign crew,
For Kentucky, she is sold.

The bones of her sons lie bleaching on
The plains of Tippecanoe,
On the field of Raisin her blood was shed,
As free as the summer's dew;
In Mexico her McRee and Clay
Were first of the brave and bold—
A change has been in her bosom wrought,
For Kentucky, she is sold.

Pride of the free, was that noble State,
And her banner still were so,
Had the iron heel of the despot not
Her prowess sunk so low;
Her valleys once were the freeman's home,
Her valor unbought with gold,

But now the pride of her life is fled,
  For Kentucky, she is sold

Her brave would once have scorned to wear
  The yoke that crushes her now,
And the tyrant grasp, and the vandal tread,
  Would sullen have made her brow ;
Her spirit yet will be wakened up,
  And her saddened fate be told,
Her gallant sons to the world yet prove
  That Kentucky is not sold.

---

## SONNET—THE SHIP OF STATE.

Here lie the peril and necessity
  That need a race of giants—a great realm,
  With not one noble leader at the helm ;
And the great Ship of State still driving high,
  'Midst breakers, on a lee shore—to the rocks.
  With ever and anon most terrible shocks—
The crew aghast, and fear in every eye.
Yet is the gracious Providence still nigh ;
  And, if our cause be just, our hearts be true,
  We shall save goodly ship and gallant crew,
Nor suffer shipwreck of our liberty !
  It needs that as a people we arise,
  With solemn purpose that even fate defies,
And brave all perils with unblenching eye !

CHARLESTON MERCURY.

## "IN HIS BLANKET ON THE GROUND."

BY CAROLINE H. GERVAIS, CHARLESTON.

WEARY, weary lies the soldier,
In his blanket on the ground
With no sweet "Good-night" to cheer him,
And no tender voice's sound,
Making music in the darkness,
Making light his toilsome hours,
Like a sunbeam in the forest,
Or a tomb wreathed o'er with flowers.

Thoughtful, hushed, he lies, and tearful,
As his memories sadly roam
To the "cozy little parlor"
And the loved ones of his home ;
And his waking and his dreaming
Softly braid themselves in one,
As the twilight is the mingling
Of the starlight and the sun.

And when sleep descends upon him,
*Still* his thought within his dream
Is of home, and friends, and loved ones,
And his busy fancies seem
To be *real*, as they wander
To his mother's cherished form.

As she gently said, in parting
"Thine in sunshine and in storm ;
Thine in helpless childhood's morning,
And in boyhood's joyous time,
Thou must leave me now—*God* watch thee
In thy manhood's ripened prime."

Or, mayhap, amid the phantoms
Teeming thick within his brain,
His dear father's locks, o'er-silvered,
Come to greet his view again ;
And he hears his trembling accents,
Like a clarion ringing high,
"Since *not mine* are youth and strength, boy,
*Thou* must victor prove, or die."

Or perchance he hears a whisper
Of the faintest, faintest sigh,
Something deeper than word-spoken,
Something breathing of a tie
Near his soul as bounding heart-blood :
It is hers, that patient wife—
And again that parting seemeth
Like the taking leave of life :
And her last kiss he remembers,
And the agonizing thrill,
And the "*Must you go?*" and answer,
"*I but know my Country's will.*"

Or the little children gather,
  Half in wonder, round his knees ;
And the faithful dog, mute, watchful,
  In the mystic glass he sees ;
And the voice of song, and pictures,
  And the simplest homestead flowers,
Unforgotten, crowd before him
  In the solemn midnight hours.

Then his thoughts in Dreamland wander
  To a sister's sweet caress,
And he feels her dear lips quiver
  As his own they fondly press ;
And he hears her proudly saying,
  (Though sad tears are in her eyes),
"Brave men fall, but live in story,
  *For the Hero never dies!"*

Or, perhaps, his brown cheek flushes,
  And his heart beats quicker now,
As he thinks of one who gave him,
  Him, the loved one, love's sweet vow ;
And, ah, fondly he remembers
  He is *still* her dearest care,
Even in his star-watched slumber
  That she pleads for him in prayer.

Oh, the soldier *will* be dreaming,
  Dreaming *often* of us all,
(When the damp earth is his pillow,
  And the snow and cold sleet fall),
Of the dear, familiar faces,
  Of the cozy, curtained room,
Of the flitting of the shadows
  In the twilight's pensive gloom.

Or when summer suns burn o'er him,
  Bringing drought and dread disease,
And the throes of wasting fever
  Come his weary frame to seize—
In the restless sleep of sickness,
  Doomed, perchance, to martyr death,
Hear him whisper "*Home*"—sweet cadence,
  With his quickened, labored breath.

Then God bless him, bless the soldier,
  And God nerve him for the fight;
May He lend his arm new prowess
  To do battle for the right.
Let him feel that while he's dreaming
  In his fitful slumber bound,
That we're praying—*God watch o'er him*
  *In his blanket on the ground.*

## THE MOUNTAIN PARTISAN.

I.

My rifle, pouch, and knife!
My steed! And then we part!
One loving kiss, dear wife,
One press of heart to heart!
Cling to me yet awhile,
But stay the sob, the tear!
Smile—only try to smile—
And I go without a fear.

II.

Our little cradled boy,
He sleeps—and in his sleep,
Smiles, with an angel joy,
Which tells thee not to weep.
I'll kneel beside, and kiss—
He will not wake the while,
Thus dreaming of the bliss,
That bids thee, too, to smile.

III.

Think not, dear wife, I go,
With a light thought at my heart:
'Tis a pang akin to woe,
That fills me as we part;

But when the wolf was heard
  To howl around our lot,
Thou know'st, dear mother-bird,
  I slew him on the spot!

IV.

Aye, panther, wolf, and bear,
  Have perish'd 'neath my knife;
Why tremble, then, with fear,
  When now I go, my wife?
Shall I not keep the peace,
  That made our cottage dear;
And 'till these wolf-curs cease
  Shall I be housing here?

V.

One loving kiss, dear wife,
  One press of heart to heart;
Then for the deadliest strife,
  For freedom I depart!
I were of little worth,
  Were these Yankee wolves left free
To ravage 'round our hearth,
  And bring one grief to thee!

VI

God's blessing on thee, wife,
  God's blessing on the young:

Pray for me through the strife,
And teach our infant's tongue.
Whatever haps in fight,
I shall be true to thee—
To the home of our delight—
To my people of the free.

---

## THE CAMEO BRACELET.

BY JAMES R. RANDALL, OF MARYLAND.

Eva sits on the ottoman there,
Sits by a Psyche carved in stone,
With just such a face, and just such an air,
As Esther upon her throne.

She's sifting lint for the brave who bleed,
And I watch her fingers float and flow
Over the linen, as, thread by thread,
It flakes to her lap like snow.

A bracelet clinks on her delicate wrist,
Wrought, as Cellini's were at Rome,
Out of the tears of the amethyst,
And the wan Vesuvian foam.

And full on the bauble-crest alway—
A cameo image keen and fine—

Glares thy impetuous knife, Corday,
  And the lava-locks are thine!

I thought of the war-wolves on our trail,
  Their gaunt fangs sluiced with gouts of blood;
Till the Past, in a dead, mesmeric veil,
  Drooped with a wizard flood

Till the surly blaze through the iron bars
  Shot to the hearth with a pang and cry—
And a lank howl plunged from the Champ de Mars
  To the Column of July—

Till Corday sprang from the gem, I swear,
  And the dove-eyed damsel I knew had flown—
For Eva was not on the ottoman there,
  By the Psyche carved in stone.

She grew like a Pythoness flushed with fate,
  With the incantation in her gaze,
A lip of scorn—an arm of hate—
  And a dirge of the "Marseillaise!"

Eva, the vision was not wild,
  When wreaked on the tyrants of the land—
For you were transfigured to Nemesis, child,
  With the dagger in your hand!

## ZOLLICOFFER.

BY H. L. FLASH, OF ALABAMA.

FIRST in the fight, and first in the arms
Of the white-winged angels of glory,
With the heart of the South at the feet of God,
And his wounds to tell the story :

And the blood that flowed from his hero heart,
On the spot where he nobly perished,
Was drunk by the earth as a sacrament
In the holy cause he cherished.

In Heaven a home with the brave and blessed,
And, for his soul's sustaining,
The apocalyptic eyes of Christ—
And nothing on earth remaining,

But a handful of dust in the land of his choice,
A name in song and story,
And Fame to shout with her brazen voice,
"Died on the Field of Glory!"

## BEAUREGARD.

BY CATHARINE A. WARFIELD, OF MISSISSIPPI.

Let the trumpet shout once more,
Beauregard!
Let the battle-thunders roar,
Beauregard!
And again by yonder sea,
Let the swords of all the free
Leap forth to fight with thee,
Beauregard!

Old Sumter loves thy name,
Beauregard!
Grim Moultrie guards thy fame,
Beauregard!
Oh! first in Freedom's fight!
Oh! steadfast in the right!
Oh! brave and Christian Knight!
Beauregard!

St. Michael with his host,
Beauregard!
Encamps by yonder coast,
Beauregard!

And the Demon's might shall quail,
And the Dragon's terrors fail,
Were he trebly clad in mail,
Beauregard!

Not a leaf shall fall away,
Beauregard!
From the laurel won to-day,
Beauregard!
While the ocean breezes blow,
While the billows lapse and flow
O'er the Northman's bones below,
Beauregard!

Let the trumpet shout once more,
Beauregard!
Let the battle-thunders roar,
Beauregard!
From the centre to the shore,
From the sea to the land's core
Thrills the echo, evermore,
Beauregard!

---

## SOUTH CAROLINA.

1719. Colonial Revolution.
1763. Colonial History—Progress.
1776. American Revolution.
1812–15. Second War with Great Britain
1830–32. Nullification for State Rights.
1835–40. Florida War.
1847. Mexican War—Palmetto Regiment.
1860–61. Secession, and Third War for Independence.

My brave old Country! I have watched thee long
Still ever first to rise against the wrong;
To check the usurper in his giant stride,
And brave his terrors and abase his pride;
Foresee the insidious danger ere it rise,
And warn the heedless and inform the wise;
Scorning the lure, the bribe, the selfish game,
Which, through the office, still becomes the shame;
Thou stood'st aloof—superior to the fate
That would have wrecked thy freedom as a State.
In vain the despot's threat, his cunning lure;
Too proud thy spirit, and thy heart too pure;
Thou hadst no quest but freedom, and to be
In conscience well-assured, and people free.
The statesman's lore was thine, the patriot's aim,
These kept thee virtuous, and preserved thy fame;
The wisdom still for council, the brave voice,
That thrills a people till they all rejoice.
These were thy birthrights; and two centuries pass'd,
As, at the first, still find thee at the last;

Supreme in council, resolute in will,
Pure in thy purpose—independent still !

The great good counsels, the examples brave,
Won from the past, not buried in its grave,
Still warm your soul with courage—still impar
Wisdom to virtue, valor to the heart !
Still first to check th' encroachment—to declare
"Thus far ! no further, shall the assailant dare ;"
Thou keep'st thy ermine white, thy State secure,
Thy fortunes prosperous, and thy freedom sure ;
No glozing art deceives thee to thy bane ;
The tempter and the usurper strive in vain !
Thy spear's first touch unfolds the fiendish form,
And first, with fearless breast, thou meet'st the storm ;
Though hosts assail thee, thou thyself a host,
Prepar'st to meet the invader on the coast :
Thy generous sons contending which shall be
First in the phalanx, gathering by the sea ;
No dastard fear appals them, as they teach
How best to hurl the bolt, or man the breach !

Great Soul in little frame !—the hope of man
Exults, when such as thou art in the van !
Unshaken, unbeguiled, unslaved, unbought,
Thy fame shall brighten with each battle fought ;
True to the examples of the past, thou'lt be,
For the long future, best security.

CHARLESTON MERCURY. GOSSYPIUM.

# CAROLINA.

BY HENRY TIMROD.

I.

The despot treads thy sacred sands,
Thy pines give shelter to his bands,
Thy sons stand by with idle hands,
Carolina!
He breathes at ease thy airs of balm,
He scorns the lances of thy palm;
Oh! who shall break thy craven calm,
Carolina!
Thy ancient fame is growing dim,
A spot is on thy garment's rim;
Give to the winds thy battle hymn,
Carolina!

Call on thy children of the hill,
Wake swamp and river, coast and rill,
Rouse all thy strength and all thy skill,
Carolina!
Cite wealth and science, trade and art,
Touch with thy fire the cautious mart,
And pour thee through the people's heart,
Carolina!

Till even the coward spurns his fears,
And all thy fields, and fens, and meres,
Shall bristle like thy palm, with spears,
Carolina !

III.

Hold up the glories of thy dead ;
Say how thy elder children bled,
And point to Eutaw's battle-bed,
Carolina !
Tell how the patriot's soul was tried,
And what his dauntless breast defied ;
How Rutledge ruled, and Laurens died,
Carolina !
Cry ! till thy summons, heard at last,
Shall fall, like Marion's bugle-blast,
Re-echoed from the haunted past,
Carolina !

IV.

I hear a murmur, as of waves
That grope their way through sunless caves,
Like bodies struggling in their graves,
Carolina !
And now it deepens ; slow and grand
It swells, as rolling to the land
An ocean broke upon the strand,
Carolina !

Shout ! let it reach the startled Huns !
And roar with all thy festal guns !
It is the answer of thy sons,
Carolina !

V.

They will not wait to hear thee call ;
From Sachem's head to Sumter's wall
Resounds the voice of hut and hall,
Carolina !
No ! thou hast not a stain, they say,
Or none save what the battle-day
Shall wash in seas of blood away,
Carolina !
Thy skirts, indeed, the foe may part,
Thy robe be pierced with sword and dart,
They shall not touch thy noble heart,
Carolina !

VI.

Ere thou shalt own the tyrant's thrall,
Ten times ten thousand men must fall ;
Thy corpse may hearken to his call,
Carolina !
When by thy bier, in mournful throngs,
The women chant thy mortal wrongs,
'Twill be their own funereal songs,
Carolina !

From thy dead breast, by ruffians trod,
No helpless child shall look to God ;
All shall be safe beneath thy sod,
Carolina !

VII.

Girt with such wills to do and bear,
Assured in right, and mailed in prayer,
Thou wilt not bow thee to despair,
Carolina !
Throw thy bold banner to the breeze !
Front with thy ranks the threatening seas,
Like thine own proud armorial trees,
Carolina !
Fling down thy gauntlet to the Huns,
And roar the challenge from thy guns ;
Then leave the future to thy sons,
Carolina !

## MY MOTHER-LAND.

BY PAUL H. HAYNE.

"*Animis, Opibusque Parati.*"

My Mother-land! thou wert the first to fling
Thy virgin flag of freedom to the breeze,
The first to humble, in thy neighboring seas,
The imperious despot's power;
But long before that hour,
While yet, in false and vain imagining,
Thy sister nations would not own their foe,
And turned to jest thy warnings, though the low,
Deep, awful mutterings, that precede the throe
Of earthquakes, burdened all the ominous air;
While yet they paused in scorn,
Of fatal madness born,—
Thou, oh, my Mother! like a priestess bless'd
With wondrous vision of the things to come,
Thou couldst not calmly rest
Secure and dumb—
But from thy borders, with the sounds of drum
And trumpet, came the thrilling note, "Prepare!"
"Prepare for what?" thy careless sisters said;
"We see no threatening tempest overhead,
Only a few pale clouds, the west wind's breath
Will sweep away, or melt in watery death."

"Prepare!" the time grows ripe to meet our doom!
Alas! it was not till the thunder-boom
Of shell and cannon shocked the vernal day,
Which shone o'er Charleston Bay—
When the tamed "Stars and Stripes" before us bowed—
That startled, roused, the last scale fallen away
From blinded eyes, our SOUTH, erect and proud,
Fronted the issue, and, though lulled too long,
Felt her great spirit nerved, her patriot valor strong.

But darker days have found us—'gainst the horde
Of robber Northmen, who, with torch and sword,
Approach to desecrate
The sacred hearthstone and the Temple-gate—
Who would defile our fathers' graves, and cast
Their ashes to the blast—
Yea! who declare, "we will annihilate
The very bound-lines of your sovereign State"—
Against this ravening flood
Of foul invaders, drunk with lust and blood,
Oh! we,
Strong in the strength of God-supported might,
Go forth to give our foe no paltry fight,
Nor basely yield
To venal legions a scarce blood-dewed field—
But witness, Heaven! if such the need should be,
To make our fated land one vast Thermopylæ!

Death ! What of Death ?—
Can he who once drew honorable breath
In liberty's pure sphere,
Foster a sensual fear,
When death and slavery meet him face to face,
Saying : " Choose thou between us ; here, the grace
Which follows patriot martyrdom, and there,
Black degradation, haunted by despair."

Death ! What of Death ?—
The vilest reptiles, brutes or men, who crawl
Across their portion of this earthly ball,
Share life and motion with us ; would we strive
Like such to creep alive,
Polluted, loathsome, only that with sin
We still might keep our mortal breathings in ?

The very thought brings blushes to the cheek !
I hear all 'round about me murmurs run,
Hot murmurs, but soon merging into ONE
Soul-stirring utterance—hark ! the people speak :

" Our course is righteous, and our aims are just !
Behold, we seek
Not merely to preserve for noble wives
The virtuous pride of unpolluted lives,

To shield our daughters from the ruffian's hand,
And leave our sons their heirloom of command,
    In generous perpetuity of trust;
Not only to defend those ancient laws,
Which Saxon sturdiness and Norman fire
Welded forevermore with freedom's cause,
And handed scathless down from sire to sire—
Nor yet, our grand religion, and our Christ,
Undecked by upstart creeds and vulgar charms,
(Though these had sure sufficed
To urge the feeblest Sybarite to arms)—
But more than all, because embracing all,
Insuring all, SELF-GOVERNMENT, the boon
Our patriot statesmen strove to win and keep,
From prescient Pinckney and the wise Calhoun
    To him, that gallant Knight,
The youngest champion in the Senate hall,
Who, led and guarded by a luminous fate,
His armor, Courage, and his war-horse, Right,
Dared through the lists of eloquence to sweep
Against the proud Bois Guilbert of debate!*

---

* Everybody must remember the famous tournament scene in "Ivanhoe." Of course the author, in drawing a comparison between that chivalric battle and the contest upon "Foote's Resolutions" in the great Senatorial debate of 1832, would be understood as *not* pushing the comparison further than the *first* shock of arms between Bois Guilbert and his youthful opponent, which Scott tells us was the most spirited encounter of the day. Both the knights' lances were fairly broken, and they parted, with no decisive advantage on either side.

"There's not a tone from out the teeming past,
Uplifted once in such a cause as ours,
Which does not smite our souls
In long reverberating thunder-rolls,
From the far mountain-steeps of ancient story.
Above the shouting, furious Persian mass,
Millions arrayed in pomp of Orient powers,
Rings the wild war-cry of Leonidas
Pent in his rugged fortress of the rock;
And o'er the murmurous seas,
Compact of hero-faith and patriot bliss,
(For conquest crowns the Athenian's hope at last),
Come the clear accents of Miltiades,
Mingled with cheers that drown the battle-shock
Beside the wave-washed strand of Salamis.

"Where'er on earth the self-devoted heart
Hath been by worthy deeds exalted thus,
We look for proud exemplars; yet for us
    It is enough to know
*Our fathers left us freemen;* let us show
The will to hold our lofty heritage,
The patient strength to act our fathers' part—
Brothers on history's page,
We wait to write our autographs in gore,
To cast the morning brightness of our glory
    Beyond our day and hope,
The narrow limit of *one* age's scope,
    On Time's remotest shore!

"Yea! though our children's blood
Rain 'round us in a crimson-swelling flood,
Why pause or falter?—that red tide shall bear
The Ark that holds our shrined liberty,
Nearer, and yet more near
Some height of promise o'er the ensanguined sea.

"At last, the conflict done,
The fadeless meed of final victory won—
Behold! emerging from the rifted dark
Athwart a shining summit high in heaven,
That delegated Ark!
No more to be by vengeful tempests driven,
But poised upon the sacred mount, whereat
The congregated nations gladly gaze,
Struck by the quiet splendor of the rays
That circle Freedom's blood-bought Ararat!"

Thus spake the people's wisdom; unto me
Its voice hath come, a passionate augury!
Methinks the very aspect of the world
Changed to the mystic music of its hope.
For, lo! about the deepening heavenly cope
The stormy cloudland banners all are furled,
And softly borne above
Are brooding pinions of invisible love,
Distilling balm of rest and tender thought
From fairy realms, by fairy witchery wrought:

O'er the hushed ocean steal celestial gleams
  Divine as light that haunts a poet's dreams ;
  And universal nature, wheresoever
My vision strays—o'er sky, and sea, and river—
  Sleeps, like a happy child,
  In slumber undefiled,
A premonition of sublimer days,
  When war and warlike lays
  At length shall cease,
  Before a grand Apocalypse of Peace,
  Vouchsafed in mercy to all human kind—
  A prelude and a prophecy combined !

---

## JOE JOHNSTON.

BY JOHN R. THOMPSON.

ONCE more to the breach for the land of the West !
And a leader we give of our bravest and best,
  Of his State and his army the pride ;
Hope shines like the plume of Navarre on his crest,
  And gleams in the glaive at his side.

For his courage is keen, and his honor is bright
As the trusty Toledo* he wears to the fight,

---

* General Johnston carries with him a beautiful blade, recently presented to him, bearing the mark of the Royal Manufactory of Toledo, 1862.

Newly wrought in the forges of Spain ;
And this weapon, like all he has brandished for right,
Will never be dimmed by a stain.

He leaves the loved soil of Virginia behind,
Where the dust of his fathers is fitly enshrined,
Where lie the fresh fields of his fame ;
Where the murmurous pines, as they sway in the wind,
Seem ever to whisper his name.

The Johnstons have always borne wings on their spurs,
And their motto a noble distinction confers—
" Ever ready !" for friend or for foe—
With a patriot's fervor the sentiment stirs
The large, manly heart of our Joe.

We read that a former bold chief of the clan,
Fell, bravely defending the West, in the van,
On Shiloh's illustrious day ;
And with reason we reckon our Johnston's the man
The dark, bloody debt to repay.

There is much to be done ; if not glory to seek,
There's a just and terrible vengeance to wreak
For crimes of a terrible dye ;
While the plaint of the helpless, the wail of the weak,
In a chorus rise up to the sky.

For the Wolf of the North we once drove to his den,
That quailed with affright 'neath the stern glance of men,
With his pack has returned to the spoil;
Then come from the mountain, the hamlet, the glen,
And drive him again from your soil.

Brave-born Tennesseeans, so loyal, so true,
Who have hunted the beast in your highlands, of you
Our leader had never a doubt;
You will troop by the thousand the chase to renew,
The day that his bugles ring out.

But ye "Hunters," so famed, "of Kentucky" of yore,
Where now are the rifles that kept from your door
The wolf and the robber as well?
Of a truth, you have never been laggard before
To deal with a savage so fell.

Has the love you once bore to your country grown cold?
Has the fire on the altar died out? do you hold
Your lives than your freedom more dear?
Can you shamefully barter your birthright for gold,
Or basely take counsel of fear?

We will not believe it; Kentucky, the land
Of a Clay, will not tamely submit to the brand
That disgraces the dastard, the slave;

The hour of redemption draws nigh, is at hand,
Her own sons her own honor shall save!

Mighty men of Missouri, come forth to the call,
When the rush of your rivers, when tempests appal,
And the torrents their sources unseal;
And this be the watchword of one and of all—
"Remember the butcher, McNeil!"

Then once more to the breach for the land of the West;
Strike home for your hearths—for the lips you love best;
Follow on where your leader you see;
One flash of his sword, when the foe is hard pressed,
And the land of the West shall be free!

---

## OVER THE RIVER.

BY JANE T. H. CROSS.

PUBLISHED IN THE NASHVILLE CHRISTIAN ADVOCATE, 1861.

We hail your "stripes" and lessened "stars,"
As one may hail a neighbor;
Now forward move! no fear of jars,
With nothing but free labor;
And we will mind our slaves and farm,
And never wish you any harm,
But greet you—*over the river.*

The self-same language do we speak,
  The same dear words we utter;
Then let's not make each other weak,
  Nor 'gainst each other mutter;
But let each go his separate way,
And each will doff his hat, and say:
  "I greet you—over the river!"

Our flags, almost the same, unfurl,
  And nod across the border;
Ohio's waves between them curl—
  *Our stripe's a little broader;*
May yours float out on every breeze,
And, *in our wake,* traverse all seas—
  We greet you—over the river!

We part, as friends of years should part,
  With pleasant words and wishes,
And no desire is in our heart
  For Lincoln's loaves and fishes;
"Farewell," we wave you from afar,
We like you best—just where you are—
  And greet you—over the river!

## THE CONFEDERACY.

BY JANE T. H. CROSS.

PUBLISHED IN THE SOUTHERN CHRISTIAN ADVOCATE, 1864.

Born in a day, full-grown, our Nation stood,
  The pearly light of heaven was on her face ;
Life's early joy was coursing in her blood ;
  A thing she was of beauty and of grace.

She stood, a stranger on the great broad earth,
  No voice of sympathy was heard to greet
The glory-beaming morning of her birth,
  Or hail the coming of the unsoiled feet.

She stood, derided by her passing foes ;
  Her heart beat calmly 'neath their look of scorn ;
Their rage in blackening billows round her rose—
  Her brow, meanwhile, as radiant as the morn.

Their poisonous coils about her limbs are cast,
  She shakes them off in pure and holy ire,
As quietly as Paul, in ages past,
  Shook off the serpent in the crackling fire.

She bends not to her foes, nor to the world,
  She bears a heart for glory, or for gloom ;

But with her starry cross, her flag unfurled,
  She kneels amid the sweet magnolia bloom.

She kneels to Thee, O God, she claims her birth,
  She lifts to Thee her young and trusting eye,
She asks of Thee her place upon the earth—
  For it is Thine to give or to deny.

Oh, let *Thine* eye but recognize her right!
  Oh, let *Thy* voice but justify her claim!
Like grasshoppers are nations in Thy sight,
  And all their power is but an empty name.

Then listen, Father, listen to her prayer!
  Her robes are dripping with her children's blood;
Her foes around "like bulls of Bashan stare,"
  They fain would sweep her off, "as with a flood."

The anguish wraps her close around, like death,
  Her children lie in heaps about her slain;
Before the world she bravely holds her breath,
  Nor gives one utterance to a note of pain.

But 'tis not like Thee to forget the oppressed,
  Thou feel'st within her heart the stifled moan—
Thou Christ! Thou Lamb of God! oh, give her rest!
  For Thou hast called her!—is she not Thine own?

## PRESIDENT DAVIS.

BY JANE T. H. CROSS.

PUBLISHED IN THE NEW YORK NEWS, 1865.

The cell is lonely, and the night
Has filled it with a darker gloom;
The little rays of friendly light,
Which through each crack and chink found room
To press in with their noiseless feet,
All merciful and fleet,
And bring, like Noah's trembling dove,
God's silent messages of love—
These, too, are gone,
Shut out, and gone,
And that great heart is left alone.

Alone, with darkness and with woe,
Around him Freedom's temple lies,
Its arches crushed, its columns low,
The night-wind through its ruin sighs;
Rash, cruel hands that temple razed,
Then stood the world amazed!
And now those hands—ah, ruthless deeds!
Their captive pierce—his brave heart bleeds;
And yet no groan
Is heard, no groan!
He suffers silently, alone.

For all his bright and happy home,
He has that cell, so drear and dark,
The narrow walls, for heaven's blue dome,
The clank of chains, for song of lark;
And for the grateful voice of friends—
That voice which ever lends
Its charm where human hearts are found—
He hears the key's dull, grating sound;
No heart is near,
No kind heart near,
No sigh of sympathy, no tear!

Oh, dream not thus, thou true and good!
Unnumbered hearts on thee await,
By thee invisibly have stood,
Have crowded through thy prison-gate;
Nor dungeon bolts, nor dungeon bars,
Nor floating "stripes and stars,"
Nor glittering gun or bayonet,
Can ever cause us to forget
Our faith to thee,
Our love to thee,
Thou glorious soul! thou strong! *thou free!*

## THE RIFLEMAN'S "FANCY SHOT."

"RIFLEMAN, shoot me a fancy shot,
 Straight at the heart of yon prowling vidette;
Ring me a ball on the glittering spot
 That shines on his breast like an amulet."

"Ah, captain! here goes for a fine-drawn bead;
 There's music around when my barrel's in tune."
Crack! went the rifle; the messenger sped,
 And dead from his horse fell the ringing dragoon.

"Now, rifleman, steal through the bushes, and snatch
 From your victim some trinket to handsel first blood:
A button, a loop, or that luminous patch
 That gleams in the moon like a diamond stud."

"Oh, captain! I staggered, and sank in my track,
 When I gazed on the face of the fallen vidette;
For he looked so like you, as he lay on his back,
 That my heart rose upon me, and masters me yet.

"But I snatched off the trinket—this locket of gold;
 An inch from the centre my lead broke its way,
Scarce grazing the picture, so fair to behold,
 Of a beautiful lady in bridal array."

"Ha! rifleman! fling me the locket—'tis she!
My brother's young bride; and the fallen dragoon
Was her husband. Hush, soldier!—'twas heaven's decr
We must bury him there, by the light of the moon.

"But hark! the far bugles their warning unite;
War is a virtue, and weakness a sin;
There's a lurking and lopping around us to-night:
Load again, rifleman, keep your hand in!"

---

## "ALL QUIET ALONG THE POTOMAC TO-NIGHT."

BY LAMAR FONTAINE.

[The claim to the authorship of this poem, which Fontaine alleges, has been disputed in behalf of a lady of New York, but she herself continues silent on the subject.]

"All quiet along the Potomac to-night!"
Except here and there a stray picket
Is shot, as he walks on his beat, to and fro,
By a rifleman hid in the thicket.

'Tis nothing! a private or two now and then
Will not count in the news of a battle;

Not an officer lost! only one of the men
  Moaning out, all alone, the death-rattle.

All quiet along the Potomac to-night!
  Where soldiers lie peacefully dreaming;
And their tents in the rays of the clear autumn moon,
  And the light of their camp-fires are gleaming.

A tremulous sigh, as a gentle night-wind
  Through the forest leaves slowly is creeping;
While the stars up above, with their glittering eyes,
  Keep guard o'er the army while sleeping.

There's only the sound of the lone sentry's tread,
  As he tramps from the rock to the fountain,
And thinks of the two on the low trundle bed,
  Far away, in the cot on the mountain.

His musket falls slack, his face, dark and grim,
  Grows gentle with memories tender,
As he mutters a prayer for the children asleep,
  And their mother—"may heaven defend her!"

The moon seems to shine forth as brightly as then—
  That night, when the love, yet unspoken,

Leaped up to his lips, and when low-murmured vows
Were pledged to be ever unbroken.

Then drawing his sleeve roughly over his eyes,
He dashes off tears that are welling ;
And gathers his gun closer up to his breast,
As if to keep down the heart's swelling.

He passes the fountain, the blasted pine-tree,
And his footstep is lagging and weary ;
Yet onward he goes, through the broad belt of light,
Towards the shades of the forest so dreary.

Hark ! was it the night-wind that rustled the leaves ?
Was it moonlight so wondrously flashing ?
It looked like a rifle : "Ha ! Mary, good-by !"
And his life-blood is ebbing and splashing.

"All quiet along the Potomac to-night !"
No sound save the rush of the river ;
While soft falls the dew on the face of the dead,
And the picket's off duty forever !

## ADDRESS

DELIVERED AT THE OPENING OF THE NEW THEATRE AT RICHMOND.

A PRIZE POEM.—BY HENRY TIMROD.

A FAIRY ring
Drawn in the crimson of a battle-plain—
From whose weird circle every loathsome thing
And sight and sound of pain
Are banished, while about it in the air,
And from the ground, and from the low-hung skies,
Throng, in a vision fair
As ever lit a prophet's dying eyes,
Gleams of that unseen world
That lies about us, rainbow-tinted shapes
With starry wings unfurled,
Poised for a moment on such airy capes
As pierce the golden foam
Of sunset's silent main—
Would image what in this enchanted dome,
Amid the night of war and death
In which the armed city draws its breath,
We have built up!
For though no wizard wand or magic cup
The spell hath wrought,
Within this charmed fane we ope the gates
Of that divinest fairy-land
Where, under loftier fates

Than rule the vulgar earth on which we stand,
Move the bright creatures of the realm of thought.

Shut for one happy evening from the flood
That roars around us, here you may behold—
As if a desert way
Could blossom and unfold
A garden fresh with May—
Substantialized in breathing flesh and blood,
Souls that upon the poet's page
Have lived from age to age,
And yet have never donned this mortal clay.
A golden strand
Shall sometimes spread before you like the isle
Where fair Miranda's smile
Met the sweet stranger whom the father's art
Had led unto her heart,
Which, like a bud that waited for the light,
Burst into bloom at sight!
Love shall grow softer in each maiden's eyes
As Juliet leans her cheek upon her hand,
And prattles to the night.
Anon, a reverend form
With tatterèd robe and forehead bare,
That challenge all the torments of the air,
Goes by!
And the pent feelings choke in one long sigh,
While, as the mimic thunder rolls, you hear

The noble wreck of Lear
Reproach like things of life the ancient skies,
And commune with the storm!
Lo! next a dim and silent chamber, where
Wrapt in glad dreams, in which, perchance, the Moor
Tells his strange story o'er,
The gentle Desdemona chastely lies,
Unconscious of the loving murderer nigh.
Then through a hush like death
Stalks Denmark's mailed ghost!
And Hamlet enters with that thoughtful breath
Which is the trumpet to a countless host
Of reasons, but which wakes no deed from sleep;
For while it calls to strife,
He pauses on the very brink of fact
To toy as with the shadow of an act,
And utter those wise saws that cut so deep
Into the core of life!

Nor shall be wanting many a scene
Where forms of more familiar mien,
Moving through lowlier pathways, shall present
The world of every day,
Such as it whirls along the busy quay,
Or sits beneath a rustic orchard wall,
Or floats about a fashion-freighted hall,
Or toils in attics dark the night away.
Love, hate, grief, joy, gain, glory, shame, shall meet,

As in the round wherein our lives are pent;
    Chance for a while shall seem to reign,
While goodness roves like guilt about the street,
    And guilt looks innocent.
But all at last shall vindicate the right,
Crime shall be meted with its proper pain,
Motes shall be taken from the doubter's sight,
And fortune's general justice rendered plain.
Of honest laughter there shall be no dearth,
Wit shall shake hands with humor grave and sweet,
Our wisdom shall not be too wise for mirth,
Nor kindred follies want a fool to greet.
As sometimes from the meanest spot of earth
A sudden beauty unexpected starts,
So you shall find some germs of hidden worth
    Within the vilest hearts;
And now and then, when in those moods that turn
To the cold Muse that whips a fault with sneers,
You shall, perchance, be strangely touched to learn
    You've struck a spring of tears!

But while we lead you thus from change to change,
Shall we not find within our ample range
Some type to elevate a people's heart—
Some haro who shall teach a hero's part
    In this distracted time?
Rise from thy sleep of ages, noble Tell!
And, with the Alpine thunders of thy voice,

As if across the billows unenthralled,
Thy Alps unto the Alleghanies called,
          Bid liberty rejoice!
Proclaim upon this trans-Atlantic strand
The deeds which, more than their own awful mien,
Make every crag of Switzerland sublime!
And say to those whose feeble souls would lean
Not on themselves, but on some outstretched hand,
That once a single mind sufficed to quell
The malice of a tyrant; let them know
That each may crowd in every well-aimed blow,
Not the poor strength alone of arm and brand,
But the whole spirit of a mighty land!

Bid liberty rejoice! Aye, though its day
Be far or near, these clouds shall yet be red
With the large promise of the coming ray.
Meanwhile, with that calm courage which can smile
Amid the terrors of the wildest fray,
Let us among the charms of art awhile
          Fleet the deep gloom away;
Nor yet forget that on each hand and head
Rest the dear rights for which we fight and pray.

# THE BATTLE OF RICHMOND.

BY GEORGE HERBERT SASS, CHARLESTON, S. C.

"For they gat not the land in possession by their own sword; neither was it their own arm that helped them; but Thy right hand, and Thine arm, and the light of Thy countenance, because Thou hadst a favor unto them."—*Psalm* xliv. 3, 4.

I.

Now blessed be the Lord of Hosts through all our Southern land,
And blessed be His holy name, in whose great might we stand;
For He who loves the voice of prayer hath heard His people's cry,
And with His own almighty arm hath won the victory!
Oh, tell it out through hearth and home, from blue Potomac's wave
To those far waters of the West which hide De Soto's grave.

II.

Now let there be through all the land one grand triumphant cry,
Wherever beats a Southern heart, or glows a Southern sky;
For He who ruleth every fight hath been with us to-day,
And the great God of battles hath led the glorious fray;

Oh, then unto His holy name ring out the joyful song,
The race hath not been to the swift, the battle to the
strong.

*   *   *   *   *   *   *

III.

From royal Hudson's cliff-crowned banks, from proud Ohio's
flood,
From that dark rock in Plymouth's bay where erst the
pilgrims stood,
From East and North, from far and near, went forth the
gathering cry,
And the countless hordes came swarming on with fierce
and lustful eye.
In the great name of Liberty each thirsty sword is drawn;
In the great name of Liberty each tyrant presseth on.

IV.

Alas, alas! her sacred name is all dishonored now,
And blood-stained hands are tearing off each laurel from
her brow;
But ever yet rings out the cry, in loud and mocking tone,
Still in her holy shrine they strive to rear a despot's throne;
And pressing on with eager tread, they sweep across the
land,
To burn and havoc and destroy—a fierce and ruthless
band.

V.

I looked on fair Potomac's shore, and at my feet the while
The sparkling waves leaped gayly up to meet glad summer's smile;
And pennons gay were floating there, and banners fair to see,
A mighty host arrayed, I ween, in war's proud panoply;
And as I gazed a cry arose, a low, deep-swelling hum,
And loud and stern along the line broke in the sullen drum.

VI.

Onward, o'er fair Virginia's fields, through ranks of nodding grain,
With shout and song they sweep along, a gay and gallant train.
Oh, ne'er, I ween, had those broad plains beheld a fairer sight,
And clear and glad those skies of June shed forth their glorious light.
Onwards, yea, ever onwards, that mighty host hath passed,
And "On to Richmond!" is the cry which echoes on the blast.

VII.

I looked again, the rising sun shines down upon the moors,
And 'neath his beams rise ramparts high and frowning embrasures,

And on each proud abattis yawn, with menace stern and dread,
Grim-visaged messengers of death: the watchful sentry's tread
In measured cadence slowly falls; all Nature seems at ease,
And over all the Stars and Stripes are floating in the breeze.

VIII.

But far away another line is stretching dark and long,
Another flag is floating free where armed legions throng;
Another war-cry's on the air, as wakes the martial drum,
And onward still, in serried ranks, the Southern soldiers come,
And up to that abattis high the charging columns tread,
And bold and free the Stars and Bars are waving at their head.

IX.

They are on it! they are o'er it! who can stay that living flood?
Lo, ever swelling, rolleth on the weltering tide of blood.
Yet another and another is full boldly stormed and won,
And forward to the spoiler's camp the column presseth on.
Hurrah! hurrah! the field is won! we've met them man to man,
And ever still the Stars and Bars are riding in the van.

X.

They are flying! they are flying! and close upon their track
Comes our glorious "Stonewall" Jackson, with ten thousand at his back;
And Longstreet, too, and gallant Hill, and Rhodes, and brave Huger,*
And he whose name is worth a host, our bold, devoted Lee;
And back to where the lordly James his scornful billow rolls,
The recreant foe is fleeing fast—those men of dastard souls.

XI.

They are flying! they are flying! horse and foot, and bold dragoon,
In one refluent mass are mingled, 'neath the slowly waning moon;
And louder still the cry is heard, as borne upon the blast,
The shouts of the pursuing host are rising full and fast:
"On, on unto the river, 'tis our only chance for life!
We needs must reach the gunboats, or we perish in the strife!"

XII.

'Tis done! the gory field is ours; we've conquered in the fight!
And yet once more our tongues can tell the triumph of the right;

---

* Pronounced *Eujee.*

And humbled is the haughty foe, who our destruction
 sought,
For God's right hand and holy arm have great deliverance
 wrought.
Oh, then, unto His holy name ring out the joyful song—
The race has not been to the swift, the battle to the strong.

---

## THE GUERRILLAS: A SOUTHERN WAR-SONG.

BY S. TEACKLE WALLIS, OF MARYLAND.

"Awake! and to horse, my brothers!
 For the dawn is glimmering gray;
And hark! in the crackling brushwood
 There are feet that tread this way.

"Who cometh?" "A friend." "What tidings?"
 "O God! I sicken to tell,
For the earth seems earth no longer,
 And its sights are sights of hell!

"There's rapine and fire and slaughter,
 From the mountain down to the shore;
There's blood on the trampled harvest—
 There's blood on the homestead floor.

"From the far-off conquered cities
 Comes the voice of a stifled wail;
And the shrieks and moans of the houseless
 Ring out, like a dirge, on the gale.

"I've seen, from the smoking village,
 Our mothers and daughters fly;
I've seen where the little children
 Sank down, in the furrows, to die.

"On the banks of the battle-stained river
 I stood, as the moonlight shone,
And it glared on the face of my brother,
 As the sad wave swept him on.

"Where my home was glad, are ashes,
 And horror and shame had been there—
For I found, on the fallen lintel,
 This tress of my wife's torn hair.

"They are turning the slave upon us,
 And, with more than the fiend's worst art,
Have uncovered the fires of the savage
 That slept in his untaught heart.

"The ties to our hearths that bound him,
 They have rent, with curses, away,
And maddened him, with their madness,
 To be almost as brutal as they.

"With halter and torch and Bible,
 And hymns to the sound of the drum,
They preach the gospel of Murder,
 And pray for Lust's kingdom to come.

"To saddle! to saddle! my brothers!
Look up to the rising sun,
And ask of the God who shines there,
Whether deeds like these shall be done!

"Wherever the vandal cometh,
Press home to his heart with your steel,
And when at his bosom you cannot,
Like the serpent, go strike at his heel!

"Through thicket and wood go hunt him,
Creep up to his camp fireside,
And let ten of his corpses blacken
Where one of our brothers hath died.

"In his fainting, foot-sore marches,
In his flight from the stricken fray,
In the snare of the lonely ambush,
The debts that we owe him pay.

"In God's hand, alone, is judgment;
But He strikes with the hands of men,
And His blight would wither our manhood
If we smote not the smiter again.

"By the graves where our fathers slumber,
By the shrines where our mothers prayed,
By our homes and hopes and freedom,
Let every man swear on his blade,—

"That he will not sheath nor stay it,
Till from point to heft it glow
With the flush of Almighty vengeance,
In the blood of the felon foe."

They swore—and the answering sunlight
Leapt red from their lifted swords,
And the hate in their hearts made echo
To the wrath in their burning words.

There's weeping in all New England,
And by Schuylkill's banks a knell,
And the widows there, and the orphans,
How the oath was kept can tell.

---

## A FAREWELL TO POPE.

BY JOHN R. THOMPSON, OF VIRGINIA.

"Hats off" in the crowd, "Present arms" in the line!
Let the standards all bow, and the sabres incline—
Roll, drums, the Rogue's March, while the conqueror goes,
Whose eyes have seen only "the backs of his foes"—
Through a thicket of laurel, a whirlwind of cheers,
His vanishing form from our gaze disappears;
Henceforth with the savage Dacotahs to cope,
*Abiit, evasit, erupit*—John Pope.

He came out of the West, like the young Lochinvar,
Compeller of fate and controller of war,
*Videre et vincere,* simply to see,
And straightway to conquer Hill, Jackson and Lee ,
And old Abe at the White House, like Kilmansegg *père*,
With a monkeyish grin and beatified air,
" Seemed washing his hands with invisible soap,"
As with eager attention he listened to Pope.

He *came*—and the poultry was swept by his sword,
Spoons, liquors, and furniture went by the board ;
He *saw*—at a distance, the rebels appear,
And " rode to the front," which was strangely the rear ;
He *conquered*—truth, decency, honor full soon,
Pest, pilferer, puppy, pretender, poltroon ;
And was fain from the scene of his triumphs to slope.
Sure there never was fortunate hero like Pope.

He has left us his shining example to note,
And Stuart has captured his uniform coat ;
But 'tis puzzling enough, as his deeds we recall,
To tell on whose shoulders his mantle should fall ;
While many may claim to deserve it, at least,
From Hunter, the Hound, down to Butler, the Beast,
None else, we can say, without risking the trope,
But himself can be parallel ever to Pope.

Like his namesake the poet of genius and fire,
He gives new expression and force to *the lyre ;*

But in one little matter they differ, the two,
And differ, indeed, very widely, 'tis true—
While his verses gave great Alexaader his fame,
'Tis our hero's *re*verses accomplish the same ;
And fate may decree that the end of a rope
Shall award yet his highest position to Pope.

---

## SONNET.

### ON READING A PROCLAMATION FOR PUBLIC PRAYER.

SOUTH CAROLINIAN.

Oh ! terrible, this prayer in the market-place,
These advertised humilities—decreed
By proclamation, that we may be freed,
And mercy find for once, and saving grace,
Even while we forfeit all that made the race
Worthy of Heavenly favor—and profess
Our faith and homage only through duress,
And dread of danger which we dare not face.

All working that's done worthily is prayer—
And honest thought is prayer—the wish, the will
To mend our wnys, maintain our virtues still,
And, losing life, still keep our bosoms fair
In sight of God—with whom humility
And patient working can alone make free.

## BATTLE OF BELMONT.

BY J. AUGUSTINE SIGNAIGO.

FROM THE MEMPHIS APPEAL, DEC. 21, 1861.

I.

Now glory to our Southern cause, and praises be to God,
That He hath met the Southron's foe, and scourged him with his rod:
On the tented plains of Belmont, in their might the Vandals came,
And they gave unto destruction all they found, with sword and flame;
But they met a stout resistance from a little band that day,
Who swore nobly they would conquer, or return to mother clay.

II.

But the Vandals with presumption—for they came in all their might—
Gave free vent unto their *feelings*, for they thought to win the fight;
And they forced our little cohorts to the very river's brink,
With a breath between destruction and of life's remaining link:
When the cannon of McCown, belching fire from out its mouth,
Brought destruction to the Vandals and protection to the South.

III.

There was Pillow, Polk and Cheatham, who had sworn that
day on high
That field should see them conquer, or that field should see
them die ;
And amid the groan of dying and amid the battle's din,
Came the echo back from heaven, that they should that
battle win :
And amid the boom of cannons, and amid the clash of swords,
Came destruction to the foeman—and the vengeance was
the Lord's !

IV.

When the fight was raging hottest, came the wild and
cheering cry,
That brought terror to the foeman, and that raised our spirits
high !
It was "Cheatham !" "Cheatham !" "Cheatham !" that the
Vandals' ears did sting,
And our boys caught up the echo till it made the welkin ring ;
And the moment that the Hessians thought the fight was
surely won,
From the crackling of our rifles—*bravely* then they had to
run !

V.

Then they ran unto their transports in deep terror and dismay,
And their great grandchildren's children will be shamed to
name that day ;

For the woe they came to bring to the people of the South
Was returned tenfold to them at the cannon's booming
mouth:
And the proud old Mississippi ran that day a horrid flood,
For its banks were deeply crimsoned with the hireling
Northman's blood.

VI.

Let us think of those who fell there, fighting foremost with
the foe,
And who nobly struck for Freedom, dealing Tyranny a blow:
Like the ocean beating wildly 'gainst a prow of adamant,
Or the storm that keeps on bursting, but cannot destroy the
plant;
Brave Lieutenant Walker, wounded, still fought on the
bloody field,
Cheering on his noble comrades, ne'er unto the foe to yield!

VII.

None e'er knew him but to love him, the brave martyr to
his clime—
Now his name belongs to Freedom, to the very end of Time:
And the last words that he uttered will forgotten be by few:
"I have bravely fought them, mother—I have bravely
fought for you!"
Let his memory be green in the hearts who love the South,
And his noble deeds the theme that shall dwell in every
mouth.

VIII.

In the hottest of the battle stood a Vandal bunting rag,
Proudly to the breeze 'twas floating in defiance to our flag;
And our Southern boys knew well that, to bring that bunting down,
They would meet the angel death in his sternest, maddest frown;
But it could not gallant Armstrong, dauntless Vollmer, or brave Lynch,
Though ten thousand deaths confronted, from the task of honor flinch!

IX.

And they charged upon that bunting, guarded by grim-visaged Death,
Who had withered all around it with the blister of his breath;
But they plucked it from his grasp, and brave Vollmer waved it high,
On the gory field of battle, where the three were doomed to die;
But before their spirits fled came the death-shout of the three,
Cheering for the sunny South and beloved old Tennessee!

X.

Let the horrors of this day to the foe a warning be,
That the Lord is with the South, that His arm is with the free;
That her soil is pure and spotless, as her clear and sunny sky.
And that he who dare pollute it on her soil shall basely die;

For His fiat hath gone forth, e'en among the Hessian horde,
That the South has got His blessing, for the South is of the
Lord.

XI.

Then glory to our Southern cause, and praises give to God,
That He hath met the Southron's foe and scourged him with
His rod;
That He hath been upon our side, with all His strength and
might,
And battled for the Southern cause in every bloody fight;
Let us, in meek humility, to all the world proclaim,
We bless and glorify the Lord, and battle in His name.

---

## VICKSBURG—A BALLAD.

BY PAUL H. HAYNE.

I.

For sixty days and upwards,
A storm of shell and shot
Rained 'round us in a flaming shower,
But still we faltered not!
"If the noble city perish,"
Our grand young leader said,
"Let the only walls the foe shall scale
Be the ramparts of the dead!

II.

For sixty days and upwards
  The eye of heaven waxed dim,
And even throughout God's holy morn,
  O'er Christian's prayer and hymn,
Arose a hissing tumult,
  As if the fiends of air
Strove to ingulf the voice of faith
  In the shrieks of their despair.

III.

There was wailing in the houses,
  There was trembling on the marts,
While the tempest raged and thundered,
  'Mid the silent thrill of hearts ;
But the Lord, our shield, was with us,
  And ere a month had sped
Our very women walked the streets
  With scarce one throb of dread.

IV.

And the little children gambolled—
  Their faces purely raised,
Just for a wondering moment,
  As the huge bomb whirled and blazed !

Then turned with silvery laughter
To the sports which children love,
Thrice mailed in the sweet, instinctive thought,
That the good God watched above.

V.

Yet the hailing bolts fell faster,
From scores of flame-clad ships,
And about us, denser, darker,
Grew the conflict's wild eclipse,
Till a solid cloud closed o'er us,
Like a type of doom and ire,
Whence shot a thousand quivering tongues
Of forked and vengeful fire.

VI.

But the unseen hands of angels
Those death-shafts turned aside,
And the dove of heavenly mercy
Ruled o'er the battle tide ;
In the houses ceased the wailing,
And through the war-scarred marts
The people trode with the step of hope,
To the music in their hearts.

Columbia, S. C., August 6, 1862.

## A BALLAD OF THE WAR.

PUBLISHED ORIGINALLY IN THE SOUTHERN FIELD AND FIRESIDE.

BY GEORGE HERBERT SASS, OF CHARLESTON, S. C.

WATCHMAN, what of the night?
  Through the city's darkening street,
Silent and slow, the guardsmen go
  On their long and lonely beat.

Darkly, drearily down,
  Falleth the wintry rain ;
And the cold, gray mist hath the roof-tops kissed,
  As it glides o'er town and plain.

Beating against the windows,
  The sleet falls heavy and chill,
And the children draw nigher 'round hearth and fire,
  As the blast shrieks loud and shrill.

Silent is all without,
  Save the sentry's challenge grim,
And a hush sinks down o'er the weary town,
  And the sleeper's eyes are dim.

Watchman, what of the night?
  Hark ! from the old church-tower

Rings loud and clear, on the misty air,
The chime of the midnight hour.

But another sound breaks in,
A summons deep and rude,
The roll of the drum, and the rush and hum
Of a gathering multitude.

And the dim and flickering torch
Sheds a red and lurid glare,
O'er the long dark line, whose bayonets shine
Faintly, yet sternly there.

A low, deep voice is heard :
"Rest on your arms, my men."
Then the muskets clank through each serried rank,
And all is still again.

Pale faces and tearful eyes
Gaze down on that grim array,
For a rumor hath spread that that column dread
Marcheth ere break of day.

Marcheth against "the rebels,"
Whose camp lies heavy and still,
Where the driving sleet and the cold rain beat
On the brow of a distant hill.

And the mother's heart grows faint,
As she thinks of her darling one,
Who perchance may lie 'neath that wintry sky,
Ere the long, dark night be done.

Pallid and haggard, too,
Is the cheek of the fair young wife ;
And her eye grows dim as she thinks of him
She loveth more than life.

For fathers, husbands, sons,
Are the "rebels" the foe would smite,
And earnest the prayer for those lives so dear,
And a bleeding country's right.

And where their treasure is,
There is each loving heart ;
And sadly they gaze by the torches' blaze,
And the tears unbidden start.

Is there none to warn the camp,
None from that anxious throng ?
Ah, the rain beats down o'er plain and town—
The way is dark and long.

No *man* is left behind,
None that is brave and true,

And the bayonets, bright in the lurid light
With menace stern shine through.

Guarded is every street,
Brutal the hireling foe ;
Is there one heart here will boldly dare
So brave a deed to do?

Look ! in her still, dark room,
Alone a woman kneels,
With Care's deep trace on her pale, worn face,
And Sorrow's ruthless seals.

Wrinkling her placid brow,
A matron, she, and fair,
Though wan her cheek, and the silver streak
Gemming her glossy hair.

A moment in silent prayer
Her pale lips move, and then,
Through the dreary night, like an angel bright,
On her mission of love to men.

She glideth upon her way,
Through the lonely, misty street,
Shrinking with dread as she hears the tread
Of the watchman on his beat.

Onward, aye, onward still,
  Far past the weary town,
Till languor doth seize on her feeble knees,
  And the heavy hands hang down.

But bravely she struggles on,
  Breasting the cold, dank rain,
And, heavy and chill, the mist from the hill
  Sweeps down upon the plain.

Hark ! far behind she hears
  A dull and muffled tramp,
But before her the gleam of the watch-fire's beam
  Shines out from the Southern camp.

She hears the sentry's challenge,
  Her work of love is done ;
She has fought a good fight, and on Fame s proud height
  Hath a crown of glory won.

Oh, they tell of a Tyrol maiden,
  Who saved from a ruthless foe
Her own fair town, 'mid its mountains brown,
  Three hundred years ago.

And I've read in tales heroic
  How a noble Scottish maid

Her own life gave, her king to save
From the foul assassin's blade.

But if these, on the rolls of honor,
Shall live in lasting fame,
Oh, close beside, in grateful pride,
We'll write this matron's name.

And when our fair-haired children
Shall cluster round our knee,
With wondering gaze, as we tell of the days
When we swore that we would be free,

We'll tell them the thrilling story,
And we'll say to each childish heart,
"By this gallant deed, at thy country's need,
Be ready to do thy part."

---

## THE TWO ARMIES.

BY HENRY TIMROD.

Two armies stand enrolled beneath
The banner with the starry wreath:
One, facing battle, blight, and blast,
Through twice a hundred fields has passed;
Its deeds against a ruffian foe,
Stream, valley, hill, and mountain know,

Till every wind that sweeps the land
Goes, glory-laden, from the strand.

The other, with a narrower scope,
Yet led by not less grand a hope,
Hath won, perhaps, as proud a place,
And wears its fame with meeker grace.
Wives march beneath its glittering sign,
Fond mothers swell the lovely line:
And many a sweetheart hides her blush
In the young patriot's generous flush.

No breeze of battle ever fanned
The colors of that tender band;
Its office is beside the bed,
Where throbs some sick or wounded head.
It does not court the soldier's tomb,
But plies the needle and the loom;
And, by a thousand peaceful deeds,
Supplies a struggling nation's needs.

Nor is that army's gentle might
Unfelt amid the deadly fight;
It nerves the son's, the husband's hand,
It points the lover's fearless brand;
It thrills the languid, warms the cold,
Gives even new courage to the bold;

And sometimes lifts the veriest clod
To its own lofty trust in God.

When Heaven shall blow the trump of peace,
And bid this weary warfare cease,
Their several missions nobly done,
The triumph grasped, and freedom won,
Both armies, from their toils at rest,
Alike may claim the victor's crest,
But each shall see its dearest prize
Gleam softly from the other's eyes.

---

## THE LEGION OF HONOR.

BY H. L. FLASH.

Why are we forever speaking
Of the warriors of old?
Men are fighting all around us,
Full as noble, full as bold.

Ever working, ever striving,
Mind and muscle, heart and soul,
With the reins of judgment keeping
Passions under full control.

Noble hearts are beating boldly
As they ever did on earth ;
Swordless heroes are around us,
Striving ever from their birth.

Tearing down the old abuses,
Building up the purer laws,
Scattering the dust of ages,
Searching out the hidden flaws.

Acknowledging no "right divine"
In kings and princes from the rest ;
In their creed he is the noblest
Who has worked and striven best.

Decorations do not tempt them—
Diamond stars they laugh to scorn—
Each will wear a "Cross of Honor"
On the Resurrection morn.

Warriors they in fields of wisdom—
Like the noble Hebrew youth,
Striking down Goliath's error
With the God-blessed stone of truth.

Marshalled 'neath the Right's broad banner,
Forward rush these volunteers,

Beating olden wrong away
  From the fast advancing years.

Contemporaries do not see them,
  But the *coming* times will say
(Speaking of the slandered present),
  "There *were* heroes in that day."

Why are we then idly lying
  On the roses of our life,
While the noble-hearted struggle
  In the world-redeeming strife.

Let us rise and join the legion,
  Ever foremost in the fray—
Battling in the name of Progress
  For the nobler, purer day.

---

## CLOUDS IN THE WEST.

BY A. J. REQUIER, OF ALABAMA.

HARK! on the wind that whistles from the West
  A manly shout for instant succor comes,
From men who fight, outnumbered, breast to breast,
  With rage-indented drums!

Who dare for child, wife, country—stream and strand,
  Though but a fraction to the swarming foe,
There—at the flooded gateways of the land,
  To stem a torrent's flow.

To arms! brave sons of each embattled State,
  Whose queenly standard is a Southern star:
Who would be free must ride the lists of Fate
  On Freedom's victor-car!

Forsake the field, the shop, the mart, the hum
  Of craven traffic for the mustering clan:
The dead themselves are pledged that you shall come
  And prove yourself—a man.

That sacred turf where first a thrilling grief
  Was felt which taught you Heaven alone disposes—
God! can you live to see a foreign thief
  Contaminate its roses?

Blow, summoning trumpets, a compulsive stave
  Through all the bounds, from Beersheba to Dan;
Come out! come out! who scorns to be a slave,
  Or claims to be a man!

Hark! on the breezes whistling from the West
  A manly shout for instant succor comes,

From men who fight, outnumbered, breast to breast,
With rage-indented drums!

Who charge and cheer amid the murderous din,
Where still your battle-flags unbended wave,
Dying for what your fathers died to win
And you must fight to save.

Ho! shrilly fifes that stir the vales from sleep,
Ho! brazen thunders from the mountains hoar;
The very waves are marshalling on the deep,
While tempests tread the shore.

Arise and swear, your palm-engirdled land
Shall burial only yield a bandit foe;
Then spring upon the caitiffs, steel in hand,
And strike the fated blow.

---

## GEORGIA, MY GEORGIA!

BY CARRIE BELL SINCLAIR.

Hark! 'tis the cannon's deafening roar,
That sounds along thy sunny shore,
And thou shalt lie in chains no more,
My wounded, bleeding Georgia!
Then arm each youth and patriot sire,
Light up the patriotic fire,

And bid the zeal of those ne'er tire,
Who strike for thee, my Georgia !

On thee is laid oppression's hand,
Around thy altars foemen stand,
To scatter freedom's gallant band,
And lay thee low, my Georgia !
But thou hast noble sons, and brave,
The Stars and Bars above thee wave,
And here we'll make oppression's grave,
Upon the soil of Georgia !

We bow at Liberty's fair shrine,
And kneel in holy love at thine,
And while above our stars still shine,
We'll strike for them and Georgia !
Thy woods with victory shall resound,
Thy brow shall be with laurels crowned,
And peace shall spread her wings around
My own, my sunny Georgia !

Yes, these shall teach thy foes to feel
That Southern hearts, and Southern steel,
Will make them in submission kneel
Before the sons of Georgia !
And thou shalt see thy daughters, too,
With pride and patriotism true,

Arise with strength to dare and do,
Ere they shall conquer Georgia !

Thy name shall be a name of pride—
Thy heroes all have nobly died,
That thou mayst be the spotless bride
Of Liberty, my Georgia !
Then wave thy sword and banner high,
And louder raise the battle-cry,
'Till shouts of victory reach the sky,
And thou art free, my Georgia !

---

## SONG OF THE TEXAS RANGERS.

AIR—*The Yellow Rose of Texas.*

THE morning star is paling,
The camp-fires flicker low,
Our steeds are madly neighing,
For the bugle bids us go.
So put the foot in stirrup,
And shake the bridle free,
For to-day the Texas Rangers
Must cross the Tennessee.
With Wharton for our leader,
We'll chase the dastard foe,
Till our horses bathe their fetlocks
In the deep blue Ohio.

Our men are from the prairies,
  That roll broad and proud and free,
From the high and craggy mountains
  To the murmuring Mexic' sea ;
And their hearts are open as their plains,
  Their thoughts as proudly brave
As the bold cliffs of the San Bernard,
  Or the Gulf's resistless wave.

Then quick ! into the saddle,
  And shake the bridle free,
To-day, with gallant Wharton,
  We cross the Tennessee.

'Tis joy to be a Ranger !
  To fight for dear Southland ;
'Tis joy to follow Wharton,
  With his gallant, trusty band !
'Tis joy to see our Harrison,
  Plunge like a meteor bright
Into the thickest of the fray,
  And deal his deathly might.

Oh ! who'd not be a Ranger,
  And follow Wharton's cry !
To battle for his country—
  And, if it needs be—die !

By the Colorado's waters,
  On the Gulf's deep murmuring shore,
On our soft green peaceful prairies
  Are the homes we may see no more;
But in those homes our gentle wives,
  And mothers with silv'ry hairs,
Are loving us with tender hearts,
  And shielding us with prayers.

So, trusting in our country's God,
  We draw our stout, good brand,
For those we love at home,
  Our altars and our land.

Up, up with the crimson battle-flag—
  Let the blue pennon fly;
Our steeds are stamping proudly—
  They hear the battle-cry!
The thundering bomb, the bugle's call,
  Proclaim the foe is near;
We strike for God and native land,
  And all we hold most dear.

Then spring into the saddle,
  And shake the bridle free—
For Wharton leads, through fire and blood,
  For Home and Victory!

## KENTUCKY REQUIRED TO YIELD HER ARMS.

BY —— BOONE.

Ho ! will the despot trifle,
  In dwellings of the free ;
Kentuckians yield the rifle,
  Kentuckians bend the knee !
With dastard fear of danger;
  And trembling at the strife ;
Kentucky, to the stranger,
  Yield liberty for life !
Up ! up ! each gallant ranger,
  With rifle and with knife !

The bastard and the traitor,
  The wolfcub and the snake,
The robber, swindler, hater,
  Are in your homes—awake !
Nor let the cunning foeman
  Despoil your liberty;
Yield weapon up to no man,
  While ye can strike and see,
Awake, each gallant yeoman,
  If still ye would be free !

Aye, see to sight the rifle,
  And smite with spear and knife,

Let no base cunning stifle
  Each lesson of your life:
How won your gallant sires
  The country which ye keep?
By soul, which still inspires
  The soil on which ye weep!
Leap up! their spirit fires,
  And rouse ye from your sleep!

"What!" cry the sires so famous,
  In Orleans' ancient field,
"Will ye, our children, shame us,
  And to the despot yield?
What! each brave lesson stifle
  We left to give you life?
Let apish despots trifle
  With home and child and wife?
And yield, O shame! the rifle,
  And sheathe, O shame! the knife?"

---

## "THERE'S LIFE IN THE OLD LAND YET."

FIRST PUBLISHED IN THE NEW ORLEANS DELTA, ABOUT SEPTEMBER 1, 1861.

By blue Patapsco's billowy dash
  The tyrant's war-shout comes,
Along with the cymbal's fitful clash
  And the growl of his sullen drums;

We hear it, we heed it, with vengeful thrills,
  And we shall not forgive or forget—
There's faith in the streams, there's hope in the hills,
  "There's life in the Old Land yet!"

Minions! we sleep, but we are not dead,
  We are crushed, we are scourged, we are scarred—
We crouch—'tis to welcome the triumph-tread
  Of the peerless Beauregard.
Then woe to your vile, polluting horde,
  When the Southern braves are met;
There's faith in the victor's stainless sword,
  "There's life in the Old Land yet!"

Bigots! ye quell not the valiant mind
  With the clank of an iron chain;
The spirit of Freedom sings in the wind
  O'er Merryman, Thomas, and Kane;
And we—though we smite not—are not thralls,
  We are piling a gory debt;
While down by McHenry's dungeon walls
  "There's life in the Old Land yet!"

Our women have hung their harps away
  And they scowl on your brutal bands,
While the nimble poignard dares the day
  In their dear defiant hands;

They will strip their tresses to string our bows
  Ere the Northern sun is set—
There's faith in their unrelenting woes—
  "There's life in the Old Land yet!"

There's life, though it throbbeth in silent veins,
  'Tis vocal without noise;
It gushed o'er Manassas' solemn plains
  From the blood of the Maryland boys.
That blood shall cry aloud and rise
  With an everlasting threat—
By the death of the brave, by the God in the skies,
  "There's life in the Old Land yet!"

---

## TELL THE BOYS THE WAR IS ENDED.

BY EMILY J. MOORE.

While in the first ward of the Quintard Hospital, Rome, Georgia, a young soldier from the Eighth Arkansas Regiment, who had been wounded at Murfreesboro', called me to his bedside. As I approached I saw that he was dying, and when I bent over him he was just able to whisper, "Tell the boys the war is ended."

"Tell the boys the war is ended,"
  These were all the words he said;
"Tell the boys the war is ended,"
  In an instant more was dead.

Strangely bright, serene, and cheerful
  Was the smile upon his face,
While the pain, of late so fearful,
  Had not left the slightest trace.

"Tell the boys the war is ended,"
  And with heavenly visions bright
Thoughts of comrades loved were blended,
  As his spirit took its flight.
"Tell the boys the war is ended,"
  "Grant, O God, it may be so,"
Was the prayer which then ascended,
  In a whisper deep, though low.

"Tell the boys the war is ended,"
  And his warfare then was o'er,
As, by angel bands attended,
  He departed from earth's shore.
Bursting shells and cannons roaring
  Could not rouse him by their din;
He to better worlds was soaring,
  Far from war, and pain, and sin.

## "THE SOUTHERN CROSS."

BY ST. GEORGE TUCKER, OF VIRGINIA.

Oh! say can you see, through the gloom and the storm,
More bright for the darkness, that pure constellation?
Like the symbol of love and redemption its form,
As it points to the haven of hope for the nation.
How radiant each star, as the beacon afar,
Giving promise of peace, or assurance in war!
'Tis the Cross of the South, which shall ever remain
To light us to freedom and glory again!

How peaceful and blest was America's soil,
'Till betrayed by the guile of the Puritan demon,
Which lurks under virtue, and springs from its coil
To fasten its fangs in the life-blood of freemen.
Then boldly appeal to each heart that can feel,
And crush the foul viper 'neath Liberty's heel!
And the Cross of the South shall in triumph remain,
To light us to freedom and glory again!

'Tis the emblem of peace, 'tis the day-star of hope,
Like the sacred *Labarum* that guided the Roman;
From the shores of the Gulf to the Delaware's slope,
'Tis the trust of the free and the terror of foemen.
Fling its folds to the air, while we boldly declare
The rights we demand or the deeds that we dare!

While the Cross of the South shall in triumph remain,
To light us to freedom and glory again !

And if peace should be hopeless and justice denied,
And war's bloody vulture should flap its black pinions,
Then gladly "to arms," while we hurl, in our pride,
Defiance to tyrants and death to their minions !
With our front in the field, swearing never to yield,
Or return, like the Spartan, in death on our shield !
And the Cross of the South shall triumphantly wave,
As the flag of the free or the pall of the brave !

SOUTHERN LITERARY MESSENGER.

---

## ENGLAND'S NEUTRALITY.

### A PARLIAMENTARY DEBATE.

BY JOHN R. THOMPSON, OF RICHMOND, VIRGINIA.

ALL ye who with credulity the whispers hear of fancy,
Or yet pursue with eagerness hope's wild extravagancy,
Who dream that England soon will drop her long miscalled
neutrality,
And give us, with a hearty shake, the hand of nationality,

Read, as we give, with little fault of statement or omission,
The *next* debate in parliament on Southern Recognition ;

They're all so much alike, indeed, that one can write it off
I see,
As truly as the *Times'* report, without the gift of prophecy.

Not yet, not yet to interfere does England see occasion,
But treats our good commissioner with coolness and evasion;
Such coolness in the premises, that really 'tis refrigerant
To think that two long years ago she called us a belligerent.

But, further, Downing-street is dumb, the premier deaf to
reason,
As deaf as is the *Morning Post*, both in and out of season;
The working men of Lancashire are all reduced to beggary,
And yet they will not listen unto Roebuck or to Gregory,

"Or any other man," to-day, who counsels interfering,
While all who speak on t'other side obtain a ready hearing—
As, *par exemple*, Mr. Bright, that pink of all propriety,
That meek and mild disciple of the blessed Peace Society.

"Why, let 'em fight," says Mr. Bright, "those Southerners,
I hate 'em,
And hope the Black Republicans will soon exterminate 'em;

If freedom can't rebellion crush, pray tell me what's the use
of her?"
And so he chuckles o'er the fray as gleefully as Lucifer.

Enough of him—an abler man demands our close atten-
tion—
The Maximus Apollo of strict *non*-intervention—
With pitiless severity, though decorous and calm his tone,
Thus spake the "old man eloquent," the puissant Earl of
Palmerston :

"What though the land run red with blood, what though
the lurid flashes
Of cannon light, at dead of night, a mournful heap of ashes
Where many an ancient mansion stood—what though the
robber pillages
The sacred home, the house of God, in twice a hundred vil-
lages.

"What though a fiendish, nameless wrong, that makes re-
venge a duty,
Is daily done" (O Lord, how long!) "to tenderness and
beauty!"
(And who shall tell this deed of hell, how deadlier far a
curse it is
Than even pulling temples down and burning universities)?

"Let arts decay, let millions fall, aye, let freedom perish,
With all that in the western world men fain would love
and cherish;
Let universal ruin there become a sad reality:
We cannot swerve, we must preserve our rigorous neutrality."

Oh, Pam! oh, Pam! hast ever read what's writ in holy
pages,
How blessed the peace-makers are, God's children of the
ages?
Perhaps you think the promise sweet was nothing but a
platitude;
'Tis clear that *you* have no concern in that divine beatitude.

But "hear! hear! hear!" another peer, that mighty man
of muscle,
Is on his legs, what slender pegs! "ye noble Earl" of
Russell;
Thus might he speak, did not of speech his shrewd reserve
the folly see,
And thus unfold the subtle plan of England's secret policy.

"John Bright was right, yes, let 'em fight, these fools
across the water,
'Tis no affair at all of ours, their carnival of slaughter;

The Christian world, indeed, may say we ought not to allow
it, sirs,
But still 'tis music in our ears, this roar of Yankee howitzers.

"A word or two of sympathy, that costs us not a penny,
We give the gallant Southerners, the few against the many;
We say their noble fortitude of final triumph presages,
And praise, in Blackwood's Magazine, Jeff. Davis and his
messages.

"Of course we claim the shining fame of glorious Stonewall Jackson,
Who typifies the English race, a sterling Anglo-Saxon;
To bravest song his deeds belong, to Clio and Melpomene"—
(And why not for a British stream demand the Chickahominy?)

"But for the cause in which he fell we cannot lift a finger,
'Tis idle on the question any longer here to linger;
'Tis true the South has freely bled, her sorrows are Homeric, oh!
Her case is like to his of old who journeyed unto Jericho.

"The thieves have stripped and bruised, although as yet
they have not bound her,
We'd like to see her slay 'em all to right and left around her;

We shouldn't cry in parliament if Lee should cross the Raritan,
But England never yet was known to play the Good Samaritan.

"And so we pass the other side, and leave them to their glory,
To give new proofs of manliness, new scenes for song and story;
These honeyed words of compliment may possibly bamboozle 'em,
But ere we intervene, you know, we'll see 'em in—Jerusalem.

"Yes, let 'em fight, till both are brought to hopeless desolation,
Till wolves troop round the cottage door in one and t'other nation,
Till, worn and broken down, the South shall prove no more refractory,
And rust eats up the silent looms of every Yankee factory.

"Till bursts no more the cotton boll o'er fields of Carolina,
And fills with snowy flosses the dusky hands of Dinah;
Till war has dealt its final blow, and Mr. Seward's knavery
Has put an end in all the land to freedom and to slavery.

"The grim Bastile, the rack, the wheel, without remorse or
pity,
May flourish with the guillotine in every Yankee city;
No matter should old Abe revive the brazen bull of Phalaris,
'Tis no concern at all of ours"—(sensation in the galleries.)

"So shall our 'merry England' thrive on trans-Atlantic
troubles,
While India, on her distant plains, her crop of cotton
doubles;
And just so long as North or South shall show the least
vitality,
We cannot swerve, we must preserve our rigorous neutrality."

Your speech, my lord, might well become a Saxon legislator,
When the "fine old English gentleman" lived in a state of
natur',
When Vikings quaffed from human skulls their fiery
draughts of honey mead,
Long, long before the barons bold met tyrant John at Runnymede.

But 'tis a speech so plain, my lord, that all may understand it,
And so we quickly turn again to fight the Yankee bandit,
Convinced that we shall fairly win at last our nationality,
Without the help of Britain's arm, *in spite of* her neutrality.

ILLUSTRATED NEWS.

## CLOSE THE RANKS.

BY JOHN L. O'SULLIVAN.

THE fell invader is before!
  Close the ranks! Close up the ranks!
We'll hunt his legions from our shore,
  Close the ranks! Close up the ranks!
Our wives, our children are behind,
Our mothers, sisters, dear and kind,
Their voices reach us on the wind,
  Close the ranks! Close up the ranks!

Are we to bend to slavish yoke?
  Close the ranks! Close up the ranks!
We'll bend when bends our Southern oak.
  Close the ranks! Close up the ranks!
On with the line of serried steel,
We all can die, we none can kneel
To crouch beneath the Northern heel.
  Close the ranks! Close up the ranks!

We kneel to God, and God alone.
  Close the ranks! Close up the ranks!
One heart in all—all hearts as one.
  Close the ranks! Close up the ranks!

For home, for country, truth and right,
We stand or fall in freedom's fight :
In such a cause the right is might.
Close the ranks ! Close up the ranks !

We're here from every southern home.
Close the ranks ! Close up the ranks !
Fond, weeping voices bade us come.
Close the ranks ! Close up the ranks
The husband, brother, boy, and sire,
All burning with one holy fire—
Our country's love our only hire.
Close the ranks ! Close up the ranks !

We cannot fail, we will not yield !
Close the ranks ! Close up the ranks !
Our bosoms are our country's shield.
Close the ranks ! Close up the ranks !
By Washington's immortal name,
By Stonewall Jackson's kindred fame,
Their souls, their deeds, their cause the same,
Close the ranks ! Close up the ranks !

By all we hope, by all we love,
Close the ranks ! Close up the ranks !
By home on earth, by Heaven above,
Close the ranks ! Close up the ranks !

By all the tears, and heart's blood shed,
By all our hosts of martyred dead,
We'll conquer, or we'll share their bed.
  Close the ranks! Close up the ranks!

The front may fall, the rear succeed,
  Close the ranks! Close up the ranks!
We smile in triumph as we bleed,
  Close the ranks! Close up the ranks!
Our Southern Cross above us waves,
Long shall it bless the sacred graves
Of those who died, but were not slaves.
  Close the ranks! Close up the ranks!

---

## THE SEA-KINGS OF THE SOUTH.

BY EDWARD C. BRUCE, OF WINCHESTER, VA.

FULL many have sung of the victories our warriors have won,
From Bethel, by the eastern tide, to sunny Galveston,
On fair Potomac's classic shore, by sweeping Tennessee,
Hill, rock, and river shall tell forever the vengeance of the free.

The air still rings with the cannon-shot, with battle's breath is warm;
Still on the hills their swords have saved our legions wheel and form;

And Johnston, Beauregard, and Lee, with all their gallant
train,
Wait yet at their head, in silence dread, the hour to charge
again.

But a ruggeder field than the mountain-side—a broader field
than the plain,
Is spread for the fight in the stormy wave and the globe-
embracing main.
'Tis there the keel of the goodly ship must trace the fate of
the land,
For the name ye write in the sea-foam white shall first and
longest stand.

For centuries on centuries, since first the hallowed tree
Was launched by the lone mariner on some primeval sea,
No stouter stuff than the heart of oak, or tough elastic pine,
Had floated beyond the shallow shoal to pass the burning
Line.

The Naiad and the Dryad met in billow and in spar;
The forest fought at Salamis, the grove at Trafalgar.
Old Tubalcain had sweated amain to forge the brand and
ball;
But failed to frame the mighty hull that held enfortressed all.

Six thousand years had waited for our gallant tars to show
That iron was to ride the wave and timber sink below.

The waters bland that welcomed first the white man to our shore,
Columbus, of an iron world, the brave Buchanan bore.

Not gun for gun, but thirty to one, the odds he had to meet!
One craft, untried of wind or tide, to beard a haughty fleet!
Above her shattered relics now the billows break and pour;
But the glory of that wondrous day shall be hers for evermore.

See yonder speck on the mist afar, as dim as in a dream!
Anear it speeds, there are masts like reeds and a tossing plume of steam!
Fleet, fierce, and gaunt, with bows aslant, she dashes proudly on,
Whence and whither, her prey to gather, the foe shall learn anon.

Oh, broad and green is her hunting-park, and plentiful the game!
From the restless bay of old Biscay to the Carib' sea she came.
The catchers of the whale she caught; swift *Ariel* overhauled;
And made *Hatteras* know the hardest *blow* that ever a tar appalled.

She bears the name of a noble State, and sooth she bears it
well.
To us she hath made it a word of pride, to the Northern ear
a knell.
To the Puritan in the busy mart, the Puritan on his deck,
With "Alabama" visions start of ruin, woe, and wreck.

In vain his lubberly squadrons round her magic pathway
swoop—
Admiral, captain, commodore, in gunboat, frigate, sloop.
Save to snatch a prize, or a foe chastise, as their feeble art
she foils,
She will scorn a point from her course to veer, to baffle all
their toils.

And bravely doth her sister-ship begin her young career.
Already hath her gentle name become a name of fear;
The name that breathes of the orange-bloom, of soft lagoons
that roll
Round the home of the Roman of the West—the uncon-
quered Seminole.

Like the albatross and the tropic-bird, forever on the wing,
For them nor night nor breaking morn may peace nor
shelter bring.
All drooping from the weary cruise or shattered from the fight,
No dear home-haven opes to them its arms with welcome
bright.

Then side by side, in our love and pride, be our men of the
land and sea ;
The fewer these, the sterner task, the greater their guerdon
be !
The fairest wreaths of amaranth the fairest hands shall
twine
For the brows of our preux chevaliers, the Bayards of the
brine !

The "stars and bars" of our sturdy tars as gallantly shall
wave
As long shall live in the storied page, or the spirit-stirring
stave,
As hath the red cross of St. George or the raven-flag of
Thor,
Or flag of the sea, whate'er it be, that ever unfurled to war.

Then flout full high to their parent sky those circled stars
of ours,
Where'er the dark-hulled foeman floats, where'er his emblem
towers !
Speak for the right, for the truth and light, from the gun's
unmuzzled mouth,
And the fame of the Dane revive again, ye Vikings of the
South !

Richmond Sentinel, March 30, 1863.

## THE RETURN.

THREE years! I wonder if she'll know me?
  I limp a little, and I left one arm
At Petersburg; and I am grown as brown
  As the plump chestnuts on my little farm:
And I'm as shaggy as the chestnut burrs—
But ripe and sweet within, and wholly hers.

The darling! how I long to see her!
  My heart outruns this feeble soldier pace,
For I remember, after I had left,
  A little Charlie came to take my place.
Ah! how the laughing, three-year old, brown eyes—
His mother's eyes—will stare with pleased surprise!

Surely, they will be at the corner watching!
  I sent them word that I should come to-night:
The birds all know it, for they crowd around,
  Twittering their welcome with a wild delight;
And that old robin, with a halting wing—
I saved her life, three years ago last spring.

Three years! perhaps I am but dreaming!
  For, like the pilgrim of the long ago,
I've tugged, a weary burden at my back,
  Through summer's heat and winter's blinding snow;

Till now, I reach my home, my darling's breast,
There I can roll my burden off, and rest.
* * * * *

When morning came, the early rising sun
  Laid his light fingers on a soldier sleeping—
Where a soft covering of bright green grass
  Over two mounds was lightly creeping ;
But waked him not : his was the rest eternal,
Where the brown eyes reflected love supernal.

---

## OUR CHRISTMAS HYMN.

BY JOHN DICKSON BRUNS, M. D., OF CHARLESTON, S. C.

"Good-will and peace ! peace and good-will !"
  The burden of the Advent song,
What time the love-charmed waves grew still
  To hearken to the shining throng ;
The wondering shepherds heard the strain
  Who watched by night the slumbering fleece,
The deep skies echoed the refrain,
  "Peace and good-will, good-will and peace !"

And wise men hailed the promised sign,
  And brought their birth-gifts from the East,
Dear to that Mother as the wine
  That hallowed Cana's bridal feast ;

But what to these are myrrh or gold,
And what Arabia's costliest gem,
Whose eyes the Child divine behold,
The blessed Babe of Bethlehem.

"Peace and good-will, good-will and peace!"
They sing, the bright ones overhead;
And scarce the jubilant anthems cease
Ere Judah wails her first-born dead;
And Rama's wild, despairing cry
Fills with great dread the shuddering coast,
And Rachel hath but one reply,
"Bring back, bring back my loved and lost."

So, down two thousand years of doom
That cry is borne on wailing winds,
But never star breaks through the gloom,
No cradled peace the watcher finds;
And still the Herodian steel is driven,
And breaking hearts make ceaseless moan,
And still the mute appeal to heaven
Man answers back with groan for groan.

How shall we keep our Christmas tide?
With that dread past, its wounds agape,
Forever walking by our side,
A fearful shade, an awful shape;

Can any promise of the spring
  Make green the faded autumn leaf?
Or who shall say that time will bring
  Fair fruit to him who sows but grief?

Wild bells! that shake the midnight air
  With those dear tones that custom loves,
You wake no sounds of laughter here,
  Nor mirth in all our silent groves;
On one broad waste, by hill or flood,
  Of ravaged lands your music falls,
And where the happy homestead stood
  The stars look down on roofless halls.

At every board a vacant chair
  Fills with quick tears some tender eye,
And at our maddest sports appear
  Those well-loved forms that will not die.
We lift the glass, our hand is stayed–
  We jest, a spectre rises up—
And weeping, though no word is said,
  We kiss and pass the silent cup,

And pledge the gallant friend who keeps
  His Christmas-eve on Malvern's height,
And him, our fair-haired boy, who sleeps
  Beneath Virginian snows to-night;

While, by the fire, she, musing, broods
  On all that was and might have been,
If Shiloh's dank and oozing woods
  Had never drunk that crimson stain.

O happy Yules of buried years !
  Could ye but come in wonted guise,
Sweet as love's earliest kiss appears,
  When looking back through wistful eyes,
Would seem those chimes whose voices tell
  His birth-night with melodious burst,
Who, sitting by Samaria's well,
  Quenched the lorn widow's life-long thirst.

Ah ! yet I trust that all who weep,
  Somewhere, at last, will surely find
His rest, if through dark ways they keep
  The child-like faith, the prayerful mind :
And some far Christmas morn shall bring
  From human ills a sweet release
To loving hearts, while angels sing
  "Peace and good-will, good-will and peace !"

## CHARLESTON.

WRITTEN FOR THE CHARLESTON COURIER IN 1863.

BY MISS E. B. CHEESBOROUGH.

PROUDLY she stands by the crystal sea,
With the fires of hate around her,
But a cordon of love as strong as fate,
With adamant links surround her.
Let them hurl their bolts through the azure sky,
And death-bearing missiles send her,
She finds in our God a mighty shield,
And in heaven a sure defender.

Her past is a page of glory bright,
Her present a blaze of splendor,
You may turn o'er the leaves of the jewell'd tome,
You'll not find the word *surrender;*
For sooner than lay down her trusty arms,
She'd build her own funeral pyre,
And the flames that give her a martyr's fate
Will kindle her glory higher.

How the demons glare as they see her stand
In majestic pride serenely,
And gnash with the impotent rage of hate,
Creeping up slowly, meanly;

While she cries, "Come forth from your covered dens,
  All your hireling legions send me,
I'll bare my breast to a million swords,
  Whilst God and my sons defend me."

Oh, brave old town, o'er thy sacred form
  Whilst the fiery rain is sweeping,
May He whose love is an armor strong
  Embrace thee in tender keeping;
And when the red war-cloud has rolled away,
  Anoint thee with holy chrism,
And sanctified, chastened, regenerate, true,
  Thou surviv'st this fierce baptism.

---

## GATHERING SONG.

Air—Bonnie Blue Flag

BY ANNIE CHAMBERS KETCHUM.

Come, brothers! rally for the right!
  The bravest of the brave
Sends forth her ringing battle-cry
  Beside the Atlantic wave!
She leads the way in honor's path!
  Come, brothers, near and far,
Come rally 'round the Bonnie Blue Flag
  That bears a single star!

We've borne the Yankee trickery,
The Yankee gibe and sneer,
Till Yankee insolence and pride
Know neither shame nor fear ;
But ready now with shot and steel
Their brazen front to mar,
We hoist aloft the Bonnie Blue Flag
That bears a single star !

Now Georgia marches to the front,
And close beside her come
Her sisters by the Mexique Sea,
With pealing trump and drum !
Till, answering back from hill and glen
The rallying cry afar,
A Nation hoists the Bonnie Blue Flag
That bears a single star !

By every stone in Charleston Bay,
By each beleaguered town,
We swear to rest not, night nor day,
But hunt the tyrants down !
Till, bathed in valor's holy blood
The gazing world afar
Shall greet with shouts the Bonnie Blue Flag
That bears the cross and star !

## CHRISTMAS.

BY HENRY TIMROD, OF SOUTH CAROLINA.

How grace this hallowed day?
Shall happy bells, from yonder ancient spire,
Send their glad greetings to each Christmas fire
Round which the children play?

Alas! for many a moon,
That tongueless tower hath cleaved the Sabbath air,
Mute as an obelisk of ice aglare
Beneath an Arctic noon.

Shame to the foes that drown
Our psalms of worship with their impious drum.
The sweetest chimes in all the land lie dumb
In some far rustic town.

There, let us think, they keep,
Of the dead Yules which here beside the sea
They've ushered in with old-world, English glee,
Some echoes in their sleep.

How shall we grace the day?
With feast, and song, and dance, and antique sports,
And shout of happy children in the courts,
And tales of ghost and fay?

Is there indeed a door
Where the old pastimes, with their lawful noise,
And all the merry round of Christmas joys,
Could enter as of yore?

Would not some pallid face
Look in upon the banquet, calling up
Dread shapes of battle in the wassail cup,
And trouble all the place?

How could we bear the mirth,
While some loved reveller of a year ago
Keeps his mute Christmas now beneath the snow,
In cold Virginian earth?

How shall we grace the day?
Ah! let the thought that on this holy morn
The Prince of Peace—the Prince of Peace was born,
Employ us, while we pray!

Pray for the peace which long
Hath left this tortured land, and haply now
Holds its white court on some far mountain's brow,
There hardly safe from wrong.

Let every sacred fane
Call its sad votaries to the shrine of God,

And, with the cloister and the tented sod,
Join in one solemn strain !

With pomp of Roman form,
With the grave ritual brought from England's shore,
And with the simple faith which asks no more
Than that the heart be warm.

He, who till time shall cease,
Shall watch that earth, where once, not all in vain,
He died to give us peace, will not disdain
A prayer whose theme is—peace.

Perhaps, ere yet the spring
Hath died into the summer, over all
The land, the peace of His vast love shall fall
Like some protecting wing.

Oh, ponder what it means !
Oh, turn the rapturous thought in every way !
Oh, give the vision and the fancy play,
And shape the coming scenes !

Peace in the quiet dales,
Made rankly fertile by the blood of men ;
Peace in the woodland, and the lonely glen,
Peace in the peopled vales !

Peace in the crowded town,
Peace in a thousand fields of waving grain,
Peace in the highway and the flowery lane,
Peace on the wind-swept down!

Peace on the furthest seas,
Peace in our sheltered bays and ample streams,
Peace wheresoe'er our starry garland gleams,
And peace in every breeze!

Peace on the whirring marts,
Peace where the scholar thinks, the hunter roams,
Peace, God of Peace! peace, peace in all our homes,
And peace in all our hearts!

---

## A PRAYER FOR PEACE.

BY S. TEACKLE WALLIS, OF MARYLAND.

Peace! Peace! God of our fathers, grant us Peace!
Unto our cry of anguish and despair
Give ear and pity! From the lonely homes,
Where widowed beggary and orphaned woe
Fill their poor urns with tears; from trampled plains,
Where the bright harvest Thou has sent us rots—
The blood of them who should have garnered it
Calling to Thee—from fields of carnage, where

The foul-beaked vultures, sated, flap their wings
O'er crowded corpses, that but yesterday
Bore hearts of brothers, beating high with love
And common hopes and pride, all blasted now—
Father of Mercies ! not alone from these
Our prayer and wail are lifted. Not alone
Upon the battle's seared and desolate track,
Nor with the sword and flame, is it, O God,
That Thou hast smitten us. Around our hearths,
And in the crowded streets and busy marts,
Where echo whispers not the far-off strife
That slays our loved ones ; in the solemn halls
Of safe and quiet counsel—nay, beneath
The temple-roofs that we have reared to Thee,
And 'mid their rising incense—God of Peace !
The curse of war is on us. Greed and hate
Hungering for gold and blood ; Ambition, bred
Of passionate vanity and sordid lusts,
Mad with the base desire of tyrannous sway
Over men's souls and thoughts, have set their price
On human hecatombs, and sell and buy
Their sons and brothers for the shambles. Priests,
With white, anointed, supplicating hands,
From Sabbath unto Sabbath clasped to Thee,
Burn, in their tingling pulses, to fling down
Thy censers and Thy cross, to clutch the throats
Of kinsmen, by whose cradles they were born,
Or grasp the brand of Herod, and go forth
Till Rachel hath no children left to slay.

The very name of Jesus, writ upon
Thy shrines beneath the spotless, outstretched wings,
Of Thine Almighty Dove, is wrapt and hid
With bloody battle-flags, and from the spires
That rise above them angry banners flout
The skies to which they point, amid the clang
Of rolling war-songs tuned to mock Thy praise.

All things once prized and honored are forgot:
The freedom that we worshipped next to Thee;
The manhood that was freedom's spear and shield;
The proud, true heart; the brave, outspoken word,
Which might be stifled, but could never wear
The guise, whate'er the profit, of a lie;
All these are gone, and in their stead have come
The vices of the miser and the slave—
Scorning no shame that bringeth gold or power,
Knowing no love, or faith, or reverence,
Or sympathy, or tie, or aim, or hope,
Save as begun in self, and ending there.
With vipers like to these, oh! blessed God!
Scourge us no longer! Send us down, once more,
Some shining seraph in Thy glory glad,
To wake the midnight of our sorrowing
With tidings of good-will and peace to men;
And if the star, that through the darkness led
Earth's wisdom then, guide not our folly now,
Oh, be the lightning Thine Evangelist,

With all its fiery, forked tongues, to speak
The unanswerable message of Thy will.

Peace ! Peace ! God of our fathers, grant us peace !
Peace in our hearts, and at Thine altars ; Peace
On the red waters and their blighted shores ;
Peace for the 'leaguered cities, and the hosts
That watch and bleed around them and within ,
Peace for the homeless and the fatherless ;
Peace for the captive on his weary way,
And the mad crowds who jeer his helplessness ;
For them that suffer, them that do the wrong
Sinning and sinned against.—O God ! for all ;
For a distracted, torn, and bleeding land—
Speed the glad tidings ! Give us, give us Peace !

---

## THE BAND IN THE PINES.

(HEARD AFTER PELHAM DIED.)

BY JOHN ESTEN COOKE.

Oh, band in the pine-wood, cease !
Cease with your splendid call ;
The living are brave and noble,
But the dead were bravest of all !

They throng to the martial summons,
To the loud, triumphant strain ;

And the dear bright eyes of long-dead friends
  Come to the heart again !

They come with the ringing bugle,
  And the deep drum's mellow roar ;
Till the soul is faint with longing
  For the hands we clasp no more !

Oh, band in the pine-wood, cease !
  Or the heart will melt in tears,
For the gallant eyes and the smiling lips,
  And the voices of old years !

---

## AT FORT PILLOW.

FIRST PUBLISHED IN THE WILMINGTON JOURNAL, APRIL 25, 1864.

You shudder as you think upon
  The carnage of the grim report,
The desolation when we won
  The inner trenches of the fort.

But there are deeds you may not know,
  That scourge the pulses into strife ;
Dark memories of deathless woe
  Pointing the bayonet and knife.

The house is ashes where I dwelt,
  Beyond the mighty inland sea ;
The tombstones shattered where I knelt,
  By that old church at Pointe Coupee.

The Yankee fiends, that came with fire,
  Camped on the consecrated sod,
And trampled in the dust and mire
  The Holy Eucharist of God !

The spot where darling mother sleeps,
  Beneath the glimpse of yon sad moon,
Is crushed, with splintered marble heaps,
  To stall the horse of some dragoon.

God ! when I ponder that black day
  It makes my frantic spirit wince ;
I marched—with Longstreet—far away,
  But have beheld the ravage since

The tears are hot upon my face,
  When thinking what bleak fate befell
The only sister of our race—
  A thing too horrible to tell.

They say that, ere her senses fled,
  She rescue of her brothers cried ;

Then feebly bowed her stricken head,
  Too pure to live thus—so she died.

Two of those brothers heard no plea;
  With their proud hearts forever still—
John shrouded by the Tennessee,
  And Arthur there at Malvern Hill.

But I have heard it everywhere,
  Vibrating like a passing knell;
'Tis as perpetual as the air,
  And solemn as a funeral bell.

By scorched lagoon and murky swamp
  My wrath was never in the lurch;
I've killed the picket in his camp,
  And many a pilot on his perch.

With steady rifle, sharpened brand,
  A week ago, upon my steed,
With Forrest and his warrior band,
  I made the hell-hounds writhe and bleed.

You should have seen our leader go
  Upon the battle's burning marge,
Swooping, like falcon, on the foe,
  Heading the gray line's iron charge!

All outcasts from our ruined marts,
We heard th' undying serpent hiss,
And in the desert of our hearts
The fatal spell of Nemesis.

The Southern yell rang loud and high
The moment that we thundered in,
Smiting the demons hip and thigh,
Cleaving them to the very chin.

My right arm bared for fiercer play,
The left one held the rein in slack;
In all the fury of the fray
I sought the white man, not the black.

The dabbled clots of brain and gore
Across the swirling sabres ran;
To me each brutal visage bore
The front of one accursed man.

Throbbing along the frenzied vein,
My blood seemed kindled into song—
The death-dirge of the sacred slain,
The slogan of immortal wrong.

It glared athwart the dripping glaves,
It blazed in each avenging eye—
*The thought of desecrated graves,*
*And some lone sister's desperate cry!*

## FROM THE RAPIDAN—1864.

A LOW wind in the pines!
And a dull pain in the breast!
And oh! for the sigh of her lips and eyes—
One touch of the hand I pressed!

The slow, sad lowland wind,
It sighs through the livelong day,
While the splendid mountain breezes blow,
And the autumn is burning away.

Here the pines sigh ever above,
And the broomstraw sighs below;
And far from the bare, bleak, windy fields
Comes the note of the drowsy crow.

There the trees are crimson and gold,
Like the tints of a magical dawn,
And the slender form, in the dreamy days,
By the slow stream rambles on.

Oh, day that weighs on the heart!
Oh, wind in the dreary pines!
Does she think on me 'mid the golden hours,
Past the mountain's long blue lines?

The old house, lonely and still,
By the sad Shenandoah's waves,
Must be touched to-day by the sunshine's gleam,
As the spring flowers bloom on graves.

Oh, sunshine, flitting and sad,
Oh, wind, that forever sighs!
The hall may be bright, but my life is dark
For the sunshine of her eyes!

---

## SONG OF OUR GLORIOUS SOUTHLAND.

BY MRS. MARY WARE.

FROM THE SOUTHERN FIELD AND FIRESIDE.

I.

Oh, sing of our glorious Southland,
The pride of the golden sun!
'Tis the fairest land of flowers
The eye e'er looked upon.

Sing of her orange and myrtle
That glitter like gems above;
Sing of her dark-eyed maidens
As fair as a dream of love.

Sing of her flowing rivers—
  How musical their sound !
Sing of her dark green forests,
  The Indian hunting-ground.

Sing of the noble nation
  Fierce struggling to be free ;
Sing of the brave who barter
  Their lives for liberty !

II.

Weep for the maid and matron
  Who mourn their loved ones slain ;
Sigh for the light departed,
  Never to shine again :

'Tis the voice of Rachel weeping,
  That never will comfort know ;
'Tis the wail of desolation,
  The breaking of hearts in woe !

III.

Ah ! the blood of Abel crieth
  For vengeance from the sod !
'Tis a brother's hand that's lifted
  In the face of an angry God !

Oh! brother of the Northland,
We plead from our father's grave;
We strike for our homes and altars,
He fought to build and save!

A smouldering fire is burning,
The Southern heart is steeled—
Perhaps 'twill break in dying,
But never will it yield.

---

## SONNET.

BY PAUL H. HAYNE.

Rise from your gory ashes stern and pale,
Ye martyred thousands! and with dreadful ire,
A voice of doom, a front of gloomy fire,
Rebuke those faithless souls, whose querulous wail
Disturbs your sacred sleep!—"The withering hail
Of battle, hunger, pestilence, despair,
Whatever of mortal anguish man may bear,
We bore unmurmuring! strengthened by the mail
Of a most holy purpose!—then we died!—
Vex not our rest by cries of selfish pain,
But to the noblest measure of your powers
Endure the appointed trial! Griefs defied,
But launch their threatening thunderbolts in vain,
And angry storms pass by in gentlest showers!"

## HOSPITAL DUTIES.

CHARLESTON COURIER.

Fold away all your bright-tinted dresses,
  Turn the key on your jewels to-day,
And the wealth of your tendril-like tresses
  Braid back in a serious way ;
No more delicate gloves, no more laces,
  No more trifling in boudoir or bower,
But come with your souls in your faces
  To meet the stern wants of the hour.

Look around. By the torchlight unsteady
  The dead and the dying seem one—
What ! trembling and paling already,
  Before your dear mission's begun ?
These wounds are more precious than ghastly—
  Time presses her lips to each scar,
While she chants of that glory which vastly
  Transcends all the horrors of war.

Pause here by this bedside. How mellow
  The light showers down on that brow !
Such a brave, brawny visage, poor fellow !
  Some homestead is missing him now.

Some wife shades her eyes in the clearing,
  Some mother sits moaning distressed,
While the loved one lies faint but unfearing,
  With the enemy's ball in his breast.

Here's another—a lad—a mere stripling,
  Picked up in the field almost dead,
With the blood through his sunny hair rippling
  From the horrible gash in the head.
They say he was first in the action :
  Gay-hearted, quick-headed, and witty :
He fought till he dropped with exhaustion
  At the gates of our fair southern city.

Fought and fell 'neath the guns of that city,
  With a spirit transcending his years—
Lift him up in your large-hearted pity,
  And wet his pale lips with your tears.
Touch him gently ; most sacred the duty
  Of dressing that poor shattered hand !
God spare him to rise in his beauty,
  And battle once more for his land !

Pass on ! it is useless to linger
  While others are calling your care ;
There is need for your delicate finger,
  For your womanly sympathy there.

There are sick ones athirst for caressing,
  There are dying ones raving at home,
There are wounds to be bound with a blessing,
  And shrouds to make ready for some.

They have gathered about you the harvest
  Of death in its ghastliest view ;
The nearest as well as the furthest
  Is there with the traitor and true.
And crowned with your beautiful patience,
  Made sunny with love at the heart,
You must balsam the wounds of the nations,
  Nor falter nor shrink from your part.

And the lips of the mother will bless you,
  And angels, sweet-visaged and pale,
And the little ones run to caress you,
  And the wives and the sisters cry hail!
But e'en if you drop down unheeded,
  What matter? God's ways are the best:
You have poured out your life where 'twas needed,
  And he will take care of the rest.

## THEY CRY PEACE, PEACE, WHEN THERE IS NO PEACE.

BY MRS. ALETHEA S. BURROUGHS, OF GEORGIA.

THEY are ringing peace on my heavy ear—
No peace to my heavy heart!
They are ringing peace, I hear! I hear!
O God! how my hopes depart!

They are ringing peace from the mountain side;
With a hollow voice it comes—
They are ringing peace o'er the foaming tide,
And its echoes fill our homes.

They are ringing peace, and the spring-time blooms
Like a garden fresh and fair;
But our martyrs sleep in their silent tombs—
Do *they* hear that sound—do they hear?

They are ringing peace, and the battle-cry
And the bayonet's work are done,
And the armor bright they are laying by,
From the brave sire to the son.

And the musket's clang, and the soldier's drill,
And the tattoo's nightly sound;

We shall hear no more, with a joyous thrill,
Peace, peace, they are ringing round!

There are women, still as the stifled air
On the burning desert's track,
Not a cry of joy, not a welcome cheer—
And their brave ones coming back!

There are fair young heads in their morning pride,
Like the lilies pale they bow;
Just a memory left to the soldier's bride—
Ah, God! sustain her now!

There are martial steps that we may not hear!
There are forms we may not see!
Death's muster roll they have answered clear,
*They are free! thank God, they are free!*

Not a fetter fast, nor a prisoner's chain
For the noble army gone—
No conqueror comes o'er the heavenly plain—
Peace, *peace to the dead alone!*

They are ringing peace, but strangers tread
O'er the land where our fathers trod,
And our birthright joys, like a dream, have fled,
And *Thou!* where art *Thou,* O God!

They are ringing peace ! *not here, not here,*
  Where the victor's mark is set ;
Roll back to the North its mocking cheer—
  No peace to the Southland yet !

We may sheathe the sword, and the rifle-gun
  We may hang on the cottage wall,
And the bayonet brave, sharp duty done,
  From the soldier's arm it may fall.

But peace !—no peace ! till the same good sword,
  Drawn out from its scabbard be,
And the wide world list to my country's word,
  And the South ! oh, the South, be free !

CHARLESTON BROADSIDE.

---

## BALLAD—"WHAT ! HAVE YE THOUGHT ?"

CHARLESTON MERCURY.

I.

WHAT ! have ye thought to pluck
Victory from chance and luck,
Triumph from clamorous shout, without a will ?
Without the heart to brave
All peril to the grave,
And battle on its brink, unshrinking still ?

II.

And did ye dream success
Would still unvarying bless
Your arms, nor meet reverse in some dread field?
And shall an adverse hour
Make ye mistrust the power
Of virtue, in your souls, to make your enemy yield?

III.

Oh! from this dreary sleep
Arise, and upward leap,
Nor let your hearts grow palsied with dismay!
Fling out your banner high,
Still challenging the sky,
While thousand strong arms bear it on its way.

IV.

Forth, as a sacred band,
Sworn saviours of the land,
Chosen by God, the champions of the right!
And never doubt that *He*
Who *made* will *keep* ye free,
If thus your souls resolve to triumph in the fight!

V.

The felon foe, no more
Trampling the sacred shore,

Shall leave defiling footprint on the sod ;
Where, desperate in the strife,
Reckless of wounds and life,
Ye brave your myriad foes beneath the eye of God !

VI.

On brothers, comrades, men,
Rush to the field again ;
Home, peace, love, safety—freedom—are the prize !
Strike ! while an arm can bear
Weapon—and do not spare—
Ye break a felon bond in every foe that dies !

---

## MISSING.

In the cool, sweet hush of a wooded nook,
Where the May buds sprinkle the green old mound,
And the winds, and the birds, and the limpid brook,
Murmur their dreams with a drowsy sound ;
Who lies so still in the plushy moss,
With his pale cheek pressed on a breezy pillow,
Couched where the light and the shadows cross
Through the flickering fringe of the willow ?
Who lies, alas !
So still, so chill, in the whispering grass ?

A soldier clad in the Zouave dress,
  A bright-haired man, with his lips apart,
One hand thrown up o'er his frank, dead face,
  And the other clutching his pulseless heart,
Lies here in the shadows, cool and dim,
  His musket swept by a trailing bough,
With a careless grace in each quiet limb,
  And a wound on his manly brow ;
        A wound, alas !
Whence the warm blood drips on the quiet grass.

The violets peer from their dusky beds,
  With a tearful dew in their great, pure eyes ;
The lilies quiver their shining heads,
  Their pale lips full of a sad surprise ;
And the lizard darts through the glistening fern—
  And the squirrel rustles the branches hoary ;
Strange birds fly out, with a cry, to bathe
  Their wings in the sunset glory ;
        While the shadows pass
O'er the quiet face and the dewy grass.

God pity the bride who waits at home,
  With her lily cheeks and her violet eyes,
Dreaming the sweet old dreams of love,
  While her lover is walking in Paradise ;
God strengthen her heart as the days go by,
  And the long, drear nights of her vigil follow,

Nor bird, nor moon, nor whispering wind,
May breathe the tale of the hollow ;
Alas ! alas !
The secret is safe with the woodland grass.

---

## ODE—"SOULS OF HEROES."

CHARLESTON MERCURY.

Souls of heroes, ascended from fields ye have won,
Still smile on the conflict so greatly begun ;
Bring succor to comrade, to brother, to son
Now breasting the battle in ranks of the brave ;
And the dastard that loiters, the conflict to shun,
Pursue him with scorn to the grave !

II.

Pursue him with furies that goad to despair,
Hunt him out, where he crouches in crevice and lair,
Drive him forth, while the wife of his bosom cries—" There
Goes the coward that skulks, though his sister and wife
Tremble, nightly, in sleep, overshadowed by fear
Of a sacrifice dearer than life."

III.

There are thousands that loiter, of historied claim,
Who boast of the heritage shrined in each name—

Sting their souls to the quick, till they shrink from the shame
Which dishonors the names and the past of their boast;
Even now they may win the best guerdon of fame,
And retrieve the bright honors they've lost!

IV.

Even now, while their country is torn in the toils,
While the wild boar is raging to raven the spoils,
While the boa is spreading around us the coils
Which would strangle the freedom our ancestors gave;
But each soul must be quickened until it o'er-boils,
Every muscle be corded to save!

V.

Still the cause is the same which, in long ages gone,
Roused up your great sires, so gallantly known,
When, braving the tyrant, the sceptre and throne,
They rushed to the conflict, despising the odds;
Armed with bow, spear, and scythe, and with sling and with stone,
For their homes and their family gods

VI.

Shall we be less worthy the sacrifice grand,
The heritage noble we took at their hand,

The peace and the comfort, the fruits of the land ;
  And, sunk in a torpor as hopeless as base,
Recoil from the shock of the Sodomite band,
  That would ruin the realm and the race ?

VII.

Souls of heroes, ascended from fields ye have won,
Your toils are not closed in the deeds ye have done ;
Touch the souls of each laggard and profligate son,
  The greed and the sloth, and the cowardice shame ;
Till we rise to complete the great work ye've begun,
  And with freedom make conquest of fame !

---

## JACKSON.

BY H. L. FLASH, OF GALVESTON, FORMERLY OF MOBILE.

Not midst the lightning of the stormy fight,
Nor in the rush upon the vandal foe,
Did kingly death, with his resistless might,
        Lay the great leader low.

His warrior soul its earthly shackles broke,
In the full sunshine of a peaceful town :
When all the storm was hushed, the trusty oak
        That propped our cause went down.

Though his alone the blood that flecks the ground,
Recalling all his grand heroic deeds,
Freedom herself is writhing with the wound,
And all the country bleeds.

He entered not the nation's promised land,
At the red belching of the cannon's mouth:
But broke the house of bondage with his hand—
The Moses of the South!

O gracious God! not gainless in the loss;
A glorious sunbeam gilds the sternest frown;
And while his country staggers with the cross,
He rises with the crown!

MOBILE ADVERTISER AND REGISTER.

---

## CAPTAIN MAFFIT'S BALLAD OF THE SEA.

CHARLESTON MERCURY.

I.

THOUGH winds are high and skies are dark,
And the stars scarce show us a meteor spark;
Yet buoyantly bounds our gallant barque,
Through billows that flash in a sea of blue;
We are coursing free, like the Viking shark,
And our prey, like him, pursue!

II.

At each plunge of our prow we bare the graves,
Where, heedless of roar among winds and waves,
The dead have slept in their ocean caves,
Never once dreaming—as if no more
They hear, though the Storm-God ramps and raves
From the deeps to the rock-bound shore.

III.

Brave sailors were they in the ancient times,
Heroes or pirates—men of all climes,
That had never an ear for the Sabbath chimes,
Never once called on the priest to be shriven;
They died with the courage that still sublimes,
And, haply, may fit for Heaven.

IV.

Never once asking the when or why,
But ready, all hours, to battle and die,
They went into fight with a terrible cry,
Counting no odds, and, victors or slain,
Meeting fortune or fate with an equal eye,
Defiant of death and pain.

V.

Dread are the tales of the wondrous deep,
And well do the billows their secrets keep,

And sound should those savage old sailors sleep,
    If sleep they may after such a life;
Where every dark passion, alert and aleap,
    Made slumber itself a strife.

VI.

What voices of horror, through storm and surge,
Sang in the perishing ear its dirge,
As, raging and rending, o'er Hell's black verge,
    Each howling soul sank to its doom;
And what thunder-tones from the deeps emerge,
    As yawns for its prey the tomb!

VII.

We plough the same seas which the rovers trod,
But with better faith in the saving God,
And bear aloft and carry abroad
    The starry cross, our sacred sign,
Which, never yet sullied by crime or fraud,
    Makes light o'er the midnight brine.

VIII.

And we rove not now on a lawless quest,
With passions foul in the hero's breast,
Moved by no greed at the fiend's behest,
    Gloating in lust o'er a bloody prey;

But from tyrant robber the spoil to wrest,
And tear down his despot sway!

IX.

'Gainst the spawn of Europe, and all the lands,
British and German—Norway's sands,
Dutchland and Irish—the hireling bands
Bought for butchery—recking no rede,
But, flocking like vultures, with felon hands,
To fatten the rage of greed.

X.

With scath they traverse both land and sea,
And with sacred wrath we must make them flee;
Making the path of the nations free,
And planting peace in the heart of strife;
In the star of the cross, our liberty
Brings light to the world, and life!

XI.

Let Christendom cower 'neath Stripes and Stars,
Cloaking her shame under legal bars,
Not too moral for traffic, but shirking wars,
While the Southern cross, floating topmast high,
Though torn, perchance, by a thousand scars,
Shall light up the midnight sky!

## MELT THE BELLS.

F. Y. ROCKETT.—*Memphis Appeal.*

The following lines were written on General Beauregard's appeal to the people to contribute their bells, that they may be melted into cannon.

MELT the bells, melt the bells,
Still the tinkling on the plains,
And transmute the evening chimes
Into war's resounding rhymes,
That the invaders may be slain
By the bells.

Melt the bells, melt the bells,
That for years have called to prayer,
And, instead, the cannon's roar
Shall resound the valleys o'er,
That the foe may catch despair
From the bells.

Melt the bells, melt the bells,
Though it cost a tear to part
With the music they have made,
Where the friends we love are laid,
With pale cheek and silent heart,
'Neath the bells.

Melt the bells, melt the bells,
Into cannon, vast and grim,

And the foe shall feel the ire
From each heaving lungs of fire,
And we'll put our trust in Him
    And the bells.

Melt the bells, melt the bells,
And when foes no more attack,
And the lightning cloud of war
Shall roll thunderless and far,
We will melt the cannon back
    Into bells.

Melt the bells, melt the bells,
And they'll peal a sweeter chime,
And remind of all the brave
Who have sunk to glory's grave,
And will sleep thro' coming time
    'Neath the bells.

---

## JOHN PELHAM.

BY JAMES R. RANDALL.

JUST as the spring came laughing through the strife,
  With all its gorgeous cheer;
In the bright April of historic life
  Fell the great cannoneer.

The wondrous lulling of a hero's breath
His bleeding country weeps—
Hushed in the alabaster arms of death,
Our young Marcellus sleeps.

Nobler and grander than the Child of Rome,
Curbing his chariot steeds ;
The knightly scion of a Southern home
Dazzled the land with deeds.

Gentlest and bravest in the battle brunt,
The champion of the truth,
He bore his banner to the very front
Of our immortal youth.

A clang of sabres 'mid Virginian snow,
The fiery pang of shells—
And there's a wail of immemorial woe
In Alabama dells.

The pennon drops that led the sacred band
Along the crimson field ;
The meteor blade sinks from the nerveless hand
Over the spotless shield.

We gazed and gazed upon that beauteous face,
While 'round the lips and eyes,

Couched in the marble slumber, flashed the grace
  Of a divine surprise.

Oh, mother of a blessed soul on high!
  Thy tears may soon be shed—
Think of thy boy with princes of the sky,
  Among the Southern dead.

How must he smile on this dull world beneath,
  Fevered with swift renown—
He—with the martyr's amaranthine wreath
  Twining the victor's crown!

---

## "YE BATTERIES OF BEAUREGARD."

BY J. R. BARRICK, OF KENTUCKY.

"Ye batteries of Beauregard!"
  Pour your hail from Moultrie's wall;
Bid the shock of your deep thunder
  On their fleet in terror fall:
Rain your storm of leaden fury
  On the black invading host—
Teach them that their step shall never
  Press on Carolina's coast.

"Ye batteries of Beauregard!"
  Sound the story of our wrong;
Let your tocsin wake the spirit
  Of a people brave and strong;
Her proud names of old remember—
  Marion, Sumter, Pinckney, Greene;
Swell the roll whose deeds of glory
  Side by side with theirs are seen.

"Ye batteries of Beauregard!"
  From Savannah on them frown;
By the majesty of Heaven
  Strike their "grand armada" down;
By the blood of many a freeman,
  By each dear-bought battle-field,
By the hopes we fondly cherish,
  Never ye the victory yield.

"Ye batteries of Beauregard!"
  All along our Southern coast,
Let, in after-time, your triumphs,
  Be a nation's pride and boast;
Send each missile with a greeting
  To the vile, ungodly crew;
Make them feel they ne'er can conquer
  People to themselves so true.

"Ye batteries of Beauregard!"
By the glories of the past,
By the memory of old Sumter,
Whose renown will ever last,
Speed upon their vaunted legions
Volleys thick of shot and shell,
Bid them welcome, in your glory,
To their own appointed hell.

---

## "WHEN PEACE RETURNS."

PUBLISHED IN THE GRANADA PICKET.

BY OLIVIA TULLY THOMAS.

When "war has smoothed his wrinkled front,"
And meek-eyed peace returning,
Has brightened hearts that long were wont
To sigh in grief and mourning—
How blissful then will be the day
When, from the wars returning,
The weary soldier wends his way
To dear ones that are yearning.

To clasp in true love's fond embrace,
To gaze with looks so tender
Upon the war-worn form and face
Of Liberty's defender;

To count with pride each cruel scar,
That mars the manly beauty,
Of him who proved so brave in war,
So beautiful in duty.

When peace returns, throughout our land,
Glad shouts of welcome render
The gallant few of Freedom's band
Whose cry was "no surrender;"
Who battled bravely to be free
From tyranny's oppressions,
And won, for Southern chivalry,
The homage of all nations!

And when, again, in Southern bowers
The ray of peace is shining,
Her maidens gather fairest flowers,
And honor's wreaths are twining,
To bind the brows victorious
On many a field so gory,
Whose names, renowned and glorious,
Shall live in song and story,

Then will affection's tear be shed,
And pity, joy restraining,
For those, the lost, lamented dead,
Are all beyond our plaining;

They fell in manhood's prime and might;
    And we should not weep the story
That tells of Fame, a sacred light,
    Above each grave of glory!

---

## THE RIGHT ABOVE THE WRONG.

BY JOHN W. OVERALL.

In other days our fathers' love was loyal, full, and free,
For those they left behind them in the Island of the Sea;
They fought the battles of King George, and toasted him in song,
For then the Right kept proudly down the tyranny of Wrong.

But when the King's weak, willing slaves laid tax upon the tea,
The Western men rose up and braved the Island of the Sea;
And swore a fearful oath to God, those men of iron might,
That in the end the Wrong should die, and up should go the Right.

The King sent over hireling hosts—the Briton, Hessian, Scot—
And swore in turn those Western men, when captured, should be shot;

While Chatham spoke with earnest tongue against the hireling throng,
And mournfully saw the Right go down, and place given to the Wrong.

But God was on the righteous side, and Gideon's sword was out,
With clash of steel, and rattling drum, and freeman's thunder-shout;
And crimson torrents drenched the land through that long, stormy fight,
But in the end, hurrah! the Wrong was beaten by the Right!

And when again the foemen came from out the Northern Sea,
To desolate our smiling land and subjugate the free,
Our fathers rushed to drive them back, with rifles keen and long,
And swore a mighty oath, the Right should subjugate the Wrong.

And while the world was looking on, the strife uncertain grew,
But soon aloft rose up our stars amid a field of blue;
For Jackson fought on red Chalmette, and won the glorious fight,
And then the Wrong went down, hurrah! and triumph crowned the Right!

The day has come again, when men who love the beauteous South,
To speak, if needs be, for the Right, though by the cannon's mouth ;
For foes accursed of God and man, with lying speech and song,
Would bind, imprison, hang the Right, and deify the Wrong.

But canting knave of pen and sword, nor sanctimonious fool,
Shall never win this Southern land, to cripple, bind, and rule ;
We'll muster on each bloody plain, thick as the stars of night,
And, through the help of God, the Wrong shall perish by the Right.

---

## CARMEN TRIUMPHALE.

BY HENRY TIMROD.

Go forth and bid the land rejoice,
Yet not too gladly, oh my song !
Breathe softly, as if mirth would wrong
The solemn rapture of thy voice.

Be nothing lightly done or said
This happy day ! Our joy should flow
Accordant with the lofty woe
That wails above the noble dead.

Let him whose brow and breast were calm
While yet the battle lay with God,
Look down upon the crimson sod
And gravely wear his mournful palm ;

And him, whose heart still weak from fear
Beats all too gayly for the time,
Know that intemperate glee is crime
While one dead hero claims a tear.

Yet go thou forth, my song ! and thrill,
With sober joy, the troubled days ;
A nation's hymn of grateful praise
May not be hushed for private ill.

Our foes are fallen ! Flash, ye wires !
The mighty tidings far and nigh !
Ye cities ! write them on the sky
In purple and in emerald fires !

They came with many a haughty boast ;
Their threats were heard on every breeze ;
They darkened half the neighboring seas,
And swooped like vultures on the coast.

False recreants in all knightly strife,
Their way was wet with woman's tears ;

Behind them flamed the toil of years,
And bloodshed stained the sheaves of life.

They fought as tyrants fight, or slaves ;
God gave the dastards to our hands ;
Their bones are bleaching on the sands,
Or mouldering slow in shallow graves.

What though we hear about our path
The heavens with howls of vengeance rent ;
The venom of their hate is spent ;
We need not heed their fangless wrath.

Meantime the stream they strove to chain
Now drinks a thousand springs, and sweeps
With broadening breast, and mightier deeps,
And rushes onward to the main ;

While down the swelling current glides
Our ship of state before the blast,
With streamers poured from every mast,
Her thunders roaring from her sides.

Lord ! bid the frenzied tempest cease,
Hang out thy rainbow on the sea !
Laugh round her, waves ! in silver glee,
And speed her to the ports of peace !

## THE FIEND UNBOUND.

CHARLESTON MERCURY.

I.

No more, with glad and happy cheer,
And smiling face, doth Christmas come,
But usher'd in with sword and spear,
And beat of the barbarian drum!
No more, with ivy-circled brow,
And mossy beard all snowy white,
He comes to glad the children now,
With sweet and innocent delight.

II.

The merry dance, the lavish feast,
The cheery welcome, all are o'er:
The music of the viol ceased,
The gleesome ring around the floor.
No glad communion greets the hour,
That welcomes in a Saviour's birth,
And Christmas, to a hostile power,
Yields all the sway that made its mirth.

III.

The Church, like some deserted bride,
In trembling, at the Altar waits,

While, raging fierce on every side,
  The foe is thundering at her gates.
No ivy green, nor glittering leaves,
  Nor crimson berries, deck her walls :
But blood, red dripping from her eaves,
  Along the sacred pavement falls.

IV.

Her silver bells no longer chime
  In summons to her sacred home ;
Nor holy song at matin prime,
  Proclaims the God within the dome.
Nor do the fireside's happy bands
  Assemble fond, with greetings dear,
While Patriarch Christmas spreads his hands
  To glad with gifts and crown with cheer.

V.

In place of that belovèd form,
  Benignant, bland, and blessing all,
Comes one begirt with fire and storm,
  The raging shell, the hissing ball !
Type of the Prince of Peace, no more,
  Evoked by those who bear His name,
THE FIEND, in place of SAINT of yore,
  Now hurls around Satanic flame.

VI.

In hate,—evoked by kindred lands,
 But late beslavering with caress,
Lo, Moloch, dripping crimson, stands,
 And curses where he cannot bless.
He wings the bolt and hurls the spear,
 A *demon loosed*, that rends in rage,
Sends havoc through the homes most dear,
 And butchers youth and tramples age!

VII.

With face of Fox—with glee that grins,
 And apish arms, with fingers claw'd,
To snatch at all his brother wins,
 And straight secrete, with stealth and fraud;—
Lo! Mammon, kindred Demon, comes,
 And lurks, as dreading ill, in rear;
He blows the trumpet, beats the drums,
 Inflames the torch, and sharps the spear!

VIII.

And furious, following in their train,
 What hosts of lesser Demons rise;
Lust, Malice, Hunger, Greed and Gain,
 Each raging for its special prize.
Too base for freedom, mean for toil,
 And reckless all of just and right,

They rage in peaceful homes for spoil,
And where they cannot butcher, blight.

IX.

A Serpent lie from every mouth,
Coils outward ever,—sworn to bless ;
Yet, through the gardens of the South,
Still spreading evils numberless,
By locust swarms the fields are swept,
By frenzied hands the dwelling flames,
And virgin beds, where Beauty slept,
Polluted blush, from worst of shames.

X.

The Dragon, chain'd for thousand years,
Hath burst his bonds and rages free ;—
Yet, patience, brethren, stay your fears ;—
Loosed for "a little season,"* he

---

* "1. And I saw an Angel come down from Heaven, having the key of the bottomless pit and a great chain in his hand.

"2. And he laid hold on the Dragon, that Old Serpent, which is the Devil and Satan, and bound him a thousand years.

"And cast him into the bottomless pit, and shut him up, and set a seal upon him, that he should deceive the nations no more, till the thousand years should be fulfilled; and *after that he must be loosed a little season.*"—Rev. xx., v. 1–3.

Will soon, beneath th' Ithuriel sword,
  Of heavenly judgment, crush'd and driven,
Yield to the vengeance of the Lord,
  And crouch beneath the wrath of Heaven!

XI.

"A little season," and the Peace,
  That now is foremost in your prayers,
Shall crown your harvest with increase,
  And bless with smiles the home of tears;
Your wounds be healed; your noble sons,
  Unhurt, unmutilated—free—
Shall limber up their conquering guns,
  In triumph grand of Liberty!

XII.

A few more hours of mortal strife,—
  Of faith and patience, working still,
In struggle for the immortal life,
  With all their soul, and strength, and will;
And, in the favor of the Lord,
  And powerful grown by heavenly aid,
Your roof trees all shall be restored,
  And ye shall triumph in their shade.

## THE UNKNOWN DEAD.

BY HENRY TIMROD.

THE rain is plashing on my sill,
But all the winds of Heaven are still;
And so, it falls with that dull sound
Which thrills us in the churchyard ground,
When the first spadeful drops like lead
Upon the coffin of the dead.
Beyond my streaming window-pane,
I cannot see the neighboring vane,
Yet from its old familiar tower
The bell comes, muffled, through the shower.
What strange and unsuspected link
Of feeling touched has made me think—
While with a vacant soul and eye
I watch that gray and stony sky—
Of nameless graves on battle plains,
Washed by a single winter's rains,
Where, some beneath Virginian hills,
And some by green Atlantic rills,
Some by the waters of the West,
A myriad unknown heroes rest?
Ah! not the chiefs who, dying, see
Their flags in front of victory,
Or, at their life-blood's noblest cost
Pay for a battle nobly lost,
Claim from their monumental beds

The bitterest tears a nation sheds.
Beneath yon lonely mound—the spot,
By all save some fond few forgot—
Lie the true martyrs of the fight,
Which strikes for freedom and for right.
Of them, their patriot zeal and pride,
The lofty faith that with them died,
No grateful page shall further tell
Than that so many bravely fell ;
And we can only dimly guess
What worlds of all this world's distress,
What utter woe, despair, and dearth,
Their fate has brought to many a hearth.
Just such a sky as this should weep
Above them, always, where they sleep ;
Yet, haply, at this very hour,
Their graves are like a lover's bower ;
And Nature's self, with eyes unwet,
Oblivious of the crimson debt
To which she owes her April grace,
Laughs gayly o'er their burial place.

---

## ODE—"DO YE QUAIL?"

BY W. GILMORE SIMMS.

I.

Do ye quail but to hear, Carolinians,
The first foot-tramp of Tyranny's minions?

Have ye buckled on armor, and brandished the spear,
But to shrink with the trumpet's first peal on the ear?
Why your forts now embattled on headland and height,
Your sons all in armor, unless for the fight?
Did ye think the mere show of your guns on the wall,
And your shouts, would the souls of the heathen appal?
That his lusts and his appetites, greedy as Hell,
Led by Mammon and Moloch, would sink at a spell;—
Nor strive, with the tiger's own thirst, lest the flesh
Should be torn from his jaws, while yet bleeding afresh.

II.

For shame! To the breach, Carolinians!—
To the death for your sacred dominions!—
Homes, shrines, and your cities all reeking in flame,
Cry aloud to your souls, in their sorrow and shame;
Your greybeards, with necks in the halter—
Your virgins, defiled at the altar,—
In the loathsome embrace of the felon and slave,
Touch loathsomer far than the worm of the grave!
Ah! God! if you fail in this moment of gloom!
How base were the weakness, how horrid the doom!
With the fiends in your streets howling pæans,
And the Beast o'er another Orleans!

III.

Do ye quail, as on yon little islet
They have planted the feet that defile it?

Make its sands pure of taint, by the stroke of the sword,
And by torrents of blood in red sacrifice pour'd !
Doubts are Traitors, if once they persuade you to fear,
That the foe, in his foothold, is safe from your spear !
When the foot of pollution is set on your shores,
What sinew and soul should be stronger than yours ?
By the fame—by the shame—of your sires,
Set on, though each freeman expires ;
Better fall, grappling fast with the foe, to their graves,
Than groan in your fetters, the slaves of your slaves

IV.

The voice of your loud exultation
Hath rung, like a trump, through the nation,
How loudly, how proudly, of deeds to be done,
The blood of the sire in the veins of the son !
Old Moultrie and Sumter still keep at your gates,
And the foe in his foothold as patiently waits.
He asks, with a taunt, by your patience made bold,
If the hot spur of Percy grows suddenly cold—
Makes merry with boasts of your city his own,
And the Chivalry fled, ere his trumpet is blown ;
Upon them, O sons of the mighty of yore,
And fatten the sands with their Sodomite gore !

V.

Where's the dastard that cowers and falters
In the sight of his hearthstones and altars ?

With the faith of the free in the God of the brave,
Go forth ; ye are mighty to conquer and save !
By the blue Heaven shining above ye,
By the pure-hearted thousands that love ye,
Ye are armed with a might to prevail in the fight,
And an ægis to shield and a weapon to smite !
Then fail not, and quail not ; the foe shall prevail not :
With the faith and the will, ye shall conquer him still.
To the knife—with the knife, Carolinians,
For your homes, and your sacred dominions.

---

## ODE—"OUR CITY BY THE SEA."

BY W. GILMORE SIMMS.

I.

Our city by the sea,
As the rebel city known,
With a soul and spirit free
As the waves that make her zone,
Stands in wait for the fate
From the angry arm of hate ;
But she nothing fears the terror of his blow ;
She hath garrisoned her walls,
And for every son that falls,
She will spread a thousand palls
For the foe !

II.

Old Moultrie at her gate,
Clad in arms and ancient fame,
Grimly watching, stands elate
To deliver bolt and flame!
Brave the band, at command,
To illumine sea and land
With a glory that shall honor days of yore;
And, as racers for their goals,
A thousand fiery souls,
While the drum of battle rolls,
Line the shore.

III.

Lo! rising at his side,
As if emulous to share
His old historic pride,
The vast form of Sumter there!
Girt by waves, which he braves
Though the equinoctial raves,
As the mountain braves the lightning on his steep;
And, like tigers crouching round,
Are the tribute forts that bound
All the consecrated ground,
By the deep!

IV.

It was calm, the April noon,
When, in iron-castled towers,

Our haughty foe came on,
With his aggregated powers ;
All his might 'gainst the right,
Now embattled for the fight,
With Hell's hate and venom working in his heart ;
A vast and dread array,
Glooming black upon the day,
Hell's passions all in play,
With Hell's art.

V.

But they trouble not the souls
Of our Carolina host,*
And the drum of battle rolls,
While each hero seeks his post ;
Firm, though few, sworn to do,
Their old city full in view,
The brave city of their sires and their dead ;
There each freeman had his brood,
All the dear ones of his blood,
And he knew they watching stood,
In their dread !

VI.

To the bare embattled height,
Then our gallant colonel sprung—

* The battle of Charleston Harbor, April 7, 1863, was fought by South Carolina troops exclusively.

"Bid them welcome to the fight,"
Were the accents of his tongue—
"Music! band, pour out—grand—
The free song of Dixie Land!
Let it tell them we are joyful that they come!
Bid them welcome, drum and flute,
Nor be your cannon mute,
Give them chivalrous salute—
To their doom!"*

VII.

Out spoke an eager gun,
From the walls of Moultrie then;
And through clouds of sulph'rous dun,
Rose a shout of thousand men,
As the shot, hissing hot,
Goes in lightning to the spot—
Goes crashing wild through timber and through mail;
Then roared the storm from all,
Moultrie's ports and Sumter's wall—
Bursting bomb and driving ball—
Hell in hail!

---

* As the iron-clads approached Fort Sumter in line of battle, Col. Alfred Rhett, commandant of the post, mounting the parapet, where he remained, ordered the band to strike up the national air of "Dixie;" and at the same time, in addition to the Confederate flag, the State and regimental flags were flung out at different salients of the fort, and saluted with thirteen guns.

VIII.

Full a hundred cannon roared
The dread welcome to the foe,
And his felon spirit cowered,
As he crouched beneath the blow!
As each side opened wide
To the iron and the tide,
He lost his faith in armor and in art;
And, with the loss of faith,
Came the dread of wounds and scath—
And the felon fear of death
Wrung his heart!

IX.

Quenched then his foul desires;
In his mortal pain and fear,
How feeble grew his fires,
How stayed his fell career!
How each keel, made to reel
'Neath our thunder, seems to kneel,
Their turrets staggering wildly, to and fro, blind and lame;
Ironsides and iron roof,
Held no longer bullet-proof,
Steal away, shrink aloof,
In their shame!

X.

But our lightnings follow fast,
  With a vengeance sharp and hot;
Our bolts are on the blast,
  And they rive with shell and shot!
Huge the form which they warm
With the hot breath of the storm;
Dread the crash which follows as each Titan mass is struck—
They shiver as they fly,
While their leader, drifting nigh,
Sinks, choking with the cry—
  "Keokuk!"

XI.

To the brave old city, joy!
  For that the hostile race,
Commissioned to destroy,
  Hath fled in sore disgrace!
That our sons, at their guns,
Have beat back the modern Huns—
Have maintained their household fanes and their fires;
And free from taint and scath,
Have kept the fame and faith
(And will keep, through blood and death)
  Of their sires!

XII.

To the Lord of Hosts the glory,
For His the arm and might,
That have writ for us the story,
And have borne us through the fight!
His our shield in that field—
Voice that bade us never yield;
Oh! had he not been with us through the terrors of that day?
His strength hath made us strong,
Cheered the right and crushed the wrong,
To His temple let us throng—
PRAISE AND PRAY!

---

## THE LONE SENTRY.

BY JAMES R. RANDALL.

Previous to the first battle of Manassas, when the troops under Stonewall Jackson had made a forced march, on halting at night they fell on the ground exhausted and faint. The hour arrived for setting the watch for the night. The officer of the day went to the general's tent, and said:

"General, the men are all wearied, and there is not one but is asleep. Shall I wake them?"

"No," said the noble Jackson; "let them sleep, and I will watch the camp to-night."

And all night long he rode round that lonely camp, the one lone sentinel for that brave, but weary and silent body of Virginia heroes. And when glorious morning broke, the soldiers awoke fresh and ready for action, all unconscious of the noble vigils kept over their slumbers.

'Twas in the dying of the day,
The darkness grew so still;
The drowsy pipe of evening birds
Was hushed upon the hill;
Athwart the shadows of the vale
Slumbered the men of might,
And one lone sentry paced his rounds,
To watch the camp that night.

A grave and solemn man was he,
With deep and sombre brow;
The dreamful eyes seemed hoarding up
Some unaccomplished vow.
The wistful glance peered o'er the plains
Beneath the starry light—
And with the murmured name of God,
He watched the camp that night.

The Future opened unto him
Its grand and awful scroll:
Manassas and the Valley march
Came heaving o'er his soul—
Richmond and Sharpsburg thundered by
With that tremendous fight
Which gave him to the angel hosts
Who watched the camp that night.

We mourn for him who died for us,
  With one resistless moan;
While up the Valley of the Lord
  He marches to the Throne!
He kept the faith of men and saints
  Sublime, and pure, and bright—
He sleeps—and all is well with him
  Who watched the camp that night.

Brothers! the Midnight of the Cause
  Is shrouded in our fate;
The demon Goths pollute our halls
  With fire, and lust, and hate.
Be strong—be valiant—be assured—
  Strike home for Heaven and Right!
*The soul of Jackson stalks abroad,*
  *And guards the camp to-night!*

---

## TO MY SOLDIER BROTHER.

BY SALLIE E. BALLARD, OF TEXAS.

When softly gathering shades of ev'n
Creep o'er the prairies broad and green,
And countless stars bespangle heav'n,
And fringe the clouds with silv'ry sheen,
My fondest sigh to thee is giv'n,

My lonely wand'ring soldier boy ;
    And thoughts of thee
    Steal over me
Like ev'ning shades, my soldier boy.

My brother, though thou'rt far away,
And dangers hurtle round thy path,
And battle lightnings o'er thee play,
And thunders peal in awful wrath,
Think, whilst thou'rt in the hot affray,
Thy sister prays for thee, my boy.
    If fondest prayer
    Can shield thee there
Sweet angels guard my soldier boy.

Thy proud young heart is beating high
To clash of arms and cannons' roar ;
That firm-set lip and flashing eye
Tell how thy heart is brimming o'er.
Be free and live, be free or die ;
Be that thy motto now, my boy ;
    And though thy name's
    Unknown to fame's,
'Tis graven on my heart, my boy.

## SEA-WEEDS.

WRITTEN IN EXILE.

BY ANNIE CHAMBERS KETCHUM.

Friend of the thoughtful mind and gentle heart!
  Beneath the citron-tree—
Deep calling to my soul's profounder deep—
  I hear the Mexique Sea.

While through the night rides in the spectral surf
  Along the spectral sands,
And all the air vibrates, as if from harps
  Touched by phantasmal hands.

Bright in the moon the red pomegranate flowers
  Lean to the Yucca's bells,
While with her chrism of dew, sad Midnight fills
  The milk-white asphodels.

Watching all night—as I have done before—
  I count the stars that set,
Each writing on my soul some memory deep
  Of Pleasure or Regret;

Till, wild with heart-break, toward the East I turn,
  Waiting for dawn of day;—

And chanting sea, and asphodel and star
  Are faded, all, away.

Only within my trembling, trembling hands—
  Brought unto me by thee—
I clasp these beautiful and fragile things,
  Bright sea-weeds from the sea,

Fair bloom the flowers beneath these Northern skies,
  Pure shine the stars by night,
And grandly sing the grand Atlantic waves
  In thunder-throated might ;

But, as the sea-shell in her chambers keeps
  The murmur of the sea,
So the deep-echoing memories of my home
  Will not depart from me.

Prone on the page they lie, these gentle things !
  As I have seen them cast
Like a drowned woman's hair, along the beach,
  When storms were over-past ;

Prone, like mine own affections, cast ashore
  In Battle's storm and blight ;
Would *they* had died, like sea-weeds ! Pray forgive me,
  But I must weep to-night.

Tell me again, of Summer fields made fair
  By Spring's precursing plough ;
Of joyful reapers, gathering tear-sown harvests—
  Talk to me,—will you ?—now !

---

## THE SALKEHATCHIE.

BY EMILY J. MOORE.

Written when a garrison, at or near Salkehatchie Bridge, were threatening a raid up in the Fork of Big and Little Salkehatchie.

THE crystal streams, the pearly streams,
  The streams in sunbeams flashing,
The murm'ring streams, the gentle streams,
  The streams down mountains dashing,
    Have been the theme
    Of poets' dream,
  And, in wild witching story,
Have been renowned for love's fond scenes,
  Or some great deed of glory.

The Rhine, the Tiber, Ayr, and Tweed,
  The Arno, silver-flowing,
The Hudson, Charles, Potomac, Dan,
  With poesy are glowing ;

But I would praise
In artless lays,
A stream which well may match ye,
Though dark its waters glide along
The swampy Salkehatchie.

'Tis not the beauty of its stream,
Which makes it so deserving
Of honor at the Muses' hands,
But 'tis the use it's serving,
And 'gainst a raid,
We hope its aid
Will ever prove efficient,
Its fords remain still overflowed,
In water ne'er deficient.

If Vandal bands are held in check,
Their crossing thus prevented,
And we are spared the ravage wild
Their malice has invented,
Then we may well
In numbers tell
No other stream can match ye,
And grateful we shall ever be
To swampy Salkehatchie.

## THE BROKEN MUG.

ODE (SO-CALLED) ON A LATE MELANCHOLY ACCIDENT IN THE SHENANDOAH VALLEY (SO-CALLED.)

JOHN ESTEN COOKE.

My mug is broken, my heart is sad!
What woes can fate still hold in store!
The friend I cherished a thousand days
Is smashed to pieces on the floor!
Is shattered and to Limbo gone,
I'll see my Mug no more!

Relic it was of joyous hours
Whose golden memories still allure—
When coffee made of rye we drank,
And gray was all the dress we wore!
When we were paid some cents a month,
But never asked for more!

In marches long, by day and night,
In raids, hot charges, shocks of war,
Strapped on the saddle at my back
This faithful comrade still I bore—
This old companion, true and tried,
I'll never carry more!

From the Rapidan to Gettysburg—
 "Hard bread" behind, "sour krout" before—
This friend went with the cavalry
 And heard the jarring cannon roar
 In front of Cemetery Hill—
  Good heavens! how they did roar!

Then back again, the foe behind,
 Back to the "Old Virginia shore"—
Some dead and wounded left—some holes
 In flags, the sullen graybacks bore;
 This mug had made the great campaign,
  And we'd have gone once more!

Alas! we never went again!
 The red cross banner, slow but sure,
"Fell back"—we bade to sour krout
 (Like the lover of Lenore)
 A long, sad, lingering farewell—
  To taste its joys no more.

But still we fought, and ate hard bread,
 Or starved—good friend, our woes deplore!
And still this faithful friend remained—
 Riding behind me as before—
 The friend on march, in bivouac,
  When others were no more.

How oft we drove the horsemen blue
  In Summer bright or Winter frore!
How oft before the Southern charge
  Through field and wood the blue-birds tore!
  I'm "harmonized," but long to hear
    The bugles ring once more.

Oh yes! we're all "fraternal" now,
  Purged of our sins, we're clean and pure,
Congress will "reconstruct" us soon—
  But no gray people on *that* floor!
  I'm harmonized—"so-called"—but long
    To see those times once more!

Gay days! the sun was brighter then,
  And we were happy, though so poor!
That past comes back as I behold
  My shattered friend upon the floor,
  My splintered, useless, ruined mug,
    From which I'll drink no more.

How many lips I'll love for aye,
  While heart and memory endure,
Have touched this broken cup and laughed—
  How they did laugh!—in days of yore!
  Those days we'd call "a beauteous dream,
    If they had been no more!"

Dear comrades, dead this many a day,
  I saw you weltering in your gore,
After those days, amid the pines
  On the Rappahannock shore!
  When the joy of life was much to me
    But your warm hearts were more!

Yours was the grand heroic nerve
  That laughs amid the storm of war—
Souls that "loved much" your native land,
  Who fought and died therefor!
  You gave your youth, your brains, your arms,
    Your blood—you had no more!

You lived and died true to your flag!
  And now your wounds are healed—but sore
Are many hearts that think of you
  Where you have "gone before."
  Peace, comrade! God bound up those forms,
    They are "whole" forevermore!

Those lips this broken vessel touched,
  His, too!—the man's we all adore—
That cavalier of cavaliers,
  Whose voice will ring no more—
  Whose plume will float amid the storm
    Of battle never more!

Not on this idle page I write
  That name of names, shrined in the core
Of every heart !—peace ! foolish pen,
  Hush ! words so cold and poor !
  His sword is rust ; the blue eyes dust,
    His bugle sounds no more !

Never was cavalier like ours !
  Not Rupert in the years before !
And when his stern, hard work was done,
  His griefs, joys, battles o'er—
  His mighty spirit rode the storm,
    And led his men once more !

He lies beneath his native sod,
  Where violets spring, or frost is hoar :
He recks not—charging squadrons watch
  His raven plume no more !
  That smile we'll see, that voice we'll hear,
    That hand we'll touch no more !

My foolish mirth is quenched in tears :
  Poor fragments strewed upon the floor,
Ye are the types of nobler things
  That find their use no more—
  Things glorious once, now trodden down—
    That makes us smile no more !

Of courage, pride, high hopes, stout hearts—
 Hard, stubborn nerve, devotion pure,
Beating his wings against the bars,
 The prisoned eagle tried to soar!
Outmatched, o'erwhelmed, we struggled still—
 Bread failed—we fought no more!

Lies in the dust the shattered staff
 That bore aloft on sea and shore,
That blazing flag, amid the storm!
 And none are now so poor,
 So poor to do it reverence,
 Now when it flames no more!

But it is glorious in the dust,
 Sacred till Time shall be no more:
Spare it, fierce editors! your scorn—
 The dread "Rebellion's" o'er!
 Furl the great flag—hide cross and star,
 Thrust into darkness star and bar,
 But look! across the ages far
 It flames for evermore!

# CAROLINA.

BY ANNA PEYRE DINNIES.

In the hour of thy glory,
When thy name was far renowned,
When Sumter's glowing story
Thy bright escutcheon crowned;
Oh, noble Carolina! how proud a claim was mine,
That through homage and through duty, and birthright, I was thine.

Exulting as I heard thee,
Of every lip the theme,
Prophetic visions stirred me,
In a hope-illumined dream:
A dream of dauntless valor, of battles fought and won,
Where each field was but a triumph—a hero every son.

And now, when clouds arise,
And shadows round thee fall;
I lift to heaven my eyes,
Those visions to recall;
For I cannot dream that darkness will rest upon thee long,
Oh, lordly Carolina! with thine arms and hearts so strong.

Thy serried ranks of pine,
Thy live-oaks spreading wide,

Beneath the sunbeams shine,
In fadeless robes of pride ;
Thus marshalled on their native soil their gallant sons stand forth,
As changeless as thy forests green, defiant of the North.

The deeds of other days,
Enacted by their sires,
Themes long of love and praise,
Have wakened high desires
In every heart that beats within thy proud domain,
To cherish their remembrance, and live those scenes again.

Each heart the home of daring,
Each hand the foe of wrong,
They'll meet with haughty bearing,
The war-ship's thunder song ;
And though the base invader pollute thy sacred shore,
They'll greet him in their prowess as their fathers did of yore.

His feet may press their soil,
Or his numbers bear them down,
In his vandal raid for spoil,
His sordid soul to crown ;
But his triumph will be fleeting, for the hour is drawing near,
When the war-cry of thy cavaliers shall strike his startled ear.

A fearful time shall come,
  When thy gathering bands unite,
And the larum-sounding drum
  Calls to struggle for the Right ;
"*Pro aris et pro focis*," from rank to rank shall fly,
As they meet the cruel foeman, to conquer or to die.

Oh, then a tale of glory
  Shall yet again be thine,
And the record of thy story
  The Laurel shall entwine ;
Oh, noble Carolina ! oh, proud and lordly State !
Heroic deeds shall crown thee, and the Nations own thee great.

---

## OUR MARTYRS.

BY PAUL H. HAYNE.

I AM sitting lone and weary
  On the hearth of my darkened room,
And the low wind's *miserere*
  Makes sadder the midnight gloom ;
There's a terror that's nameless nigh me—
  There's a phantom spell in the air,
And methinks that the dead glide by me,
  And the breath of the grave's in my hair !

'Tis a vision of ghastly faces,
All pallid, and worn with pain,
Where the splendor of manhood's graces
Give place to a gory stain;
In a wild and weird procession
They sweep by my startled eyes,
And stern with their fate's fruition,
Seem melting in blood-red skies.

Have they come from the shores supernal,
Have they passed from the spirit's goal,
'Neath the veil of the life eternal,
To dawn on my shrinking soul?
Have they turned from the choiring angels,
Aghast at the woe and dearth
That war, with his dark evangels,
Hath wrought in the loved of earth?

Vain dream! 'mid the far-off mountains
They lie, where the dew-mists weep,
And the murmur of mournful fountains
Breaks over their painful sleep;
On the breast of the lonely meadows,
Safe, safe from the despot's will,
They rest in the star-lit shadows,
And their brows are white and still!

Alas! for the martyred heroes
  Cut down at their golden prime,
In a strife with the brutal Neroes,
  Who blacken the path of Time!
For them is the voice of wailing,
  And the sweet blush-rose departs
From the cheeks of the maidens, paling
  O'er the wreck of their broken hearts!

And alas! for the vanished glory
  Of a thousand household spells!
And alas! for the tearful story
  Of the spirit's fond farewells!
By the flood, on the field, in the forest,
  Our bravest have yielded breath,
But the shafts that have smitten sorest,
  Were launched by a viewless death!

Oh, Thou, that hast charms of healing,
  Descend on a widowed land,
And bind o'er the wounds of feeling
  The balms of Thy mystic hand!
Till the hearts that lament and languish,
  Renewed by the touch divine,
From the depths of a mortal anguish
  May rise to the calm of Thine!

## CLEBURNE.

BY M. A. JENNINGS, OF ALABAMA.

*"Another star now shines on high."*

ANOTHER ray of light hath fled, another Southern brave
Hath fallen in his country's cause and found a laurelled grave—
Hath fallen, but his deathless name shall live when stars shall set,
For, noble Cleburne, thou art one this world will ne'er forget.

'Tis true thy warm heart beats no more, that on thy noble head
Azrael placed his icy hand, and thou art with the dead;
The glancing of thine eyes are dim; no more will they be bright
Until they ope in Paradise, with clearer, heavenlier light.

No battle news disturbs thy rest upon the sun-bright shore,
No clarion voice awakens thee on earth to wrestle more,
No tramping steed, no wary foe bids thee awake, arise,
For thou art in the angel world, beyond the starry skies

Brave Cleburne, dream in thy low bed, with pulseless, deadened heart;
Calm, calm and sweet, O warrior rest! thou well hast borne thy part;

And now a glory wreath for thee the angels singing twine,
A glory wreath, not of the earth, but made by hands divine

A long farewell—we give thee up, with all thy bright renown;
A chieftain here on earth is lost, in heaven an angel found.
Above thy grave a wail is heard—a nation mourns her dead;
A nobler for the South ne'er died, a braver never bled.

A last farewell—how can we speak the bitter word farewell!
The anguish of our bleeding hearts vain words may never tell.
Sleep on, sleep on, to God we give our chieftain in his might;
And weeping, feel he lives on high, where comes no sorrow's night.

SELMA DESPATCH, 1864.

---

## THE TEXAN MARSEILLAISE.

BY JAMES HAINES, OF TEXAS.

SONS of the South, arouse to battle!
Gird on your armor for the fight!
The Northern Thugs with dread "War's rattle,"
Pour on each vale, and glen, and height;

Meet them as Ocean meets in madness
The frail bark on the rocky shore,
When crested billows foam and roar,
And the wrecked crew go down in sadness.
Arm ! Arm ! ye Southern braves !
Scatter yon Vandal hordes !
Despots and bandits, fitting food
For vultures and your swords.

Shall dastard tyrants march their legions
To crush the land of Jackson—Lee ?
Shall freedom fly to other regions,
And sons of Yorktown bend the knee ?
Or shall their "footprints' base pollution"
Of Southern soil, in blood be purged,
And every flying slave be scourged
Back to his snows in wild confusion ?
Arm ! Arm ! &c.

Vile despots, with their minions knavish,
Would drag us back to their embrace ;
Will freemen brook a chain so slavish ?
Will brave men take so low a place ?
O, Heaven ! for words—the loathing, scorning
We feel for such a Union's bands :
To paint with more than mortal hands,
And sound our loudest notes of warning.
Arm ! Arm ! &c.

What! union with a race ignoring
The charter of our nation's birth!
Union with bastard slaves adoring
The fiend that chains them to the earth!
No! we reply in tones of thunder—
No! our staunch hills fling back the sound—
No! our hoarse cannon echo round—
No! evermore remain asunder!
Arm! Arm! &c.

SOUTHERN CONFEDERACY.

---

## O, TEMPORA! O, MORES!

BY JOHN DICKSON BRUNS, M. D.

"GREAT PAN is dead!" so cried an airy tongue
To one who, drifting down Calabria's shore,
Heard the last knell, in starry midnight rung,
Of the old Oracles, dumb for evermore.

A low wail ran along the shuddering deep,
And as, far off, its flaming accents died,
The awe-struck sailors, startled from their sleep,
Gazed, called aloud: no answering voice replied;

Nor ever will—the angry Gods have fled,
Closed are the temples, mute are all the shrines,

The fires are quenched, Dodona's growth is dead,
The Sibyl's leaves are scattered to the winds.

No mystic sentence will they bear again,
Which, sagely spelled, might ward a nation's doom ;
But we have left us still some god-like men,
And some great voices pleading from the tomb.

If we would heed them, they might save us yet,
Call up some gleams of manhood in our breasts,
Truth, valor, justice, teach us to forget
In a grand cause our selfish interests.

But we have fallen on evil times indeed,
When public faith is but the common shame,
And private morals held an idiot's creed,
And old-world honesty an empty name.

And lust, and greed, and gain are all our arts !
The simple lessons which our father's taught
Are scorned and jeered at ; in our sordid marts
We sell the faith for which they toiled and fought.

Each jostling each in the mad strife for gold,
The weaker trampled by the unrecking throng
Friends, honor, country lost, betrayed, or sold,
And lying blasphemies on every tongue.

Cant for religion, sounding words for truth,
 Fraud leads to fortune, gelt for guilt atones,
No care for hoary age or tender youth,
 For widows' tears or helpless orphans' groans.

The people rage, and work their own wild will,
 They stone the prophets, drag their highest down,
And as they smite, with savage folly still
 Smile at their work, those dead eyes wear no frown.

The sage of "Drainfield" * tills a barren soil,
 And reaps no harvest where he sowed the seed,
He has but exile for long years of toil ;
 Nor voice in council, though his children bleed.

And never more shall "Redcliff's" † oaks rejoice,
 Now bowed with grief above their master's bier ;
Faction and party stilled that mighty voice,
 Which yet could teach us wisdom, could we hear.

And "Woodland's" ‡ harp is mute : the gray, old man
 Broods by his lonely hearth and weaves no song ;
Or, if he sing, the note is sad and wan,
 Like the pale face of one who's suffered long.

---

* The country-seat of R. Barnwell Rhett.

† The homestead of Jas. H. Hammond.

‡ The homestead of W. Gilmore Simms (destroyed by Sherman's army.)

So all earth's teachers have been overborne
By the coarse crowd, and fainting droop or die;
They bear the cross, their bleeding brows the thorn,
And ever hear the clamor—"Crucify!"

Oh, for a man with godlike heart and brain!
A god in stature, with a god's great will,
And fitted to the time, that not in vain
Be all the blood we've spilt and yet must spill.

Oh, brothers! friends! shake off the Circean spell!
Rouse to the dangers of impending fate!
Grasp your keen swords, and all may yet be well—
More gain, more pelf, and it will be, too late!

CHARLESTON MERCURY [1864].

---

## OUR DEPARTED COMRADES.

BY J. MARION SHIRER.

I AM sitting alone by a fire
That glimmers on Sugar Loaf's height,
But before I to rest shall retire
And put out the fast fading light—
While the lanterns of heaven are ling'ring
In silence all o'er the deep sea,

And loved ones at home are yet mingling
  Their voices in converse of me—
While yet the lone seabird is flying
  So swiftly far o'er the rough wave,
And many fond mothers are sighing
  For the noble, the true, and the brave ;
Let me muse o'er the many departed
  Who slumber on mountain and vale ;
With the sadness which shrouds the lone-hearted,
  Let me tell of my comrades a tale.
Far away in the green, lonely mountains,
  Where the eagle makes bloody his beak,
In the mist, and by Gettysburg's fountains,
  Our fallen companions now sleep !
Near Charleston, where Sumter still rises
  In grandeur above the still wave,
And always at evening discloses
  The fact that her inmates yet live—
On islands, and fronting Savannah,
  Where dark oaks o'ershadow the ground,
Round Macon and smoking Atlanta,
  How many dead heroes are found !
And out on the dark swelling ocean,
  Where vessels go, riding the waves,
How many, for love and devotion,
  Now slumber in warriors' graves !
No memorials have yet been erected
  To mark where these warriors lie,
All alone, save by angels protected,

They sleep 'neath the sea and the sky!
But think not that they are forgotten
By those who the carnage survive:
When their headboards will all have grown rotten,
And the night-winds have levelled their graves,
Then hundreds of sisters and mothers,
Whose freedom they perished to save,
And fathers, and empty-sleeved brothers,
Who surmounted the battle's red wave;
Will crowd from their homes in the Southward,
In search of the loved and the blest,
And, rejoicing, will soon return homeward
And lay our dear martyrs to rest.

---

## NO LAND LIKE OURS.

PUBLISHED IN THE MONTGOMERY ADVERTISER, JANUARY, 1863.

BY J. R. BARRICK, OF KENTUCKY.

Though other lands may boast of skies
Far deeper in their blue,
Where flowers, in Eden's pristine dyes,
Bloom with a richer hue;
And other nations pride in kings,
And worship lordly powers;
Yet every voice of nature sings,
There is no land like ours!

Though other scenes, than such as grace
  Our forests, fields, and plains,
May lend the earth a sweeter face
  Where peace incessant reigns ;
But dearest still to me the land
  Where sunshine cheers the hours,
For God hath shown, with his own hand,
  There is no land like ours !

Though other streams may softer flow
  In vales of classic bloom,
And rivers clear as crystal glow,
  That wear no tinge of gloom ;
Though other mountains lofty look,
  And grand seem olden towers,
We see, as in an open book,
  There is no land like ours !

Though other nations boast of deeds
  That live in old renown,
And other peoples cling to creeds
  That coldly on us frown ;
On pure religion, love, and law
  Are based our ruling powers—
The world but feels, with wondering awe,
  There is no land like ours !

Though other lands may boast their brave,
Whose deeds are writ in fame,
Their heroes ne'er such glory gave
As gilds our country's name ;
Though others rush to daring deeds,
Where the darkening war-cloud lowers,
Here, each alike for freedom bleeds—
There is no land like ours !

Though other lands Napoleon
And Wellington adorn,
America, her Washington,
And later heroes born ;
Yet Johnston, Jackson, Price, and Lee,
Bragg, Buckner, Morgan towers,
With Beauregard, and Hood, and Bee—
There is no land like ours !

---

## THE ANGEL OF THE CHURCH.

BY W. GILMORE SIMMS.

The enemy, from his camp on Morris Island, has, in frequent letters in the Northern papers, avowed the object at which they aim their shells in Charleston to be the spire of St. Michael's Church. Their *practice* shows that these avowals are true. Thus far, they have not succeeded in their aim. Angels of the Churches, is a phrase applied by St. John in reference to the Seven Churches of Asia. The Hebrews recognized an Angel of the Church, in their language, "Sheliack-Zibbor," whose office may be de scribed as that of a watcher or guardian of the church. Daniel says, iv. 13, "Behold, a watcher and a Holy one came down from Heaven." The practice of naming churches after tutelary saints, originated, no doubt, in the conviction that, where the church was pure, and the faith true, and the congregation pious, these guardian angels, so chosen, would accept the office assigned them. They were generally chosen from the Seraphim and Cherubim—those who, according to St. Paul (1 Colossians xvi.), represented thrones, dominions, principalities, and powers. According to the Hebrew traditions, St. Michael was the head of the first order; Gabriel, of the second; Uriel, of the third; and Raphael, of the fourth. St. Michael is the warrior angel who led the hosts of the sky against the powers of the princes of the air; who overthrew the dragon, and trampled him under foot. The destruction of the Anaconda, in his hands, would be a smaller undertaking. Assuming for our people a hope not less rational than that of the people of Nineveh, we may reasonably build upon the guardianship and protection of God, through his angels, "a great city of sixty thousand souls," which has been for so long a season the subject of his care. These notes will supply the adequate illustrations for the ode which follows.

I.

Aye, strike with sacrilegious aim
  The temple of the living God;
Hurl iron bolt and seething flame
  Through aisles which holiest feet have trod;
Tear up the altar, spoil the tomb,
  And, raging with demoniac ire,
Send down, in sudden crash of doom,
  That grand, old, sky-sustaining spire.

II.

That spire, for full a hundred years,*
  Hath been a people's point of sight;

* St. Michael's Church was opened for divine worship, February 1, 1761.

That shrine hath warmed their souls to tears,
With strains well worthy Salem's height ;
The sweet, clear music of its bells,
Made liquid soft in Southern air,
Still through the heart of memory swells,
And wakes the hopeful soul to prayer.

III.

Along the shores for many a mile,
Long ere they owned a beacon-mark,
It caught and kept the Day-God's smile,
The guide for every wandering bark ;*
Averting from our homes the scaith
Of fiery bolt, in storm-cloud driven,
The Pharos to the wandering faith,
It pointed every prayer to Heaven !

IV.

Well may ye, felons of the time,
Still loathing all that's pure and free,
Add this to many a thousand crime
'Gainst peace and sweet humanity :
Ye, who have wrapped our towns in flame,
Defiled our shrines, befouled our homes,
But fitly turn your murderous aim
Against Jehovah's ancient domes.

---

* "The height of this steeple makes it the principal land-mark for the pilots."— *Dalcho* (in 1819).

V.

Yet, though the grand old temple falls,
And downward sinks the lofty spire,
Our faith is stronger than our walls,
And soars above the storm and fire.
Ye shake no faith in souls made free
To tread the paths their fathers trod ;
To fight and die for liberty,
Believing in the avenging God !

VI.

Think not, though long his anger stays,
His justice sleeps—His wrath is spent ;
The arm of vengeance but delays,
To make more dread the punishment !
Each impious hand that lights the torch
Shall wither ere the bolt shall fall ;
And the bright Angel of the Church,
With seraph shield avert the ball !

VII.

For still we deem, as taught of old,
That where the faith the altar builds,
God sends an angel from his fold,
Whose sleepless watch the temple shields,

And to his flock, with sweet accord,
  Yields their fond choice, from THRONES and POWERS;
Thus, Michael, with his fiery sword
  And golden shield, still champions ours!

VIII.

And he who smote the dragon down,
  And chained him thousand years of time,
Need never fear the boa's frown,
  Though loathsome in his spite and slime.
He, from the topmost height, surveys
  And guards the shrines our fathers gave;
And we, who sleep beneath his gaze,
  May well believe his power to save!

IX.

Yet, if it be that for our sin
  Our angel's term of watch is o'er,
With proper prayer, true faith must win
  The guardian watcher back once more!
Faith, brethren of the Church, and prayer—
  In blood and sackcloth, if it need;
And still our spire shall rise in air,
  Our temple, though our people bleed!

## ODE—"SHELL THE OLD CITY! SHELL!"

BY W. GILMORE SIMMS.

I.

Shell the old city! shell!
Ye myrmidons of Hell;
Ye serve your master well,
With hellish arts!
Hurl down, with bolt and fire,
The grand old shrines, the spire;
But know, your demon ire
Subdues no hearts!

II.

There, we defy ye still,
With sworn and resolute will;
Courage ye cannot kill
While we have breath!
Stone walls your bolts may break,
But, ere our souls ye shake,
Of the whole land we'll make
One realm of death!

III.

Dear are our homes! our eyes
Weep at their sacrifice;

And, with each bolt that flies,
Each roof that falls,
The pang extorts the tear,
That things so precious, dear
To memory, love, and care,
Sink with our walls.

IV.

Trophies of ancient time,
When, with great souls, sublime,
Opposing force and crime,
Our fathers fought ;
Relics of golden hours,
When, for our shrines and bowers,
Genius, with magic powers,
Her triumphs wrought !

V.

Each Sabbath-hallowed dome,
Each ancient family home,
The dear old southwest room,
All trellised round ;
Where gay, bright summer vines,
Linked in fantastic twines
With the sun's blazing lines,
Rubied the ground !

VI.

Homes, sacred to the past,
Which bore the hostile blast,
Though Spain, France, Britain cast
  Their shot and shell!
Tombs of the mighty dead,
That in our battles bled,
When on our infant head
  These furies fell!

VII.

Halls which the foreign guest
Found of each charm possessed,
With cheer unstinted blessed,
  And noblest grace;
Where, drawing to her side
The stranger, far and wide,
Frank courtesy took pride
  To give him place!

VIII.

The shaded walks—the bowers
Where, through long summer hours,
Young Love first proved his powers
  To win the prize;
Where every tree has heard
Some vows of love preferred,

And, with his leaves unstirred,
Watch'd lips and eyes.

IX.

Gardens of tropic blooms,
That, through the shaded rooms,
Sent Orient-winged perfumes
With dusk and dawn ;
The grand old laurel, tall,
As sovereign over all,
And, from the porch and hall,
The verdant lawn.

X.

Oh ! when we think of these
Old homes, ancestral trees ;
Where, in the sun and breeze,
At morn and even,
Was to enjoy the play
Of hearts at holiday,
And find, in blooms of May,
Foretaste of Heaven !

XI.

Where, as we cast our eyes
On things of precious prize,

Trophies of good and wise,
Grand, noble, brave ;
And think of these, so late
Sacred to soul and state,
Doomed, as the wreck of fate,
By fiend and slave !—

XII.

The inevitable pain,
Coursing through blood and brain,
Drives forth, like winter rain,
The bitter tear !
We cannot help but weep,
From depth of hearts that keep
The memories, dread and deep,
To vengeance dear !

XIII.

Aye, for each tear we shed,
There shall be torrents red,
Not from the eye-founts fed,
But from the veins !
Bloody shall be the sweat,
Fiends, felons, that shall yet
Pay retribution's debt,
In torture's pains !

XIV.

Our tears shall naught abate,
Of what we owe to hate—
To the avenging fate—
To earth and Heaven !
And, soon or late, the hour
Shall bring th' atoning power,
When, through the clouds that lower,
The storm-bolt's driven !

XV.

Shell the old city—shell !
But, with each rooftree's knell,
Vows deep of vengeance fell,
Fire soul and eye !
With every tear that falls
Above our stricken walls
Each heart more fiercely calls,
" Avenge, or die !"

# "THE ENEMY SHALL NEVER REACH YOUR CITY."

**ANDREW JACKSON'S ADDRESS TO THE PEOPLE OF NEW ORLEANS.**

I.

NEVER, while such as ye are in the breach,
Oh! brothers, sons, and Southrons—never! never!
Shall the foul enemy your city reach!
For souls and hearts are eager with endeavor;
And God's own sanction on your cause, makes holy
Each arm that strikes for home, however lowly!—
And ye shall conquer by the rolling deep!—
And ye shall conquer on the embattled steep!—
And ye shall see Leviathan go down
A hundred fathoms, with a horrible cry
Of drowning wretches, in their agony—
While Slaughter wades in gore along the sands,
And Terror flies with pleading, outstretched hands,
All speechless, but with glassy-staring eyes—
Flying to Fate—and fated as he flies;—
Seeking his refuge in the tossing wave,
That gives him, when the shark has fed, a grave!

II.

Thus saith the Lord of Battles: "Shall it be,
That this great city, planted by the sea,
With threescore thousand souls—with fanes and spires
Reared by a race of unexampled sires—

That I have watched, now twice a hundred years,*
Nursed through long infancy of hopes and fears,
Baptized in blood at seasons, oft in tears;
Purged with the storm and fire, and bade to grow
To greatness, with a progress firm but slow—
That being the grand condition of duration—
Until it spreads into the mighty nation!
And shall the usurper, insolent of power,
O'erwhelm it with swift ruin in an hour!
And hurl his bolts, and with a dominant will,
Say to its mighty heart—'Crouch, and be still!
My foot is on your neck! I am your Fate!
Can speak your doom, and make you desolate!'

III.

"No! He shall know—I am the Lord of war;
And all his mighty hosts but pigmies are!
His hellish engines, wrought for human woe,
His arts and vile inventions, and his power,
My arm shall bring to ruin, swift and low!
Even now my bolts are aimed, my storm-clouds lower,
And I will arm my people with a faith,
Shall make them free of fear, and free of scaith;
And they shall bear from me a smiting sword,
Edged with keen lightning, at whose stroke is poured

* Charleston was originally settled in 1671. She is now near 200 years old.

A torrent of destruction and swift wrath,
Sweeping the insolent legions from their path!
The usurper shall be taught that none shall take
The right to punish and avenge from me:
And I will guard my City by the Sea,
And save its people for their fathers' sake!"

IV.

Selah!—Oh! brothers, sons, and Southrons, rise;
To prayer: and lo! the wonder in the skies!
The sunbow spans your towers, even while the foe
Hurls his fell bolt, and rains his iron blow.
Toss'd by his shafts, the spray above yon height*
God's smile hath turned into a golden light;
Orange and purple-golden! In that sign
Find ye fit promise for that voice divine!
Hark! 'tis the thunder! Through the murky air,
The solemn roll goes echoing far and near!
Go forth, and unafraid! His shield is yours!
And the great spirits of your earlier day—
Your fathers, hovering round your sacred shores—
Will guard your bosoms through the unequal fray!
Hark to their voices, issuing through the gloom:

---

* In the late engagement of Fort Sumter, with the enemy's fleet, April 7th, the spray thrown above the walls by their enormous missiles, was formed into a beautiful sunbow, seeing which, General Ripley, with the piety of Constantine, exclaimed: "*In hoc signo vinces!*"

"The cruel hosts that haunt you, march to doom:
Give them the vulture's rites—a naked tomb!
And, while ye bravely smite, with fierce endeavor,
The foe shall reach your city—never! never!"

CHARLESTON MERCURY.

---

## WAR-WAVES.

BY CATHERINE GENDRON POYAS, OF CHARLESTON.

WHAT are the war-waves saying,
As they compass us around?
The dark, ensanguined billows,
With their deep and dirge-like sound?
Do they murmur of submission;
Do they call on us to bow
Our necks to the foe triumphant
Who is riding o'er us now?

Never! No sound submissive
Comes from those waves sublime,
Or the low, mysterious voices
Attuned to their solemn chime!
For the hearts of our noble martyrs
Are the springs of its rich supply;
And those deeply mystic murmurs
Echo their dying cry!

They bid us uplift our banner
Once more in the name of God;
And press to the goal of Freedom
By the paths our Fathers trod:
*They* passed o'er their dying brothers;
From their pale lips caught the sigh—
The *flame* of their hearts heroic,
From the flash of each closing eye!

Up! Up! for the time is pressing,
The red waves close around;—
They will lift us on their billows
If our hearts are faithful found!
They will lift us high—exultant,
And the craven world shall see
The Ark of a ransomed people
Afloat on the crimson sea!

Afloat, with her glorious banner—
The cross on its field of red,
Its stars, and its white folds waving
In triumph at her head;
Emblem of all that's sacred
Heralding Faith to view;
Type of unblemished honor;
Symbol of all that's true!

*Then* what can those waves be singing
  But an anthem grand, sublime,
As they bear for our martyred heroes
  A wail to the coast of Time?
What else as they roll majestic
  To the far-off shadowy shore,
To join the Eternal chorus
  When Time shall be no more!

---

## OLD MOULTRIE.

BY CATHERINE GENDRON POYAS, OF CHARLESTON.

All lovers of poetry will know in whose liquid gold I have dipped my brush to illumine the picture.

The splendor falls on bannered walls
  Of ancient Moultrie, great in story;
And flushes now, his scar-seamed brow,
  With rays of golden glory!
        Great in his old renown;
        Great in the honor thrown
        Around him by the foe,
        Had sworn to lay him low!

The glory falls—historic walls
  Too weak to cover foes insulting,
Become a tower—a sheltering bower—
  A theme of joy exulting;

God, merciful and great,
Preserved the high estate
Of Moultrie, by His power
Through the fierce battle-hour !

The splendor fell—his banners swell
Majestic forth to catch the shower ;
Our own loved *blue* receives anew
A rich immortal dower !
Adown the triple bars
Of its companion, spars
Of golden glory stream ;
On seven-rayed circlet beam !

The glory falls—but not on walls
Of Sumter deemed *the post of duty ;*
A brilliant sphere, it circles clear
The harbor in its beauty ;
Holding in its embrace
The city's queenly grace ;
Stern battery and tower,
Of manly strength and power.

But brightest falls on Moultrie's walls,
Forever there to rest in glory,
A hallowed light—on buttress height—
Oh, fort, beloved and hoary !

Rest *there* and tell that *faith*
Shall never suffer scaith ;
*Rest there*—and glow afar—
*Hope's ever-burning star !*

Charleston Mercury

---

## ONLY ONE KILLED.

BY JULIA L. KEYES, MONTGOMERY, ALA.

Only one killed—in company B,
'Twas a trifling loss—one man !
A charge of the bold and dashing Lee—
While merry enough it was, to see
The enemy, as he ran.

Only one killed upon our side—
Once more to the field they turn.
Quietly now the horsemen ride—
And pause by the form of the one who died,
So bravely, as now we learn.

Their grief for the comrade loved and true
For a time was unconcealed ;
They saw the bullet had pierced him through ;
That his pain was brief—ah ! very few
Die thus, on the battle-field.

The news has gone to his home, afar—
Of the short and gallant fight,
Of the noble deeds of the young La Var
Whose life went out as a falling star
In the skirmish of that night.

"Only one killed! It was my son,"
The widowed mother cried.
She turned but to clasp the sinking one,
Who heard not the words of the victory won,
But of him who had bravely died.

Ah! death to her were a sweet relief,
The bride of a single year.
Oh! would she might, with her weight of grief,
Lie down in the dust, with the autumn leaf
Now trodden and brown and sere!

But no, she must bear through coming life
Her burden of silent woe,
The aged mother and youthful wife
Must live through a nation's bloody strife,
Sighing, and waiting to go.

Where the loved are meeting beyond the stars,
Are meeting no more to part,

They can smile once more through the crystal bars—
Where never more will the woe of wars
O'ershadow the loving heart.

FIELD AND FIRESIDE.

---

## LAND OF KING COTTON.*

AIR—Red, White, and Blue.

BY J. AUGUSTINE SIGNAIGO.

FROM THE MEMPHIS APPEAL, DECEMBER 18, 1861.

OH ! Dixie, dear land of King Cotton,
"The home of the brave and the free,"
A nation by freedom begotten,
The terror of despots to be ;
Wherever thy banner is streaming,
Base tyranny quails at thy feet,
And liberty's sunlight is beaming,
In splendor of majesty sweet.
CHORUS.—Three cheers for our army so true,
Three cheers for Price, Johnston, and Lee ;
Beauregard and our Davis forever,
The pride of the brave and the free !

---

* "Land of King Cotton" was the favorite song of the Tennessee troops, but especially of the Thirteenth and One Hundred and Fifty-fourth regiments.

When Liberty sounds her war-rattle,
  Demanding her right and her due,
The first land that rallies to battle
  Is Dixie, the shrine of the true ;
Thick as leaves of the forest in summer,
  Her brave sons will rise on each plain,
And then strike, until each Vandal comer
  Lies dead on the soil he would stain.
    CHORUS.—Three cheers, etc.

May the names of the dead that we cherish,
  Fill memory's cup to the brim ;
May the laurels they've won never perish,
  " Nor star of their glory grow dim ;"
May the States of the South never sever,
  But the champions of freedom e'er be ;
May they flourish Confederate forever,
  The boast of the brave and the free.
    CHORUS.—Three cheers, etc.

---

## IF YOU LOVE ME.

BY J. AUGUSTINE SIGNAIGO.

You have told me that you love me,
  That you worship at my shrine ;
That no purity above me
  Can on earth be more divine.

Though the kind words you have spoken,
  Sound to me most sweetly strange,
Will your pledges ne'er be broken?
  Will there be in you no change?

If you love me half so wildly—
  Half so madly as you say,
Listen to me, darling, mildly—
  Would you do aught I would pray?
If you would, then hear the thunder
  Of our country's cannon speak!
While by war she's rent asunder,
  Do not come my love to seek.

If you love me, do not ponder,
  Do not breathe what you would say,
Do not look at me with wonder,
  Join your country in the fray.
Go! your aid and right hand lend her,
  Breast the tyrant's angry blast;
Be her own and my defender—
  Strike for freedom to the last.

Then I'll vow to love none other,
  While you nobly dare and do;
As you're faithful to our mother,
  So I'll faithful prove to you.

But return not while the thunder
 Lives in one invading sword ;
Strike the despot's hirelings under—
 Own no master but the Lord.

---

## THE COTTON BOLL.

BY HENRY TIMROD.

While I recline
At ease beneath
This immemorial pine,
Small sphere !—
By dusky fingers brought this morning here,
And shown with boastful smiles,—
I turn thy cloven sheath,
Through which the soft white fibres peer,
That, with their gossamer bands,
Unite, like love, the sea-divided lands,
And slowly, thread by thread,
Draw forth the folded strands,
Than which the trembling line,
By whose frail help yon startled spider fled
Down the tall spear-grass from his swinging bed,
Is scarce more fine ;
And as the tangled skein

Unravels in my hands,
Betwixt me and the noonday light,
A veil seems lifted, and for miles and miles
The landscape broadens on my sight,
As, in the little boll, there lurked a spell
Like that which, in the ocean shell,
With mystic sound,
Breaks down the narrow walls that hem us round,
And turns some city lane
Into the restless main,
With all his capes and isles!

Yonder bird,—
Which floats, as if at rest,
In those blue tracts above the thunder, where
No vapors cloud the stainless air,
And never sound is heard,
Unless at such rare time
When, from the City of the Blest,
Rings down some golden chime,—
Sees not from his high place
So vast a cirque of summer space
As widens round me in one mighty field,
Which, rimmed by seas and sands,
Doth hail its earliest daylight in the beams
Of gray Atlantic dawns;
And, broad as realms made up of many lands,
Is lost afar

Behind the crimson hills and purple lawns
Of sunset, among plains which roll their streams
Against the Evening Star!
And lo!
To the remotest point of sight,
Although I gaze upon no waste of snow,
The endless field is white;
And the whole landscape glows,
For many a shining league away,
With such accumulated light
As Polar lands would flash beneath a tropic day!
Nor lack there (for the vision grows,
And the small charm within my hands—
More potent even than the fabled one,
Which oped whatever golden mystery
Lay hid in fairy wood or magic vale,
The curious ointment of the Arabian tale—
Beyond all mortal sense
Doth stretch my sight's horizon, and I see
Beneath its simple influence,
As if, with Uriel's crown,
I stood in some great temple of the Sun,
And looked, as Uriel, down)—
Nor lack there pastures rich and fields all green
With all the common gifts of God,
For temperate airs and torrid sheen
Weave Edens of the sod;
Through lands which look one sea of billowy gold
Broad rivers wind their devious ways;

A hundred isles in their embraces fold
A hundred luminous bays;
And through yon purple haze
Vast mountains lift their pluméd peaks cloud-crowned;
And, save where up their sides the ploughman creeps,
An unknown forest girds them grandly round,
In whose dark shades a future navy sleeps!
Ye stars, which though unseen, yet with me gaze
Upon this loveliest fragment of the earth!
Thou Sun, that kindlest all thy gentlest rays
Above it, as to light a favorite hearth!
Ye clouds, that in your temples in the West
See nothing brighter than its humblest flowers!
And, you, ye Winds, that on the ocean's breast
Are kissed to coolness ere ye reach its bowers!
Bear witness with me in my song of praise,
And tell the world that, since the world began,
No fairer land hath fired a poet's lays,
Or given a home to man!

But these are charms already widely blown!
His be the meed whose pencil's trace
Hath touched our very swamps with grace,
And round whose tuneful way
All Southern laurels bloom;
The Poet of "The Woodlands," unto whom
Alike are known
The flute's low breathing and the trumpet's tone,

And the soft west-wind's sighs ;
But who shall utter all the debt,
O Land ! wherein all powers are met
That bind a people's heart,
The world doth owe thee at this day,
And which it never can repay,
Yet scarcely deigns to own !
Where sleeps the poet who shall fitly sing
The source wherefrom doth spring
That mighty commerce which, confined
To the mean channels of no selfish mart,
Goes out to every shore
Of this broad earth, and throngs the sea with ships
That bear no thunders ; hushes hungry lips
In alien lands ;
Joins with a delicate web remotest strands ;
And gladdening rich and poor,
Doth gild Parisian domes,
Or feed the cottage-smoke of English homes,
And only bounds its blessings by mankind !
In offices like these, thy mission lies,
My Country ! and it shall not end
As long as rain shall fall and Heaven bend
In blue above thee ; though thy foes be hard
And cruel as their weapons, it shall guard
Thy hearthstones as a bulwark ; make thee great
In white and bloodless state ;
And, haply, as the years increase—
Still working through its humbler reach

With that large wisdom which the ages teach—
Revive the half-dead dream of universal peace !

As men who labor in that mine
Of Cornwall, hollowed out beneath the bed
Of ocean, when a storm rolls overhead,
Hear the dull booming of the world of brine
Above them, and a mighty muffled roar
Of winds and waters, and yet toil calmly on,
And split the rock, and pile the massive ore,
Or carve a niche, or shape the archéd roof ;
So I, as calmly, weave my woof
Of song, chanting the days to come,
Unsilenced, though the quiet summer air
Stirs with the bruit of battles, and each dawn
Wakes from its starry silence to the hum
Of many gathering armies. Still,
In that we sometimes hear,
Upon the Northern winds the voice of woe
Not wholly drowned in triumph, though I know
The end must crown us, and a few brief years
Dry all our tears,
I may not sing too gladly. To Thy will
Resigned, O Lord ! we cannot all forget
That there is much even Victory must regret.
And, therefore, not too long
From the great burden of our country's wrong
Delay our just release !

And, if it may be, save
These sacred fields of peace
From stain of patriot or of hostile blood !
Oh, help us Lord ! to roll the crimson flood
Back on its course, and, while our banners wing
Northward, strike with us ! till the Goth shall cling
To his own blasted altar-stones, and crave
Mercy ; and we shall grant it, and dictate
The lenient future of his fate
There, where some rotting ships and trembling quays
Shall one day mark the Port which ruled the Western seas

---

## THE BATTLE OF CHARLESTON HARBOR.

April 7th, 1863.

BY PAUL H. HAYNE.

I.

Two hours, or more, beyond the prime of a blithe April day,
The Northman's mailed "Invincibles" steamed up fair
Charleston Bay ;
They came in sullen file, and slow, low-breasted on the wave,
Black as a midnight front of storm, and silent as the grave.

II.

A thousand warrior-hearts beat high as those dread monsters drew
More closely to the game of death across the breezeless blue,

And twice ten thousand hearts of those who watched the
scene afar,
Thrill in the awful hush that bides the battle's broadening
Star!

III.

Each gunner, moveless by his gun, with rigid aspect stands,
The ready linstocks firmly grasped in bold, untrembling
hands,
So moveless in their marbled calm, their stern heroic guise,
They looked like forms of statued stone with burning human
eyes!

IV.

Our banners on the outmost walls, with stately rustling
fold,
Flash back from arch and parapet the sunlight's ruddy
gold—
They mount to the deep roll of drums, and widely-echoing
cheers,
And then—once more, dark, breathless, hushed, wait the
grim cannoneers.

V.

Onward—in sullen file, and slow, low glooming on the
wave,
Near, nearer still, the haughty fleet glides silent as the
grave,

When sudden, shivering up the calm, o'er startled flood and shore,
Burst from the sacred Island Fort the thunder-wrath of yore!*

VI.

Ha! brutal Corsairs! tho' ye come thrice-cased in iron mail,
Beware the storm that's opening now, God's vengeance guides the hail!
Ye strive the ruffian types of Might 'gainst law, and truth, and Right,
Now quail beneath a sturdier Power, and own a mightier Might!

VII.

No empty boast! for while we speak, more furious, wilder, higher,
Dart from the circling batteries a hundred tongues of fire.
The waves gleam red, the lurid vault of heaven seems rent above.
Fight on! oh! knightly Gentlemen! for faith, and home, and love!

VIII.

There's not in all that line of flame, one soul that would not rise,
To seize the Victor's wreath of blood, tho' Death must give the prize—

* Fort Moultrie fired the first gun.

There's not in all this anxious crowd that throngs the ancient Town,
A maid who does not yearn for power to strike *one* despot down.

IX.

The strife grows fiercer! ship by ship the proud Armada sweeps,
Where hot from Sumter's raging breast the volleyed lightning leaps;
And ship by ship, raked, overborne, 'ere burned the sunset bloom,
Crawls seaward, like a hangman's hearse bound to his felon tomb!

X.

Oh! glorious Empress of the Main! from out thy storied spires,
Thou well mayst peal thy bells of joy, and light thy festal fires—
Since Heaven this day hath striven for thee, hath nerved thy dauntless sons,
And thou, in clear-eyed faith hast seen God's Angels near the guns!

# FORT WAGNER.

BY W. GILMORE SIMMS.

I.

GLORY unto the gallant boys who stood
At Wagner, and, unflinching, sought the van ;
Dealing fierce blows, and shedding precious blood,
For homes as precious, and dear rights of man !
They've won the meed, and they shall have the glory ;—
Song, with melodious memories, shall repeat
The legend, which shall grow to themes for story,
Told through long ages, and forever sweet !

II.

High honor to our youth—our sons and brothers,
Georgians and Carolinians, where they stand !
They will not shame their birthrights, or their mothers,
But keep, through storm, the bulwarks of the land !
They feel that they *must* conquer ! Not to do it,
Were worse than death—perdition ! Should they fail,
The innocent races yet unborn shall rue it,
The whole world feel the wound, and nations wail !

III.

No ! They must conquer in the breach or perish !
Assured, in the last consciousness of breath,

That love shall deck their graves, and memory cherish
 Their deeds, with honors that shall sweeten death !
They shall have trophies in long future hours,
 And loving recollections, which shall be
Green as the summer leaves, and fresh as flowers,
 That, through all seasons, bloom eternally !

IV.

Their memories shall be monuments, to rise
 Next those of mightiest martyrs of the past ;
Beacons, when angry tempests sweep the skies,
 And feeble souls bend crouching to the blast !
A shrine for thee, young Cheves, well devoted,
 Most worthy of a great, illustrious sire ;—
A niche for thee, young Haskell, nobly noted,
 When skies and seas around thee shook with fire !

V.

And others as well chronicled shall be !
 What though they fell with unrecorded name—
They live among the archives of the free,
 With proudest title to undying fame !
The unchisell'd marble under which they sleep,
 Shall tell of heroes, fearless still of fate ;
Not asking if their memories shall keep,
 But if they nobly served, and saved, the State !

VI.

For thee, young Fortress Wagner—thou shalt wear
  Green laurels, worthy of the names that now,
Thy sister forts of Moultrie, Sumter, bear !
  See that thou lift'st, for aye, as proud a brow !
And thou shalt be, to future generations,
  A trophied monument ; whither men shall come
In homage ; and report to distant nations,
  A SHRINE, which foes shall never make a TOMB !

CHARLESTON MERCURY.

---

## SUMTER IN RUINS.

BY W. GILMORE SIMMS.

I.

YE batter down the lion's den,
  But yet the lordly beast goes free ;
And ye shall hear his roar again,
From mountain height, from lowland glen,
From sandy shore and reedy fen—
Where'er a band of freeborn men
  Rears sacred shrines to liberty.

II.

The serpent scales the eagle's nest,
  And yet the royal bird, in air,

Triumphant wins the mountain's crest,
And sworn for strife, yet takes his rest,
And plumes, to calm, his ruffled breast,
Till, like a storm-bolt from the west,
He strikes the invader in his lair.

III.

What's loss of den, or nest, or home,
If, like the lion, free to go ;—
If, like the eagle, wing'd to roam,
We span the rock and breast the foam,
Still watchful for the hour of doom,
When, with the knell of thunder-boom,
We bound upon the serpent foe !

IV.

Oh ! noble sons of lion heart !
Oh ! gallant hearts of eagle wing !
What though your batter'd bulwarks part,
Your nest be spoiled by reptile art—
Your souls, on wings of hate, shall start
For vengeance, and with lightning-dart,
Rend the foul serpent ere he sting !

V.

Your battered den, your shattered nest,
Was but the lion's crouching-place ;—

It heard his roar, and bore his crest,
His, or the eagle's place of rest ;—
But not the soul in either breast !
This arms the twain, by freedom bless'd,
To save and to avenge their race !

Charleston Mercury.

---

## MORRIS ISLAND.

BY W. GILMORE SIMMS.

Oh ! from the deeds well done, the blood well shed
In a good cause springs up to crown the land
With ever-during verdure, memory fed,
Wherever freedom rears one fearless band,
The genius, which makes sacred time and place,
Shaping the grand memorials of a race !

The barren rock becomes a monument,
The sea-shore sands a shrine ;
And each brave life, in desperate conflict spent,
Grows to a memory which prolongs a line !

Oh ! barren isle—oh ! fruitless shore,
Oh ! realm devoid of beauty—how the light

From glory's sun streams down for evermore,
Hallowing your ancient barrenness with bright!

Brief dates, your lowly forts; but full of glory,
Worthy a life-long story;
Remembered, to be chronicled and read,
When all your gallant garrisons are dead;
And to be sung
While liberty and letters find a tongue!

Taught by the grandsires at the ingle-blaze,
Through the long winter night;
Pored over, memoried well, in winter days,
While youthful admiration, with delight,
Hangs, breathless, o'er the tale, with silent praise;
Seasoning delight with wonder, as he reads
Of stubborn conflict and audacious deeds;
Watching the endurance of the free and brave,
Through the protracted struggle and close fight,
Contending for the lands they may not save,
Against the felon and innumerous foe;
Still struggling, though each rampart proves a grave
For home, and all that's dear to man below!

Earth reels and ocean rocks at every blow;
But still undaunted, with a martyr's might,
They make for man a new Thermopylæ;
And, perishing for freedom, still go free!

Let but each humble islet of our coast
Thus join the terrible issue to the last;
And never shall the invader make his boast
Of triumph, though with mightiest panoply
He seeks to rend and rive, to blight and blast!

---

## PROMISE OF SPRING.

The sun-beguiling breeze,
From the soft Cuban seas,
With life-bestowing kiss wakes the pride of garden bowers;
And lo! our city elms,
Have plumed with buds their helms,
And, with tiny spears salute the coming on of flowers.

The promise of the Spring,
Is in every glancing wing
That tells its flight in song which shall long survive the flight;
And mocking Winter's glooms,
Skies, air and earth grow blooms,
With change as bless'd as ever came with passage of a night!

Ah! could our hearts but share
The promise rich and rare,
That welcomes life to rapture in each happy fond caress,

That makes each innocent thing
Put on its bloom and wing,
Singing for Spring to come to the realm she still would bless!

But, alas for us, no more
Shall the coming hour restore
The glory, sweet and wonted, of the seasons to our souls ;
Even as the Spring appears,
Her smiling makes our tears,
While with each bitter memory the torrent o'er us rolls.

Even as our zephyrs sing
That they bring us in the Spring,
Even as our bird grows musical in ecstasy of flight—
We see the serpent crawl,
With his slimy coat o'er all,
And blended with the song is the hissing of his blight.

We shudder at the blooms,
Which but serve to cover tombs—
At the very sweet of odors which blend venom with the breath ;
Sad shapes look out from trees,
And in sky and earth and breeze,
We behold but the aspect of a Horror worse than Death !

SOUTH CAROLINIAN.

## SPRING.

BY HENRY TIMROD.

SPRING, with that nameless pathos in the air
Which dwells with all things fair,
Spring, with her golden suns and silver rain,
Is with us once again.

Out in the lonely woods the jasmine burns
Its fragrant lamps, and turns
Into a royal court with green festoons
The banks of dark lagoons.

In the deep heart of every forest tree
The blood is all aglee,
And there's a look about the leafless bowers
As if they dreamed of flowers.

Yet still on every side appears the hand
Of Winter in the land,
Save where the maple reddens on the lawn,
Flushed by the season's dawn;

Or where, like those strange semblances we find
That age to childhood bind,
The elm puts on, as if in Nature's scorn,
The brown of Autumn corn.

As yet the turf is dark, although you know
That, not a span below,
A thousand germs are groping through the gloom,
And soon will burst their tomb.

Already, here and there, on frailest stems
Appear some azure gems,
Small as might deck, upon a gala day,
The forehead of a fay.

In gardens you may see, amid the dearth,
The crocus breaking earth ;
And near the snowdrop's tender white and green,
The violet in its screen.

But many gleams and shadows need must pass
Along the budding grass,
And weeks go by, before the enamored South
Shall kiss the rose's mouth.

Still there 's a sense of blossoms yet unborn
In the sweet airs of morn ;
One almost looks to see the very street
Grow purple at his feet.

At times a fragrant breeze comes floating by
And brings, you know not why,

A feeling as when eager crowds await
Before a palace gate

Some wondrous pageant; and you scarce would start,
If from a beech's heart
A blue-eyed Dryad, stepping forth, should say
"Behold me! I am May!"

Ah! who would couple thoughts of war and crime
With such a blessed time!
Who in the west-wind's aromatic breath
Could hear the call of Death!

Yet not more surely shall the Spring awake
The voice of wood and brake,
Than she shall rouse, for all her tranquil charms
A million men to arms.

There shall be deeper hues upon her plains
Than all her sunlight rains,
And every gladdening influence around
Can summon from the ground.

Oh! standing on this desecrated mould,
Methinks that I behold,
Lifting her bloody daisies up to God,
Spring, kneeling on the sod,

And calling with the voice of all her rills
Upon the ancient hills,
To fall and crush the tyrants and the slaves
Who turn her meads to graves.

---

## CHICKAMAUGA—"THE STREAM OF DEATH."

RICHMOND SENTINEL.

CHICKAMAUGA ! Chickamauga !
O'er thy dark and turbid wave
Rolls the death-cry of the daring,
Rings the war-shout of the brave ;
Round thy shore the red fires flashing,
Startling shot and screaming shell—
Chickamauga, stream of battle,
Who thy fearful tale shall tell ?

Olden memories of horror,
Sown by scourge of deadly plague,
Long hath clothed thy circling forests
With a terror vast and vague ;
Now to gather further vigor
From the phantoms grim with gore,
Hurried, by war's wilder carnage,
To their graves on thy lone shore.

Long, with hearts subdued and saddened,
  As th' oppressor's hosts moved on,
Fell the arms of freedom backward,
  Till our hopes had almost flown ;
Till outspoke stern valor's fiat—
  "*Here* th' invading wave shall stay ;
*Here* shall cease the foe's proud progress ;
  *Here* be crushed his grand array !"

*Then* their eager hearts all throbbing,
  Backward flashed each battle-flag
Of the veteran corps of Longstreet,
  And the sturdy troops of Bragg ;
Fierce upon the foemen turning,
  All their pent-up wrath breaks out
In the furious battle-clangor,
  And the frenzied battle-shout.

Roll thy dark waves, Chickamauga,
  Trembles all thy ghastly shore,
With the rude shock of the onset,
  And the tumult's horrid roar ;
As the Southern battle-giants
  Hurl their bolts of death along,
Breckenridge, the iron-hearted,
  Cheatham, chivalric and strong :

Polk Preston—gallant Buckner,
 Hill and Hindman, strong in might,
Cleburne, flower of manly valor,
 Hood, the Ajax of the fight;
Benning, bold and hardy warrior,
 Fearless, resolute Kershaw;
Mingle battle-yell and death-bolt,
 Volley fierce and wild hurrah!

At the volleys bleed their bodies,
 At the fierce shout rise their souls,
While the fiery wave of vengeance
 On their quailing column rolls;
And the parched throats of the stricken
 Breathe for air the roaring flame,
Horrors of that hell foretasted,
 Who shall ever dare to name!

Borne by those who, stiff and mangled,
 Paid, upon that bloody field,
Direful, cringing, awe-struck homage
 To the sword our heroes yield;
And who felt, by fiery trial,
 That the men who *will* be free,
Though in confiict baffled often,
 Ever will *unconquered* be!

Learned, though long unchecked they spoil us,
  Dealing desolation round,
Marking, with the tracks of ruin,
  Many a rood of Southern ground ;
Yet, whatever course they follow,
  *Somewhere* in their pathway flows,
Dark and deep, a Chickamauga,
  *Stream of death* to vandal foes !

They have found it darkly flowing
  By Manassas' famous plain,
And by rushing Shenandoah
  Met the tide of woe again ;
Chickahominy, immortal,
  By the long, ensanguined fight,
Rappahannock, glorious river,
  Twice renowned for matchless fight.

Heed the story, dastard spoilers,
  Mark the tale these waters tell,
Ponder well your fearful lesson,
  And the doom that there befell ;
Learn to shun the Southern vengeance,
  Sworn upon the votive sword,
"*Every* stream a Chickamauga
  To the vile invading horde !"

15*

## IN MEMORIAM

OF OUR RIGHT-REVEREND FATHER IN GOD, LEONIDAS POLK, LIEUTENAT-GENERAL CONFEDERATE STATES ARMY.

Peace, troubled soul! The strife is done,
This life's fierce conflicts and its woes are ended:
There is no more—eternity begun,
Faith merged in sight—hope with fruition blended.
Peace, troubled soul!
The Warrior rests upon his bier,
Within his coffin calmly sleeping.
His requiem the cannon peals,
And heroes of a hundred fields
Their last sad watch are round him keeping.

Joy, sainted soul! Within the vale
Of Heaven's great temple, is thy blissful dwelling;
Bathed in a light, to which the sun is pale,
Archangels' hymns in endless transports swelling.
Joy, sainted soul!
Back to her altar which he served,
The Holy Church her child is bringing.
The organ's wail then dies away,
And kneeling priests around him pray,
As *De Profundis* they are singing.

Bring all the trophies, that are owed
  To him at once so great, so good.
His Bible and his well-used sword—
  His snowy lawn not "stained with blood!"
No! pure as when before his God,
  He laid its spotless folds aside,
War's path of awful duty trod,
  And on his country's altar died!

Oh! Warrior-bishop, Church and State
  Sustain in thee an equal loss;
But who would call thee from thy weight
  Of glory, back to bear life's cross!
The Faith was kept—thy course was run,
  Thy good fight finished; hence the word,
"Well done, oh! faithful child, well done,
  Taste thou the mercies of thy Lord!"

No dull decay nor lingering pain,
  By slow degrees, consumed thy health,
A glowing messenger of flame
  Translated thee by fiery death!
And we who in one common grief
  Are bending now beneath the rod,
In this sweet thought may find relief,
  "Our holy father walked with God,
And is not—God has taken him!"

VIOLA.

## "STONEWALL" JACKSON.

BY H. L. FLASH.

Not 'midst the lightning of the stormy fight
  Not in the rush upon the vandal foe,
Did kingly death, with his resistless might,
  Lay the great leader low!

His warrior soul its earthly shackles bore
  In the full sunshine of a peaceful town;
When all the storm was hushed, the trusty oak
  That propped our cause, went down.

Though his alone the blood that flecks the ground,
  Recording all his grand heroic deeds,
Freedom herself is writhing with his wound,
  And all the country bleeds.

He entered not the nation's "Promised Land,"
  At the red belching of the cannon's mouth;
But broke the "House of Bondage" with his hand—
  The Moses of the South!

Oh, gracious God! not gainless is our loss:
  A glorious sunbeam gilds Thy sternest frown;
And while his country staggers with the cross—
  He rises with the crown!

## "STONEWALL" JACKSON.—A DIRGE.

Go to thy rest, great chieftain!
  In the zenith of thy fame;
With the proud heart stilled and frozen,
  No foeman e'er could tame;
With the eye that met the battle
  As the eagle's meets the sun,
Rayless—beneath its marble lid,
  Repose—thou mighty one!

Yet ill our cause could spare thee;
  And harsh the blow of fate
That struck its staunchest pillar
  From 'neath our dome of state.
Of thee, as of the Douglas,
  We say, with Scotland's king,
"There is not one to take *his* place
  In all the knightly ring."

Thou wert the noblest captain
  Of all that martial host
That front the haughty Northman,
  And put to shame his boast.
Thou wert the strongest bulwark
  To stay the tide of fight;

The name thy soldiers gave thee
  Bore witness of thy might!

But we may not weep above thee;
  This is no time for tears!
Thou wouldst not brook their shedding,
  Oh! saint among thy peers!
Couldst thou speak from yonder heaven,
  Above us smiling spread,
Thou wouldst not have us pause, for grief,
  On the blood-stained path we tread!

Not—while our homes in ashes
  Lie smouldering on the sod!
Not—while our houseless women
  Send up wild wails to God!
Not—while the mad fanatic
  Strews ruin on his track!
*Dare* any Southron give the rein
  To feeling, and look back!

No! Still the cry is "onward!"
  This is no time for tears;
No! Still the word is "vengeance!"
  Leave ruth for coming years.
We will snatch thy glorious banner
  From thy dead and stiffening hand,

And high, 'mid battle's deadly storm,
We'll bear it through the land.

And all who mark it streaming—
Oh! soldier of the cross!—
Shall gird them with a fresh resolve
Sternly to avenge our loss;
Whilst thou, enrolled a martyr,
Thy sacred mission shown,
Shalt lay the record of our wrongs
Before the Eternal throne!

---

## BEAUFORT.

BY W. J. GRAYSON, OF SOUTH CAROLINA.

Old home! what blessings late were yours;
The gifts of peace, the songs of joy!
Now, hostile squadrons seek your shores,
To ravage and destroy.

The Northman comes no longer there,
With soft address and measured phrase,
With bated breath, and sainted air,
And simulated praise.

He comes a vulture to his prey;
  A wolf to raven in your streets:
Around on shining stream and bay
  Gather his bandit fleets.

They steal the pittance of the poor;
  Pollute the precincts of the dead;
Despoil the widow of her store,—
  The orphan of his bread.

Crimes like their crimes—of lust and blood,
  No Christian land has known before;
Oh, for some scourge of fire and flood,
  To sweep them from the shore!

Exiles from home, your people fly,
  In adverse fortune's hardest school;
With swelling breast and flashing eye—
  They scorn the tyrant's rule!

Away, from all their joys away,
  The sports that active youth engage;
The scenes where childhood loves to play,
  The resting-place of age.

Away, from fertile field and farm;
  The oak-fringed island-homes that seem

To sit like swans, with matchless charm,
  On sea-born sound and stream.

Away, from palm-environed coast,
  The beach that ocean beats in vain;
The Royal Port, your pride and boast,
  The loud-resounding main.

Away, from orange groves that glow
  With golden fruit or snowy flowers,
Roses that never cease to blow,
  Myrtle and jasmine bowers.

From these afar, the hoary head
  Of feeble age, the timid maid,
Mothers and nurslings, all have fled,
  Of ruthless foes afraid.

But, ready, with avenging hand,
  By wood and fen, in ambush lie
Your sons, a stern, determined band,
  Intent to do or die.

Whene'er the foe advance to dare
  The onset, urged by hate and wrath,
Still have they found, aghast with fear,
  A Lion in the path.

Scourged, to their ships they wildly rush,
Their shattered ranks to shield and save,
And learn how hard a task to crush
The spirit of the brave.

Oh, God! Protector of the right,
The widows' stay, the orphans' friend,
Restrain the rage of lawless might,
The wronged and crushed defend!

Be guide and helper, sword and shield!
From hill and vale, where'er they roam,
Bring back the yeoman to his field,
The exile to his home!

Pastors and scattered flocks restore;
Their fanes rebuild, their altars raise;
And let their quivering lips once more
Rejoice in songs of praise!

---

## THE EMPTY SLEEVE.

BY DR. J. R. BAGBY, OF VIRGINIA.

Tom, old fellow, I grieve to see
The sleeve hanging loose at your side;
The arm you lost was worth to me
Every Yankee that ever died.

But you don't mind it at all ;
  You swear you've a beautiful stump,
And laugh at that damnable ball—
  Tom, I knew you were always a trump.

A good right arm, a nervy hand,
  A wrist as strong as a sapling oak,
Buried deep in the Malvern sand—
  To laugh at that, is a sorry joke.
Never again your iron grip
  Shall I feel in my shrinking palm—
Tom, Tom, I see your trembling lip ;
  All within is not so calm.

Well ! the arm is gone, it is true ;
  But the one that is nearest the heart
Is left—and that's as good as two ;
  Tom, old fellow, what makes you start ?
Why, man, *she* thinks that empty sleeve
  A badge of honor ; so do I,
And all of us :—I do believe
  The fellow is going to cry !

" She deserves a perfect man," you say ;
  " You were not worth her in your prime :"
Tom ! the arm that has turned to clay,
  Your whole body has made sublime ;

For you have placed in the Malvern earth
  The proof and pledge of a noble life—
And the rest, henceforward of higher worth,
  Will be dearer than all to your wife.

I see the people in the street
  Look at your sleeve with kindling eyes ;
And you know, Tom, there's naught so sweet
  As homage shown in mute surmise.
Bravely your arm in battle strove,
  Freely for Freedom's sake, you gave it ;
It has perished—but a nation's love
  In proud remembrance will save it.

Go to your sweetheart, then, forthwith—
  You're a fool for staying so long—
Woman's love you'll find no myth,
  But a truth ; living, tender, strong.
And when around her slender belt
  Your left is clasped in fond embrace,
Your right will thrill, as if it felt,
  In its grave, the usurper's place.

As I look through the coming years,
  I see a one-armed married man ;
A little woman, with smiles and tears,
  Is helping as hard as she can

To put on his coat, to pin his sleeve,
  Tie his cravat, and cut his food ;
And I say, as these fancies I weave,
  "That is Tom, and the woman he wooed."

The years roll on, and then I see
  A wedding picture, bright and fair ;
I look closer, and its plain to me
  That is Tom with the silver hair.
He gives away the lovely bride,
  And the guests linger, loth to leave
The house of him in whom they pride—
  "Brave old Tom with the empty sleeve."

---

## THE COTTON-BURNERS' HYMN.

"On yesterday, all the cotton in Memphis, and throughout the country, was burned. Probably not less than 300,000 bales have been burned in the last three days, in West Tennessee and North Mississippi."—*Memphis Appeal.*

I.

Lo ! where Mississippi rolls
  Oceanward its stream,
Upward mounting, folds on folds,
  Flaming fire-tongues gleam ;
'Tis the planters' grand oblation
On the altar of the nation ;

'Tis a willing sacrifice—
Let the golden incense rise—
Pile the Cotton to the skies!
  Chorus—Lo! the sacrificial flame
          Gilds the starry dome of night!
        Nations! read the mute acclaim—
          'Tis for liberty we fight!
          Homes! Religion! Right!

II.

Never such a golden light
  Lit the vaulted sky;
Never sacrifice as bright,
  Rose to God on high:
Thousands oxen, what were they
To the offering we pay?
And the brilliant holocaust—
When the revolution's past—
In the nation's songs will last!
  Chorus—Lo! the sacrificial flame, etc.

III.

Though the night be dark above,
  Broken though the shield—
Those who love us, those we love,
  Bid us never yield:
Never! though our bravest bleed,
And the vultures on them feed;

Never! though the Serpents' race—
Hissing hate and vile disgrace—
By the million should menace!
  CHORUS—Lo! the sacrificial flame, etc.

IV.

Pile the Cotton to the skies;
  Lo! the Northmen gaze;
England! see our sacrifice—
  See the Cotton blaze!
God of nations! now to Thee,
Southrons bend th' imploring knee;
'Tis our country's hour of need—
Hear the mothers intercede—
Hear the little children plead!
  CHORUS—Lo! the sacrificial flame, etc.

---

## READING THE LIST.

"Is there any news of the war?" she said—
"Only a list of the wounded and dead,"
    Was the man's reply,
    Without lifting his eye
    To the face of the woman standing by.
"'Tis the very thing I want," she said;
"Read me a list of the wounded and dead."

He read the list—'twas a sad array
Of the wounded and killed in the fatal fray;
 In the very midst, was a pause to tell
 Of a gallant youth, who fought so well
That his comrades asked: "Who is he, pray?"
"The only son of the Widow Gray,"
  Was the proud reply
  Of his Captain nigh.
What ails the woman standing near?
Her face has the ashen hue of fear!

"Well, well, read on; is he wounded? quick!
Oh God! but my heart is sorrow-sick!"
 "Is he wounded? No! he fell, they say,
 Killed outright on that fatal day!"
 But see, the woman has swooned away!

Sadly she opened her eyes to the light;
Slowly recalled the events of the fight;
Faintly she murmured: "Killed outright!
 It has cost me the life of my only son;
 But the battle is fought, and the victory won;
 The will of the Lord, let it be done!"

God pity the cheerless Widow Gray,
And send from the halls of eternal day,
The light of His peace to illumine her way!

# HIS LAST WORDS.

"A few moments before his death (Stonewall Jackson) he called out in his delirium: 'Order A. P. Hill to prepare for action. Pass the infantry rapidly to the front. Tell Major Hawks ——.' Here the sentence was left unfinished. But, soon after, a sweet smile overspread his face, and he murmured quietly, with an air of relief: 'Let us cross the river and rest under the shade of the trees.' These were his last words; and, without any expression of pain, or sign of struggle, his spirit passed away."

I.

Come, let us cross the river, and rest beneath the trees,
And list the merry leaflets at sport with every breeze;
Our rest is won by fighting, and Peace awaits us there.
Strange that a cause so blighting produces fruit so fair!

II.

Come, let us cross the river, those that have gone before,
Crush'd in the strife for freedom, await on yonder shore;
So bright the sunshine sparkles, so merry hums the breeze,
Come, let us cross the river, and rest beneath the trees.

III.

Come, let us cross the river, the stream that runs so dark:
'Tis none but cowards quiver, so let us all embark.
Come, men with hearts undaunted, we'll stem the tide with ease,
We'll cross the flowing river, and rest beneath the trees.

IV.

Come, let us cross the river, the dying hero cried,
And God, of life the giver, then bore him o'er the tide.
Life's wars for him are over, the warrior takes his ease,
There, by the flowing river, at rest beneath the trees.

---

## CHARGE OF HAGOOD'S BRIGADE.

### WELDON RAILROAD, AUGUST 21, 1864.

The following lines were written in the summer of 1864, immediately after the charge referred to in them, which was always considered by the brigade as their most desperate encounter.

SCARCE seven hundred men they stand
In tattered, rude array,
A remnant of that gallant band,
Who erstwhile held the sea-girt strand
Of Morris' isle, with iron hand
'Gainst Yankees' hated sway.

SECESSIONVILLE their banner claims,
And SUMTER, held 'mid smoke and flames,
And the dark battle on the streams
Of POCOTALIGO :
And WALTHALL'S JUNCTION'S hard-earned fight,
And DREWRY'S BLUFF'S embattled height,

Whence, at the gray dawn of the light,
They rushed upon the foe.

Tattered and torn those banners now,
But not less proud each lofty brow,
Untaught as yet to yield:
With mien unblenched, unfaltering eye,
Forward, where bombshells shrieking fly
Flecking with smoke the azure sky
On Weldon's fated field.

Sweeps from the woods the bold array,
Not theirs to falter in the fray,
No men more sternly trained than they
To meet their deadly doom:
While, from a hundred throats agape,
A hundred sulphurous flames escape,
Round shot, and canister, and grape,
The thundering cannon's boom!

Swift, on their flank, with fearful crash
Shrapnel and ball commingling clash,
And bursting shells, with lurid flash,
Their dazzled sight confound:
Trembles the earth beneath their feet,
Along their front a rattling sheet
Of leaden hail concentric meet,
And numbers strew the ground.

On, o'er the dying and the dead,
O'er mangled limb and gory head,
With martial look, with martial tread,
March Hagood's men to bloody bed,
Honor their sole reward ;
Himself doth lead their battle line,
Himself those banners guard.

They win the height, those gallant few,
A fiercer struggle to renew,
Resolved as gallant men to do
Or sink in glory's shroud ;
But scarcely gain its stubborn crest,
Ere, from the ensign's murdered breast,
An impious foe has dared to wrest
That banner proud.

Upon him, Hagood, in thy might !
Flash on thy soul th' immortal light
Of those brave deeds that blazon bright
Our Southern Cross.
He dies. Unfurl its folds again,
Let it wave proudly o'er the plain ;
The dying shall forget their pain,
Count not their loss.

Then, rallying to your chieftain's call,
Ploughed through by cannon-shot and ball,

Hemmed in, as by a living wall,
Cleave back your way.
Those bannered deeds their souls inspire,
Borne, amid sheets of forkéd fire,
By the Two Hundred who retire
Of that array.

Ah, Carolina! well the tear
May dew thy cheek; thy clasped hands rear
In passion, o'er their tombless bier,
Thy fallen chivalry!
Malony, mirror of the brave,
And Sellers lie in glorious grave;
No prouder fate than theirs, who gave
Their lives for Liberty.

---

## CAROLINA.

APRIL 14, 1861.

BY JOHN A. WAGENER, OF S. C.

Carolina! Carolina!
Noble name in State and story,
How I love thy truthful glory,
As I love the blue sky o'er ye,
Carolina evermore!

Carolina ! Carolina !
Land of chivalry unfearing,
Daughters fair beyond comparing,
Sons of worth, and noble daring,
Carolina evermore !

Carolina ! Carolina !
Soft thy clasp in loving greeting,
Plenteous board and kindly meeting,
All thy pulses nobly beating,
Carolina evermore !

Carolina ! Carolina !
Green thy valleys, bright thy heaven,
Bold thy streams through forest riven,
Bright thy laurels, hero-given,
Carolina evermore !

Carolina ! Carolina !
Holy name, and dear forever,
Never shall thy childen, never,
Fail to strike with grand endeavor,
Carolina evermore !

# SAVANNAH.

BY ALETHEA S. BURROUGHS.

Thou hast not drooped thy stately head,
Thy woes a wondrous beauty shed !
Not like a lamb to slaughter led,
But with the lion's monarch tread,
Thou comest to thy battle bed,
Savannah ! oh, Savannah !

Thine arm of flesh is girded strong ;
The blue veins swell beneath thy wrong ;
To thee, the triple cords belong,
Of woe, ȧnd death, and shameless wrong,
And spirit vaunted long, *too* long !
Savannah ! oh, Savannah !

No blood-stains spot thy forehead fair ;
Only the martyrs' blood is there ;
It gleams upon thy bosom bier,
It moves thy deep, deep soul to prayer,
And tunes a dirge for thy sad ear,
Savannah ! oh, Savannah !

Thy clean white hand is opened wide
For weal or woe, thou Freedom Bride ;

The sword-sheath sparkles at thy side,
Thy plighted troth, whate'er betide,
Thou hast but Freedom for thy guide,
Savannah ! oh, Savannah !

What though the heavy storm-cloud lowers—
Still at thy feet the old oak towers ;
Still fragrant are thy jessamine bowers,
And things of beauty, love, and flowers
Are smiling o'er this land of ours,
My sunny home, Savannah !

There is no film before thy sight—
Thou seest woe, and death, and night—
And blood upon thy banner bright ;
But in thy full wrath's kindled might,
What carest *thou* for woe, or night ?
My rebel home, Savannah !

Come—for the crown is on thy head !
Thy woes a wondrous beauty shed,
Not like a lamb to slaughter led,
But with the lion's monarch tread,
Oh ! come unto thy battle bed,
Savannah ! oh, Savannah !

# "OLD BETSY."

BY JOHN KILLUM.

Come, with the rifle so long in your keeping,
  Clean the old gun up and hurry it forth ;
Better to die while "Old Betsy" is speaking,
  Than live with arms folded, the slave of the North.

Hear ye the yelp of the North-wolf resounding,
  Scenting the blood of the warm-hearted South ;
Quick ! or his villainous feet will be bounding
  Where the gore of our maidens may drip from his mouth.

Oft in the wildwood "Old Bess" has relieved you,
  When the fierce bear was cut down in his track—
If at that moment she never deceived you,
  Trust her to-day with this ravenous pack.

Then come with the rifle so long in your keeping,
  Clean the old girl up and hurry her forth ;
Better to die while "Old Betsy" is speaking,
  Than live with arms folded, the slave of the North.

## AWAKE—ARISE!

BY G. W. ARCHER, M. D.

Sons of the South—awake—arise!
  A million foes sweep down amain,
Fierce hatred gleaming in their eyes,
  And fire and rapine in their train,
  Like savage Hun and merciless Dane!
"We come as brothers!" Trust them not!
  By all that's dear in heaven and earth,
  By every tie that hath its birth
  Within your homes—around your hearth;
Believe me, 'tis a tyrant's plot,
  Worse for the fair and sleek disguise—
A traitor in a patriot's cloak!
      "Your country's good
        Demands your blood!"
Was it a fiend from hell that spoke?

They point us to the Stripes and Stars;
  (Our banner erst—the despot's now!)
But let not thoughts of by-gone wars,
  When beat we back the common foe,
  And felled them fast and shamed them so,
Divide us at this fearful hour;
  But think of dungeons and of chains—
  Think of your violated fanes—
  Of your loved homestead's gory stains—

Eternal thraldom for your dower!
No love of country fires their breasts—
The fell fanatics fain would free
A grovelling race,
And in their place
Would fetter us with fiendish glee!

Sons of the South—awake—awake!
And strike for rights full dear as those
For which our struggling sires did shake
Earth's proudest throne—while freedom rose,
Baptized in blood of braggart foes.
Awake—that hour hath come again!
Strike! as ye look to Heaven's high throne—
Strike! for the Christian patriot's crown—
Strike! in the name of Washington,
Who taught you once to rend the chain,
Smiles now from heaven upon our cause,
So like his own. His spirit moves
Through every fight,
And lends its might
To every heart that freedom loves.

Ye beauteous of the sunny land!
Unmatched your charms in all the earth,
'Neath freedom's banner take your stand;
And, though ye strike not, prove your worth,

As wont in days of joy and mirth :
Lavish your praises on the brave—
Pray when the battle fiercely lowers—
Smile when the victory is ours—
Frown on the wretch who basely cowers—
Mourn o'er each fallen hero's grave !
Lend thus your favors whilst we smite !
Full soon we'll crush this vandal host !—
With woman's charms
To nerve their arms,
Oh ! when have men their freedom lost !

---

## GENERAL ALBERT SIDNEY JOHNSTON.

BY MARY JERVEY, OF CHARLESTON.

In thickest fight triumphantly he fell,
While into victory's arms he led us on ;
A death so glorious our grief should quell :
We mourn him, yet his battle-crown is won.

No slanderous tongue can vex his spirit now,
No bitter taunts can stain his blood-bought fame ;
Immortal honor rests upon his brow,
And noble memories cluster round his name.

For hearts shall thrill and eyes grow dim with tears,
To read the story of his touching fate ;
How in his death the gallant soldier wears
The crown that came for earthly life too late.

Ye people ! guard his memory—sacred keep
The garlands green above his hero-grave ;
Yet weep, for praise can never wake his sleep,
To tell him he is shrined among the brave !

---

## EULOGY OF THE DEAD.

BY B. F. PORTER, OF ALABAMA.

" *Weep not for the dead ; neither bemoan him.*"—*Jeremiah.*

Oh ! weep not for the dead,
Whose blood, for freedom shed,
Is hallowed evermore !
Who on the battle-field
Could die—but never yield !
Oh, bemoan them never more—
They live immortal in their gore !

Oh, what is it to die
Midst shouts of victory,
Our rights and homes defending !
Oh ! what were fame and life
Gained in that basest strife

For tyrants' power contending,
Our country's bosom rending !

Oh ! dead of red Manassah !
Oh ! dead of Shiloh's fray !
Oh ! victors of the Richmond field !
Dead on your mother's breast,
You live in glorious rest ;
Each on* his honored shield,
Immortal in each bloody field !

Oh ! sons of noble mothers !
Oh ! youth of maiden lovers !
Oh ! husbands of chaste wives !
Though asleep in beds of gore,
You return, oh ! never more ;
Still immortal are your lives !
Immortal mothers ! lovers ! wives !

How blest is he who draws
His sword in freedom's cause !
Though dead on battle-field,
Forever to his tomb
Shall youthful heroes come,
Their hearts for freedom steeled,
And learn to die on battle-field.

---

* The Grecian mother, on sending her son to battle, pointing tc his shield, said—" With it, or on it."

As at Thermopylæ,
Grecian child of liberty ;
Swears to despot ne'er to yield—
Here, by our glorious dead,
Let's revenge the blood they've shed,
Or die on bloody field,
By the sons who scorned to yield !

Oh ! mothers ! lovers ! wives !
Oh ! weep no more—our lives
Are our country's evermore !
More glorious in your graves,
Than if living Lincoln's slaves,
Ye will perish never more,
Martyred on our fields of gore !

---

## THE BEAUFORT EXILE'S LAMENT.

Now chant me a dirge for the Isles of the Sea,
  And sing the sad wanderer's psalm—
Ye women and children in exile that flee
  From the land of the orange and palm.

Lament for your homes, for the house of your God,
  Now the haunt of the vile and the low ;
Lament for the graves of your fathers, now trod
  By the foot of the Puritan foe !

No longer for thee, when the sables of night
  Are fading like shadows away,
Does the mocking-bird, drinking the first beams of light,
  Praise God for the birth of a day.

No longer for thee, when the rays are now full,
  Do the oaks form an evergreen glade;
While the drone of the locust o'erhead, seemed to lull
  The cattle that rest in the shade.

No longer for thee does the soft-shining moon
  Silver o'er the green waves of the bay;
Nor at evening, the notes of the wandering loon
  Bid farewell to the sun's dying ray.

Nor when night drops her pall over river and shore,
  And scatters eve's merry-voiced throng,
Does there rise, keeping time to the stroke of the oar,
  The wild chant of the sacred boat-song.

Then the revellers would cease ere the red wine they'd quaff,
  The traveller would pause on his way;
And maidens would hush their low silvery laugh,
  To list to the negro's rude lay.

"Going home! going home!" methinks I now hear
  At the close of each solemn refrain;

'Twill be many a day, aye, and many a year,
  Ere ye'll sing that dear word "Home" again.

Your noble sons slain, on the battle-field lie,
  Your daughters 'mid strangers now roam;
Your aged and helpless in poverty sigh
  O'er the days when they once had a *home.*

"Going home! going home!" for the exile alone
  Can those words sweep the chords of the soul,
And raise from the grave the loved ones who are gone,
  As the tide-waves of time backward roll.

"Going home! going home!" Ah! how many who pine,
  Dear Beaufort, to press thy green sod,
Ere then will have passed to shores brighter than thine—
  Will have gone home at last to their God!

---

## SOMEBODY'S DARLING.

BY MARIE LA COSTE, OF GEORGIA.

Into a ward of the whitewashed halls,
  Where the dead and the dying lay—
Wounded by bayonets, shells, and balls,
  Somebody's darling was borne one day—

Somebody's darling, so young and so brave!
  Wearing yet on his sweet, pale face—
Soon to be hid in the dust of the grave—
  The lingering light of his boyhood's grace!

Matted and damp are the curls of gold
  Kissing the snow of that fair young brow,
Pale are the lips of delicate mould—
  Somebody's darling is dying now.
Back from his beautiful blue-veined brow
  Brush his wandering waves of gold;
Cross his hands on his bosom now—
  Somebody's darling is still and cold.

Kiss him once for somebody's sake,
  Murmur a prayer soft and low—
One bright curl from its fair mates take—
  They were somebody's pride you know.
Somebody's hand hath rested there;
  Was it a mother's, soft and white?
Or have the lips of a sister fair
  Been baptized in their waves of light?

God knows best! He has somebody's love;
  Somebody's heart enshrined him there—
Somebody wafted his name above,
  Night and morn, on the wings of prayer.

Somebody wept when he marched away,
 Looking so handsome, brave, and grand!
Somebody's kiss on his forehead lay—
 Somebody clung to his parting hand.

Somebody's watching and waiting for him,
 Yearning to hold him again to her heart;
And there he lies with his blue eyes dim,
 And the smiling child-like lips apart.
Tenderly bury the fair young dead—
 Pausing to drop on his grave a tear;
Carve on the wooden slab o'er his head—
 "Somebody's darling slumbers here."

---

## JOHN PEGRAM,

FELL AT THE HEAD OF HIS DIVISION, FEB. 6TH, 1865, ÆTAT XXXIII.

BY W. GORDON McCABE.

WHAT shall we say, now, of our gentle knight,
 Or how express the measure of our woe,
For him who rode the foremost in the fight,
 Whose good blade flashed so far amid the foe?

Of all his knightly deeds what need to tell?—
 That good blade now lies fast within its sheath;

What can we do but point to where he fell,
And, like a soldier, met a soldier's death?

We sorrow not as those who have no hope;
For he was pure in heart as brave in deed—
God pardon us, if blindly we should grope,
And love be questioned by the hearts that bleed.

And yet—oh! foolish and of little faith!
We cannot choose but weep our useless tears;
We loved him so; we never dreamed that death
Would dare to touch him in his brave young years.

Ah! dear, browned face, so fearless and so bright!
As kind to friend as thou wast stern to foe—
No more we'll see thee radiant in the fight,
The eager eyes—the flush on cheek and brow!

No more we'll greet the lithe, familiar form,
Amid the surging smoke, with deaf'ning cheer;
No more shall soar above the iron storm,
Thy ringing voice in accents sweet and clear.

Aye! he has fought the fight and passed away—
Our grand young leader smitten in the strife!
So swift to seize the chances of the fray,
And careless only of his noble life.

He is not dead, but sleepeth! well we know
The form that lies to-day beneath the sod,
Shall rise that time the golden bugles blow,
And pour their music through the courts of God.

And there amid our great heroic dead—
The war-worn sons of God, whose work is done—
His face shall shine, as they with stately tread,
In grand review, sweep past the jasper throne.

Let not our hearts be troubled! Few and brief
His days were here, yet rich in love and faith:
Lord, we believe, help thou our unbelief,
And grant thy servants such a life and death!

---

## CAPTIVES GOING HOME.

No flaunting banners o'er them wave,
No arms flash back the sun's bright ray,
No shouting crowds around them throng,
No music cheers them on their way:
They're going home. By adverse fate
Compelled their trusty swords to sheathe;
True soldiers they, even though disarmed—
Heroes, though robbed of victory's wreath.

Brave Southrons ! 'Tis with sorrowing hearts
We gaze upon them through our tears,
And sadly feel how vain were all
Their heroic deeds through weary years ;
Yet 'mid their enemies they move
With firm, bold step and dauntless mien :
Oh, Liberty ! in every age,
Such have thy chosen heroes been.

Going home ! Alas, to them the words
Bring visions fraught with gloom and woe :
Since last they saw those cherished homes
The legions of the invading foe
Have swept them, simoon-like, along,
Spreading destruction with the wind !
"They found a garden, but they left
A howling wilderness behind."

Ah ! in those desolated homes
To which the "fate of war has come,"
Sad is the welcome—poor the feast—
That waits the soldier's coming home ;
Yet loving ones will round him throng,
With smiles more tender, if less gay,
And joy will brighten pallid cheeks
At sight of the dear boys in gray.

Aye, give them welcome home, fair South,
  For you they've made a deathless name;
Bright through all after-time will glow
  The glorious record of their fame.
They made a nation. What, though soon
  Its radiant sun has seemed to set;
The past has shown what they can do,
  The future holds bright promise yet.

---

## ON THE HEIGHTS OF MISSION RIDGE.

BY J. AUGUSTINE SIGNAIGO.

When the foes, in conflict heated,
  Battled over road and bridge,
While Bragg sullenly retreated
  From the heights of Mission Ridge—
There, amid the pines and wildwood,
  Two opposing colonels fell,
Who had schoolmates been in childhood,
  And had loved each other well.

There, amid the roar and rattle,
  Facing Havoc's fiery breath,
Met the wounded two in battle,
  In the agonies of death.

But they saw each other reeling
  On the dead and dying men,
And the old time, full of feeling,
  Came upon them once again.

When that night the moon came creeping,
  With its gold streaks, o'er the slain,
She beheld two soldiers, sleeping,
  Free from every earthly pain.
Close beside the mountain heather,
  Where the rocks obscure the sand,
They had died, it seems, together,
  As they clasped each other's hand.

---

## "OUR LEFT AT MANASSAS."

From dawn to dark they stood,
  That long midsummer's day!
While fierce and fast
The battle-blast
  Swept rank on rank away!

From dawn to dark, they fought
  With legions swept and cleft,

While black and wide,
The battle-tide
  Poured ever on our "Left!"

They closed each ghastly gap!
  They dressed each shattered rank
They knew, how well!
That Freedom fell
  With that exhausted flank!

"Oh! for a thousand men,
  Like these that melt away!"
And down they came,
With steel and flame,
  *Four thousand* to the fray!

They left the laggard train;
  The panting steam might stay;
And down they came,
With steel and flame,
  Head-foremost to the fray!

Right through the blackest cloud
  Their lightning-path they cleft!
Freedom and Fame
With triumph came
  To our immortal Left.

Ye! of your living, sure!
    Ye! of your dead, bereft!
Honor the brave
Who died to save
    *Your all*, upon our Left.

---

## ON TO RICHMOND.

AFTER SOUTHEY'S "MARCH TO MOSCOW."

BY JOHN R. THOMPSON, OF VIRGINIA.

MAJOR-GENERAL SCOTT
An order had got
    To push on the columns to Richmond;
For loudly went forth,
From all parts of the North,
The cry that an end of the war must be made
In time for the regular yearly Fall Trade:
Mr. Greeley spoke freely about the delay,
The Yankees "to hum" were all hot for the fray;
The chivalrous Grow
Declared they were slow,
And therefore the order
To march from the border
    And make an excursion to Richmond.

Major-General Scott
Most likely was not
Very loth to obey this instruction, I wot;
In his private opinion
The Ancient Dominion
Deserved to be pillaged, her sons to be shot,
    And the reason is easily noted;
Though this part of the earth
Had given him birth,
And medals and swords,
Inscribed with fine words,
    It never for Winfield had voted.
Besides, you must know that our First of Commanders
Had sworn, quite as hard as the Army in Flanders,
With his finest of armies and proudest of navies,
To wreak his old grudge against Jefferson Davis.
Then "forward the column," he said to McDowell;
    And the Zouaves, with a shout,
    Most fiercely cried out,
"To Richmond or h--ll" (I omit here the vowel),
And Winfield, he ordered his carriage and four,
A dashing turn-out, to be brought to the door,
    For a pleasant excursion to Richmond.

Major-General Scott
Had there on the spot
A splendid array
To plunder and slay;

In the camp he might boast
Such a numerous host,
As he never had yet
In the battle-field set;
Every class and condition of Northern society
Were in for the trip, a most varied variety:
In the camp he might hear every lingo in vogue,
"The sweet German accent, the rich Irish brogue."
The buthiful boy
    From the banks of the Shannon,
Was there to employ
His excellent cannon;
And besides the long files of dragoons and artillery,
    The Zouaves and Hussars,
    All the children of Mars,
    There were barbers and cooks
    And writers of books,—
The *chef de cuisine* with his French bills of fare,
And the artists to dress the young officers' hair.
And the scribblers all ready at once to prepare
    An eloquent story
    Of conquest and glory;
And servants with numberless baskets of Sillery,
Though Wilson, the Senator, followed the train,
At a distance quite safe, to "conduct the *champagne*:"
While the fields were so green and the sky was so blue,
There was certainly nothing more pleasant to do
    On this pleasant excursion to Richmond.

In Congress the talk, as I said, was of action,
To crush out *instanter* the traitorous faction.
In the press, and the mess,
They would hear nothing less
Than to make the advance, spite of rhyme or of reason,
And at once put an end to the insolent treason.
There was Greeley,
And Ely,
The bloodthirsty Grow,
And Hickman (the rowdy, not Hickman the beau),
And that terrible Baker
Who would seize on the South, every acre,
And Webb, who would drive us all into the Gulf, or
Some nameless locality smelling of sulphur;
And with all this bold crew
Nothing would do,
While the fields were so green and the sky was so blue,
    But to march on directly to Richmond.

Then the gallant McDowell
Drove madly the rowel
    Of spur that had never been "won" by him,
In the flank of his steed,
To accomplish a deed,
    Such as never before had been done by him;
And the battery called Sherman's
    Was wheeled into line,
While the beer-drinking Germans.

From Neckar and Rhine,
With minie and yager,
Came on with a swagger,
Full of fury and lager,
(The day and the pageant were equally fine.)
Oh! the fields were so green and the sky was so blue,
Indeed 'twas a spectacle pleasant to view,
As the column pushed onward to Richmond.

Ere the march was begun,
In a spirit of fun,
General Scott in a speech
Said this army should teach
The Southrons the lesson the laws to obey,
And just before dusk of the third or fourth day,
Should joyfully march into Richmond.

He spoke of their drill
And their courage and skill,
And declared that the ladies of Richmond would rave
O'er such matchless perfection, and gracefully wave
In rapture their delicate kerchiefs in air
At their morning parades on the Capitol Square.
But alack! and alas!
Mark what soon came to pass,
When this army, in spite of his flatteries,
Amid war's loudest thunder
Must stupidly blunder
Upon those accursed "masked batteries."

Then Beauregard came,
Like a tempest of flame,
To consume them in wrath
On their perilous path ;
And Johnston bore down in a whirlwind to sweep
    Their ranks from the field
    Where their doom had been sealed,
As the storm rushes over the face of the deep ;
While swift on the centre our President pressed.
    And the foe might descry
    In the glance of his eye
The light that once blazed upon Diomed's crest.
McDowell ! McDowell ! weep, weep for the day
When the Southrons you meet in their battle array ;
To your confident hosts with its bullets and steel
'Twas worse than Culloden to luckless Lochiel.
Oh ! the generals were green and old Scott is now blue,
And a terrible business, McDowell, to you,
    Was that pleasant excursion to Richmond.

Richmond Whig.

---

## TURNER ASHBY.

BY JOHN R. THOMPSON, OF VIRGINIA

To the brave all homage render,
    Weep, ye skies of June !
With a radiance pure and tender,
    Shine, oh saddened moon !

"Dead upon the field of glory,"
Hero fit for song and story,
Lies our bold dragoon!

Well they learned, whose hands have slain him,
Braver, knightlier foe
Never fought with Moor nor Paynim—
Rode at Templestowe;
With a mien how high and joyous,
'Gainst the hordes that would destroy us,
Went he forth we know.

Never more, alas! shall sabre
Gleam around his crest;
Fought his fight, fulfilled his labor,
Stilled his manly breast;
All unheard sweet nature's cadence,
Trump of fame and voice of maidens—
Now he takes his rest.

Earth, that all too soon hath bound him,
Gently wrap his clay;
Linger lovingly around him,
Light of dying day;
Softly fall the summer showers,
Birds and bees among the flowers
Make the gloom seem gay.

There, throughout the coming ages,
  When his sword is rust,
And his deeds in classic pages ;
  Mindful of her trust,
    Shall Virginia, bending lowly,
    Still a ceaseless vigil holy
  Keep above his dust.

---

## CAPTAIN LATANE.

BY JOHN R. THOMPSON, OF VIRGINIA.

The combat raged not long ; but ours the day,
  And through the hosts which compassed us around
Our little band rode proudly on its way,
  Leaving one gallant spirit, glory crowned,
Unburied on the field he died to gain :
Single, of all his men, among the hostile slain !

One moment at the battle's edge he stood,
  Hope's halo, like a helmet, round his hair—
The next, beheld him dabbled in his blood,
  Prostrate in death ; and yet in death how fair !
And thus he passed, through the red gates of strife,
From earthly crowns and palms, to an eternal life.

A brother bore his body from the field,
  And gave it into strangers' hands, who closed
His calm blue eyes, on earth forever sealed,
  And tenderly the slender limbs composed ;
Strangers, but *sisters, who, with Mary's love,*
*Sat by the open tomb and, weeping, looked above.*

A little girl strewed roses on his bier,
  Pale roses—not more stainless than his soul,
Nor yet more fragrant than his life sincere,
  That blossomed with good actions—brief, but whole.
The aged matron, with the faithful slave,
Approached with reverent steps the hero's lowly grave.

No man of God might read the burial rite
  Above the rebel—thus declared the foe,
Who blanched before him in the deadly fight ;
  But woman's voice, in accents soft and low,
Trembling with pity, touched with pathos, read
Over his hallowed dust, the ritual for the dead !

" 'Tis sown in weakness ; it is raised in power."
  Softly the promise floated on the air,
And the sweet breathings of the sunset hour,
  Come back responsive to the mourner's prayer.
Gently they laid him underneath the sod,
And left him with his fame, his country, and his God.

We should not weep for him ! His deeds endure ;
 So young, so beautiful, so brave—he died
As he would wish to die. The past secure,
 Whatever yet of sorrow may betide
Those who still linger by the stormy shore ;
Change cannot hurt him now, nor fortune reach him more.

And when Virginia, leaning on her spear,
 *Vitrix et vidua*, the conflict done,
Shall raise her mailéd hand to wipe the tear
 That starts, as she recalls each martyr son ;
No prouder memory her breast shall sway
Than thine—the early lost—lamented Lat-a-nè !

---

## THE MEN.

BY MAURICE BELL.

IN the dusk of the forest shade
 A sallow and dusty group reclined ;
Gallops a horseman up the glade—
 "Where will I your leader find ?
Tidings I bring from the morning's scout—
 I've borne them o'er mound, and moor, and fen."
"Well, sir, stay not hereabout,
 Here are only a few of 'the men.'

"Here no collar has bar or star,
No rich lacing adorns a sleeve;
Further on our officers are,
Let them your report receive.
Higher up, on the hill up there,
Overlooking this shady glen,
There are their quarters—don't stop here,
We are only some of 'the men.'

"Yet stay, courier, if you bear
Tidings that the fight is near;
Tell them we're ready, and that where
They wish us to be we'll soon appear;
Tell them only to let us know
Where to form our ranks, and when;
And we'll teach the vaunting foe
That they've met a few of 'the men.'

"We're *the men*, though our clothes are worn—
We're *the men*, though we wear no lace—
We're *the men*, who the foe hath torn,
And scattered their ranks in dire disgrace;
We're the men who have triumphed before—
We're the men who will triumph again;
For the dust, and the smoke, and the cannon's roar,
And the clashing bayonets—'*we're the men.*'

"Ye who sneer at the battle-scars,
Of garments faded, and soiled and bare,
Yet who have for the 'stars and bars"
Praise, and homage, and dainty fare;
Mock the wearers and pass them on,
Refuse them kindly word—and then
Know, if your freedom is ever won
By human agents—*these are the men!*"

---

## "A REBEL SOLDIER KILLED IN THE TRENCHES BEFORE PETERSBURG, VA., APRIL 15, 1865."

BY A KENTUCKY GIRL.

Killed in the trenches! How cold and bare
The inscription graved on the white card there.
'Tis a photograph, taken last Spring, they say,
Ere the smoke of battle had cleared away—
Of a rebel soldier—just as he fell,
When his heart was pierced by a Union shell;
And his image was stamped by the sunbeam's ray,
As he lay in the trenches that April day.

Oh God! Oh God! How my woman's heart
Thrills with a quick, convulsive pain,
As I view, unrolled by the magic of Art,
One dreadful scene from the battle-plain:—

White as the foam of the storm-tossed wave,
Lone as the rocks those billows lave—
Gray sky above—cold clay beneath—
A gallant form lies stretched in death!

With his calm face fresh on the trampled clay,
And the brave hands clasped o'er the manly breast:
Save the sanguine stains on his jacket gray,
We might deem him taking a soldier's rest.
Ah no! Too red is that crimson tide—
Too deeply pierced that wounded side;
Youth, hope, love, glory—manhood's pride—
Have all in vain Death's bolt defied.

His faithful carbine lies useless there,
As it dropped from its master's nerveless ward;
And the sunbeams glance on his waving hair
Which the fallen cap has ceased to guard—
Oh Heaven! spread o'er it thy merciful shield,
No more to my sight be the battle revealed!
Oh fiercer than tempest—grim Hades as dread—
On woman's eye flashes the field of the dead!

The scene is changed: In a quiet room,
Far from the spot where the lone corse lies,
A mother kneels in the evening gloom
To offer her nightly sacrifice.

The noon is past, and the day is done,
She knows that the battle is lost or won—
Who lives? Who died? Hush! be thou still!
The boy lies dead on the trench-barred hill.

---

## BATTLE OF HAMPTON ROADS.

BY OSSIAN D. GORMAN.

NE'ER had a scene of beauty smiled
On placid waters 'neath the sun,
Like that on Hampton's watery plain,
The fatal morn the fight begun.
Far toward the silvery Sewell shores,
Below the guns of Craney Isle,
Were seen our fleet advancing fast,
Beneath the sun's auspicious smile.

Oh, fatal sight! the hostile hordes
Of Newport camp spread dire alarms:
The Cumberland for fight prepares—
The fierce marines now rush to arms.
The Merrimac, strong cladded o'er,
In quarters close begins her fire,
Nor fears the rushing hail of shot,
And deadly missiles swift and dire;
But, rushing on 'mid smoke and flame,
And belching thunder long and loud,

Salutes the ship with bow austere,
  And then withdraws in wreaths of cloud.

The work is done. The frigate turns
  In agonizing, doubtful poise—
She sinks, she sinks! along the deck
  Is heard a shrieking, wailing noise.
Engulfed beneath those placid waves
  Disturbed by battle's onward surge,
The crew is gone; the vessel sleeps,
  And whistling bombshells sing her dirge.

The battle still is raging fierce:
  The Congress, "high and dry" aground,
Maintains in vain her boasted power,
  For now the gunboats flock around,
With "stars and bars" at mainmast reared,
  And pour their lightning on the main,
While Merrimac, approaching fast
  Sends forth her shell and hot-shot rain.

Meantime the Jamestown, gallant boat,
  Engages strong redoubts at land—
While Patrick Henry glides along,
  To board the Congress, still astrand.
This done, we turn intently on
  The Minnesota, which replies,
With whizzing shell to Teaser's gun,
  Whose booming cleaves the distant skies.

The naval combat sounds anew ;
  The hostile fleets are not withdrawn,
Though night is closing earth and sea
  In twilight's pale and mystic dawn.
Strange whistling noises fill the air ;
  The powdered smoke looks dark as night,
And deadly, lurid flames, pour forth
  Their radiance on the missiles' flight ;
Grand picture on the noisy waves !
  The breezy zephyrs onward roam,
And echoing volleys float afar,
  Disturbing Neptune's coral home.
The victory's ours, and let the world
  Record Buchanan's* name with pride ;
The *crew is brave, the banner bright,*
  That ruled the day when Hutter† died.

MACON DAILY TELEGRAPH.

---

## IS THIS A TIME TO DANCE?

THE breath of evening sweeps the plain,
  And sheds its perfume in the dell,
But on its wings are sounds of pain,
  Sad tones that drown the echo's swell ;

---

* Commander of the "Merrimac."

† Midshipman on the "Patrick Henry."

And yet we hear a mirthful call,
  Fair pleasure smiles with beaming glance,
Gay music sounds in the joyous hall:
  Oh God! is this a time to dance?

Sad notes, as if a spirit sighed,
  Float from the crimson battle-plain,
As if a mighty spirit cried
  In awful agony and pain:
Our friends we know there suffering lay,
  Our brothers, too, perchance,
And in reproachful accents say,
  Loved ones, is this a time to dance?

Oh, lift your festal robes on high!
  The human gore that flows around
Will stain their hues with crimson dye;
  And louder let your music sound
To drown the dying warrior's cry!
  Let sparkling wine your joy enhance.
Forget that *blood* has tinged its dye,
  And quicker urge the maniac dance.

But stop! the floor beneath your feet
  Gives back a *coffin's* hollow moan,
And every strain of music sweet,
  Wafts forth a *dying soldier's groan.*

Oh, sisters! who have brothers dear
Exposed to every battle's chance,
Brings dark Remorse no forms of fear,
To fright you from the heartless dance?

Go, fling your festal robes away!
Go, don the mourner's sable veil!
Go, bow before your God, and pray!
If yet your prayers may aught avail.
Go, face the fearful form of Death!
And trembling meet his chilling glance,
And then, for once, with truthful breath,
Answer, *Is this a time to dance?*

---

## "THE MARYLAND LINE."

BY J. D. M'CABE, JR.

The Maryland regiments in the Confederate army have adopted the title of "The Maryland Line," which was so heroically sustained by their patriot sires of the first Revolution, and which the deeds of Marylanders at Manassas, show that the patriot Marylanders of this second Revolution are worthy to bear.

By old Potomac's rushing tide,
Our bayonets are gleaming;
And o'er the bounding waters wide
We gaze, while tears are streaming.

The distant hills of Maryland
  Rise sadly up before us—
And tyrant bands have chained our land,
  Our mother proud that bore us.

Our proud old mother's queenly head
  Is bowed in subjugation ;
With her children's blood her soil is red,
  And fiends in exultation
Taunt her with shame as they bind her chains,
  While her heart is torn with anguish ;
Old mother, on famed Manassas' plains
  Our vengeance did not languish.

We thought of your wrongs as on we rushed,
  'Mid shot and shell appalling ;
We heard your voice as it upward gush'd,
  From the Maryland life-blood falling.
No pity we knew ! Did they mercy show
  When they bound the mother that bore us ?
But we scattered death 'mid the dastard foe
  Till they, shrieking, fled before us.

We mourn for our brothers brave that fell
  On that field so stern and gory ;
But their spirits rose with our triumph yell
  To the heavenly realms of glory.

And their bodies rest on the hard-won field—
By their love so true and tender,
We'll keep the prize they would not yield,
We'll die, but we'll not surrender.

---

## THE VIRGINIANS OF THE SHENANDOAH VALLEY.

*"Sic Jurat."*

BY FRANK TICKNOR, M.D., OF GEORGIA.

The knightliest of the knightly race
Who, since the days of old,
Have kept the lamp of chivalry
Alight in hearts of gold;
The kindliest of the kindly band
Who rarely hated ease,
Yet rode with Smith around the land,
And Raleigh o'er the seas;

Who climbed the blue Virginia hills,
Amid embattled foes,
And planted there, in valleys fair,
The lily and the rose;
Whose fragrance lives in many lands,
Whose beauty stars the earth,
And lights the hearths of thousand homes
With loveliness and worth,—

We feared they slept! — the sons who kept
  The names of noblest sires,
And waked not, though the darkness crept
  Around their vigil fires;
But still the Golden Horse-shoe Knights
  Their "Old Dominion" keep:
The foe has found the enchanted ground,
  But not a knight asleep.

TORCH-HALL, GEORGIA.

---

## SONNET.—THE AVATAR OF HELL.

CHARLESTON MERCURY.

SIX thousand years of commune, God with man,—
Two thousand years of Christ; yet from such roots,
Immortal, earth reaps only bitterest fruits!
The fiends rage now as when they first began!
Hate, Lust, Greed, Vanity, triumphant still,
Yell, shout, exult, and lord o'er human will!
The sun moves back! The fond convictions felt,
That, in the progress of the race, we stood,
Two thousand years of height above the flood
Before the day's experience sink and melt,
As frost beneath the fire! and what remains
Of all our grand ideals and great gains,
With Goth, Hun, Vandal, warring in their pride,
While the meek Christ is hourly crucified!

PAX.

## "STONEWALL" JACKSON'S WAY.

These verses, according to the newspaper account, *may* have been found in the bosom of a dead rebel, after one of Jackson's battles in the Shenandoah valley; but we are pleased to state that the *author* of them is a still living rebel, and able to write even better things.

COME, stack arms, men! Pile on the rails;
Stir up the camp-fire bright;
No matter if the canteen fails,
We'll make a roaring night.
Here Shenandoah brawls along,
Here burly Blue Ridge echoes strong,
To swell the brigade's rousing song,
Of "Stonewall Jackson's way."

We see him now — the old slouched hat
Cocked o'er his eye askew —
The shrewd dry smile — the speech so pat,
So calm, so blunt, so true.
The "Blue Light Elder" knows em well:
Says he, "That's Banks; he's fond of shell.
Lord save his soul! we'll give him ——" well
That's "Stonewall Jackson's way."

Silence! Ground arms! Kneel all! Caps off!
Old "Blue Light's" going to pray.
Strangle the fool that dares to scoff!
Attention! it's his way!

Appealing from his native sod
*In forma pauperis* to God,
"Lay bare thine arm! Stretch forth thy rod!
Amen!" That's Stonewall's way.

He's in the saddle now: Fall in!
Steady! The whole brigade!
Hill's at the ford, cut off; we'll win
His way out, ball and blade.
What matter if our shoes are worn?
What matter if our feet are torn?
Quick step! we're with him before dawn!
That's Stonewall Jackson's way!

The sun's bright lances rout the mists
Of morning — and, by George!
Here's Longstreet, struggling in the lists,
Hemmed in an ugly gorge.
Pope and his Yankees, whipped before:
"Bayonets and grape!" hear Stonewall roar;
"Charge, Stuart! Pay off Ashby's score,
In Stonewall Jackson's way!"

Ah, maiden! wait, and watch, and yearn,
For news of Stonewall's band!
Ah, widow! read — with eyes that burn,
That ring upon thy hand!

Ah! wife, sew on, pray on, hope on:
Thy life shall not be all forlorn.
The foe had better ne'er been born,
That gets in Stonewall's way.

---

## THE SILENT MARCH.

On one occasion during the war in Virginia, General Lee was lying asleep by the wayside, when an army of fifteen thousand men passed by with hushed voices and footsteps, lest they should disturb his slumbers.

O'ERCOME with weariness and care,
The war-worn veteran lay
On the green turf of his native land,
And slumbered by the way;
The breeze that sighed across his brow,
And smoothed its deepened lines,
Fresh from his own loved mountain bore
The murmur of their pines;
And the glad sound of waters,
The blue rejoicing streams,
Whose sweet familiar tones were blent
With the music of his dreams:
They brought no sound of battle's din,
Shrill fife or clarion,
But only tenderest memories
Of his own fair Arlington.

While thus the chieftain slumbered,
  Forgetful of his care,
The hollow tramp of thousands
  Came sounding through the air.
With ringing spur and sabre,
  And trampling feet they come,
Gay plume and rustling banner,
  And fife, and trump, and drum;
But soon the foremost column
  Sees where, beneath the shade,
In slumber, calm as childhood,
  Their wearied chief is laid;
And down the line a murmur
  From lip to lip there ran,
Until the stilly whisper
  Had spread to rear from van;
And o'er the host a silence
  As deep and sudden fell,
As though some mighty wizard
  Had hushed them with a spell;
And every sound was muffled,
  And every soldier's tread
Fell lightly as a mother's
  'Round her baby's cradle-bed;
And rank, and file, and column,
  So softly by they swept,
It seemed a ghostly army
  Had passed him as he slept;

But mightier than enchantment
Was that with magic move—
The spell that hushed their voices—
Deep reverence and love.

---

## PRO MEMORIA.

AIR—There is rest for the weary.

BY INA M. PORTER, OF ALABAMA.

Lo! the Southland Queen, emerging
From her sad and wintry gloom,
Robes her torn and bleeding bosom
In her richest orient bloom:
CHORUS.—(Repeat first line three times.)
For her weary sons are resting
By the Edenshore;
They have won the crown immortal,
And the cross of death is o'er!
Where the Oriflamme is burning
On the starlit Edenshore!

Brightly still, in gorgeous glory,
God's great jewel lights our sky;
Look! upon the heart's white dial
There's a SHADOW flitting by!
CHORUS.—But the weary feet are resting, etc.

Homes are dark and hearts are weary,
Souls are numb with hopeless pain ;
For the footfall on the threshold
Never more to sound again !
CHORUS.—They have gone from us forever,
Aye, for evermore !
We must win the crown immortal,
Follow where they led before,
Where the Oriflamme is burning
On the starlit Edenshore.

Proudly, as our Southern forests
Meet the winter's shafts so keen :
Time-defying memories cluster
Round our hearts in living green.
CHORUS.—They have gone from us forever, etc.

May our faltering voices mingle
In the angel-chanted psalm ;
May our earthly chaplets linger
By the bright celestial palm.
CHORUS.—They have gone from us forever, etc

Crest to crest they bore our banner,
Side by side they fell asleep ;
Hand in hand we scatter flowers,
Heart to heart we kneel and weep !
CHORUS.—They have gone from us forever, etc.

When the May eternal dawneth
  At the living God's behest,
We will quaff divine Nepenthe,
  We will share the Soldier's rest.
CHORUS.—Where the weary feet are resting, etc.

Where the shadows are uplifted
  'Neath the never-waning sun,
Shout we, Gloria in Excelsis !
  We have lost, but ye have won !
CHORUS.—Our hearts are yours forever,
    Aye, for evermore !
    Ye have won the crown immortal,
    And the cross of death is o'er,
    Where the Oriflamme is burning
    On the starlit Edenshore !

---

## THE SOUTHERN HOMES IN RUIN.

BY R. B. VANCE, OF NORTH CAROLINA.

"We know a great deal about war now ; but, dear readers, the Southern women know more. Blood has not dripped on our *doorsills* yet ; shells have not burst above our *homesteads*—let us pray they never may.—*Frank Leslie's Illustrated*.

MANY a gray-haired sire has died,
  As falls the oak, to rise no more,
Because his son, his prop, his pride,
  Breathed out his last all red with gore.

No more on earth, at morn, at eve,
  Shall age and youth, entwined as one—
Nor father, son, for either grieve—
  Life's work, alas, for both is done!

Many a mother's heart has bled
  While gazing on her darling child,
As in its tiny eyes she read
  The father's image, kind and mild;
For ne'er again his voice will cheer
  The widowed heart, which mourns him dead;
Nor kisses dry the scalding tear,
  Fast falling on the orphan's head!

Many a little form will stray
  Adown the glen and o'er the hill,
And watch, with wistful looks, the way
  For him whose step is missing still;
And when the twilight steals apace
  O'er mead, and brook, and lonely home,
And shadows cloud the dear, sweet face—
  The cry will be, "Oh, papa, come!"

And many a home's in ashes now,
  Where joy was once a constant guest,
And mournful groups there are, I trow,
  With neither house nor place of rest;

And blood is on the broken *sill*,
  Where happy feet went to and fro,
And everywhere, by field and hill,
  Are sickening sights and sounds of woe!

There is a God who rules on high,
  The widow's and the orphan's friend,
Who sees each tear and hears each sigh,
  That these lone hearts to Him may send!
And when in wrath He tears away
  The reasons vain which men indite,
The record book will plainest say
  Who's in the wrong, and who is right.

---

## "RAPPAHANNOCK ARMY SONG."

BY JOHN C. M'LEMORE.

The toil of the march is over—
  The pack will be borne no more—
For we've come for the help of Richmond,
  From the Rappahannock's shore.
The foe is closing round us—
  We can hear his ravening cry;
So, ho! for fair old Richmond!
  Like soldiers we'll do or die.

We have left the land that bore us,
  Full many a league away,
And our mothers and sisters miss us,
  As with tearful eyes they pray;
But *this* will repress their weeping,
  And still the rising sigh—
For all, for fair old Richmond,
  Have come to do or die.

We have come to join our brothers
  From the proud Dominion's vales,
And to meet the dark-cheeked soldier,
  Tanned by the Tropic gales;
To greet them all full gladly,
  With hand and beaming eye,
And to swear, for fair old Richmond,
  We all will do or die.

The fair Carolina sisters
  Stand ready, lance in hand,
To fight as they did in an older war,
  For the sake of their fatherland.
The glories of Sumter and Bethel
  Have raised their fame full high,
But they'll fade, if for fair old Richmond
  They swear not to do or die.

Zollicoffer looks down on his people,
  And trusts to their hearts and arms,
To avenge the blood he has shed,
  In the midst of the battle's alarms.
Alabamians, remember the past,
  Be the "South at Manassas," their cry;
As onward for fair old Richmond,
  They marched to do or die.

Brave Bartow, from home on high,
  Calls the Empire State to the front,
To bear once more as she has borne
  With glory the battle's brunt.
Mississippians who know no surrender,
  Bear the flag of the Chief on high;
For he, too, for fair old Richmond,
  Has sworn to do or die.

Fair land of my birth—sweet Florida—
  Your arm is weak, but your soul
Must tell of a purer, holier strength,
  When the drums for the battle roll.
Look within, for your hope in the combat,
  Nor think of your few with a sigh—
If you win not for fair old Richmond,
  At least you can bravely die,

Onward all! Oh! band of brothers!
  The beat of the long roll's heard!
And the hearts of the columns advancing,
  By the sound of its music is stirred.
Onward all! and never return,
  Till our foes from the Borders fly—
To be crowned by the fair of old Richmond,
  As those who could do or die.

RICHMOND ENQUIRER.

---

## THE SOLDIER IN THE RAIN.

BY JULIA L. KEYES.

AH me! the rain has a sadder sound
  Than it ever had before;
And the wind more plaintively whistles through
  The crevices of the door.

We know we are safe beneath our roof
  From every drop that falls;
And we feel secure and blest, within
  The shelter of our walls.

Then why do we dread to hear the noise
  Of the rapid, rushing rain—

And the plash of the wintry drops, that beat
  Through the blinds, on the window-pane?

We think of the tents on the lowly ground,
  Where our patriot soldiers lie;
And the sentry's bleak and lonely march,
  'Neath the dark and starless sky.

And we pray, with a tearful heart, for those
  Who brave for us yet more—
And we wish this war, with its thousand ills
  And griefs, was only o'er.

We pray when the skies are bright and clear,
  When the winds are soft and warm—
But oh! we pray with an aching heart
  'Mid the winter's rain and storm.

We fain would lift these mantling clouds
  That shadow our sunny clime;
We can but wait—for we know there'll be
  A day, in the coming time,

When peace, like a rosy dawn, will flood
  Our land with softest light:
Then—we will scarcely hearken the rain
  In the dreary winter's night.

## MY COUNTRY.

BY W. D. PORTER, S. C.

I.

Go, read the stories of the great and free,
The nations on the long, bright roll of fame,
Whose noble rage has baffled the decree
Of tyrants to despoil their life and name;

II.

Whose swords have flashed like lightning in the eyes
Of robber despots, glorying in their might,
And taught the world, by deeds of high emprise,
The power of truth and sacredness of right:

III.

Whose people, strong to suffer and endure,
In faith have wrestled till the blessing came,
And won through woes a victory doubly sure,
As martyr wins his crown through blood and flame.

IV.

The purest virtue has been sorest tried,
Nor is there glory without patient toil;
And he who woos fair Freedom for his bride,
Through suffering must be purged of stain and soil.

V.

My country! in this hour of trial sore,
  When in the balance trembling hangs thy fate,
Brace thy great heart with courage to the core,
  Nor let one jot of faith or hope abate!

IV.

The world's bright eye is fixed upon thee still;
  *Life, honor, fame*—these all are in the scale:
*Endure! endure! endure!* with iron will,
  And by the truth of heaven, thou shalt not fail!

PATRIOT AND MOUNTAINEER.

---

## "AFTER THE BATTLE."

BY MISS AGNES LEONARD.

I.

ALL day long the sun had wandered,
  Through the slowly creeping hours,
And at last the stars were shining
  Like some golden-petalled flowers
Scattered o'er the azure bosom
  Of the glory-haunted night,
Flooding all the sky with grandeur,
  Filling all the earth with light.

II

And the fair moon, with the sweet stars,
  Gleamed amid the radiant spheres
Like "a pearl of great price" shining
  Just as it had shone for years,
On the young land that had risen,
  In her beauty and her might,
Like some gorgeous superstructure
  Woven in the dreams of night:

III.

With her "cities hung like jewels"
  On her green and peaceful breast,
With her harvest fields of plenty,
  And her quiet homes of rest.
But a change had fallen sadly
  O'er the young and beauteous land,
Brothers on the field fought madly
  That once wandered hand in hand.

IV.

And "the hearts of distant mountains
  Shuddered," with a fearful wonder,
As the echoes burst upon them
  Of the cannon's awful thunder.
Through the long hours waged the battle
  Till the setting of the sun

Dropped a seal upon the record,
  That the day's mad work was done.

V.

Thickly on the trampled grasses
  Lay the battle's awful traces,
'Mid the blood-stained clover-blossoms
  Lay the stark and ghastly faces,
With no mourners bending downward
  O'er a costly funeral pall;
And the dying daylight softly,
  With the starlight watched o'er all.

VI.

And, where eager, joyous footsteps
  Once perchance were wont to pass,
Ran a little streamlet making
  One "blue fold in the dark grass;"
And where, from its hidden fountain,
  Clear and bright the brooklet burst
Two had crawled, and each was bending
  O'er to slake his burning thirst.

VII.

Then beneath the solemn starlight
  Of the radiant jewelled skies,

Both had turned, and were intently
  Gazing in each other's eyes.
Both were solemnly forgiving—
  Hushed the pulse of passion's breath-
Calmed the maddening thirst for battle,
  By the chilling hand of death.

VIII.

Then spoke one, in bitter anguish :
  " God have pity on my wife,
And my children, in New Hampshire ;
  Orphans by this cruel strife."
And the other, leaning closer,
  Underneath the solemn sky,
Bowed his head to hide the moisture
  Gathering in his downcast eye :

IX.

" *I've* a wife and little daughter,
  'Mid the fragrant Georgia bloom,"—
Then his cry rang sharper, wilder,
  " Oh, God ! pity all their gloom."
And the wounded, in their death-hour,
  Talking of the loved ones' woes,
Nearer drew unto each other,
  Till they were no longer foes.

X.

And the Georgian listened sadly
  As the other tried to speak,
While the tears were dropping softly
  O'er the pallor of his cheek :
"How she used to stand and listen,
  Looking o'er the fields for me,
Waiting, till she saw me coming,
  'Neath the shadowy old plum-tree.
Never more I'll hear her laughter,
  As she sees me at the gate,
And beneath the plum-tree's shadows,
  All in vain for me she'll wait."

XI.

Then the Georgian, speaking softly,
  Said : "A brown-eyed little one
Used to wait among the roses,
  For *me*, when the day was done ;
And amid the early fragrance
  Of those blossoms, fresh and sweet,
Up and down the old verandah
  I would chase my darling's feet.
But on earth no more the beauty
  Of her face my eye shall greet,
Nevermore I'll hear the music
  Of those merry pattering feet—

Ah, the solemn starlight, falling
  On the far-off Georgia bloom,
Tells no tale unto my darling
  Of her absent father's doom."

XII.

Through the tears that rose between them
  Both were trying grief to smother,
As they clasped each other's fingers
  Whispering: "*Let's forgive each other.*"

* * * * *

XIII.

When the morning sun was walking
  "Up the gray stairs of the dawn,"
And the crimson east was flushing
  All the forehead of the morn,
Pitying skies were looking sadly
  On the "once proud, happy land,"
On the Southron and the Northman,
  Holding fast each other's hand.
Fatherless the golden tresses,
  Watching 'neath the old plum-tree;
Fatherless the little Georgian
  Sporting in unconscious glee.

CHICAGO JOURNAL OF COMMERCE, June, 1868.

## OUR CONFEDERATE DEAD.

WHAT THE HEART OF A YOUNG GIRL SAID TO THE DEAD SOLDIER.

BY A LADY OF AUGUSTA, GEO.

UNKNOWN to me, brave boy, but still I wreathe
For you the tenderest of wildwood flowers;
And o'er your tomb a virgin's prayer I breathe,
To greet the pure moon and the April showers.

I only know, I only care to know,
You died for me—for me and country bled;
A thousand Springs and wild December snow
Will weep for one of all the SOUTHERN DEAD.

Perchance, some mother gazes up the skies,
Wailing, like Rachel, for her martyred brave—
Oh, for her darling sake, my dewy eyes
Moisten the turf above your lowly grave.

The cause is sacred, when our maidens stand
Linked with sad matrons and heroic sires,
Above the relics of a vanquished land
And light the torch of sanctifying fires.

Your bed of honor has a rosy cope
To shimmer back the tributary stars;

And every petal glistens with a hope
Where Love hath blossomed in the disk of Mars.

Sleep! On your couch of glory slumber comes
Bosomed amid the archangelic choir;
Not with the grumble of impetuous drums
Deep'ning the chorus of embattled ire.

Above you shall the oak and cedar fling
Their giant plumage and protecting shade;
For you the song-bird pause upon his wing
And warble requiems ever undismayed.

Farewell! And if your spirit wander near
To kiss this plant of unaspiring art—
Translate it, even in the heavenly sphere,
As the libretto of a maiden's heart.

---

## YE CAVALIERS OF DIXIE.

BY BENJ. F. PORTER, OF ALABAMA.

Ye Cavaliers of Dixie
That guard our Southern shores,
Whose standards brave the battle-storm
That round the border roars;

Your glorious sabres draw again,
And charge the invading foe ;
Reap the columns deep
Where the battle tempests blow,
Where the iron hail in floods descends,
And the bloody torrents flow.

Ye Cavaliers of Dixie !
Though dark the tempest lower,
No arms will wear a tyrant's chains !
No dastard heart will cower !
Bright o'er the cloud the sign will rise,
To lead to victory ;
While your swords reap his hordes,
Where the battle-tempests blow,
And the iron hail in floods descends,
And the bloody torrents flow.

Ye Cavaliers of Dixie !
Though Vicksburg's towers fall,
Here still are sacred rights to shield !
Your wives, your homes, your all !
With gleaming arms advance again,
Drive back the raging foe,
Nor yield your native field,
While the battle-tempests blow,
And the iron hail in floods descends,
And the bloody torrents flow.

Our country needs no ramparts,
No batteries to shield!
Your bosoms are her bulwarks strong,
Breastworks that cannot yield!
The thunders of your battle-blades
Shall sweep the hated foe,
While their gore stains the shore,
Where the battle-tempests blow,
And the iron hail in floods descends,
And the bloody torrents flow.

The spirits of your fathers
Shall rise from every grave!
Our country is their field of fame,
They nobly died to save!
Where Johnson, Jackson, Tilghman fell,
Your patriot hearts shall glow;
While you reap columns deep,
Through the armies of the foe,
Where the battle-storm is raging loud,
And the bloody torrents flow.

The battle-flag of Dixie
On crimson field shall flame,
With azure cross, and silver stars,
To light her sons to fame!
When peace with olive-branch returns,
That flag's white folds shall glow,

Still bright on every height,
Where the storm has ceased to blow,
Where battle-tempests rage no more,
Nor bloody torrents flow.

The battle-flag of Dixie
Shall long triumphant wave,
Where'er the storms of battle roar,
And victory crowns the brave!
The Cavaliers of Dixie!
In woman's songs shall glow
The fame of your name,
When the storm has ceased to blow,
When the battle-tempests rage no more,
Nor the bloody torrents flow.

---

## SONG OF SPRING, (1864.)

BY JOHN A. WAGENER, OF SOUTH CAROLINA.

Spring has come! Spring has come!
The brightening earth, the sparkling dew,
The bursting buds, the sky of blue,
The mocker's carol, in tree and hedge,
Proclaim anew Jehovah's pledge—
"So long as man shall earth retain,
The seasons gone shall come again."

Spring has come! Spring has come!
We have her here, in the balmy air,
In the blossoms that bourgeon without a care;
The violet bounds from her lowly bed,
And the jasmin flaunts with a lofty head;
All nature, in her baptismal dress,
Is abroad—to win, to soothe, and bless.

Spring has come! Spring has come!
Yes, and eternal as the Lord,
Who spells her being at a word;
All blest but man, whose passions proud
Wrap Nature in her bloody shroud—
His heart is winter to the core,
His spring, alas! shall come no more!

---

## "WHAT THE VILLAGE BELL SAID."

BY JOHN C. M'LEMORE, OF SOUTH CAROLINA.*

Full many a year in the village church,
Above the world have I made my home;
And happier there, than if I had hung
High up in the air in a golden dome;
For I have tolled
When the slow hearse rolled

* Mortally wounded at the battle of Seven Pines.

Its burden sad to my door;
And each echo that woke,
With the solemn stroke,
Was a sigh from the heart of the poor.

I know the great bell of the city spire
Is a far prouder one than such as I;
And its deafening stroke, compared with mine,
Is thunder compared with a sigh:
But the shattering note
Of his brazen throat,
As it swells on the Sabbath air,
Far oftener rings
For other things
Than a call to the house of prayer.

Brave boy, I tolled when your father died,
And you wept while my tones pealed loud;
And more gently I rung when the lily-white dame,
Your mother dear, lay in her shroud:
And I sang in sweet tone
The angels might own,
When your sister you gave to your friend;
Oh! I rang with delight,
On that sweet summer night,
When they vowed they would love to the end!

But a base foe comes from the regions of crime,
With a heart all hot with the flames of hell ;
And the tones of the bell you have loved so long
No more on the air shall swell :
For the people's chief,
With his proud belief
That his country's cause is God's own,
Would change the song,
The hills have rung,
To the thunder's harsher tone.

Then take me down from the village church,
Where in peace so long I have hung ;
But I charge you, by all the loved and lost,
*Remember the songs I have sung.*
Remember the mound
Of holy ground,
Where your father and mother lie ;
And swear by the love
For the dead above
To beat your foul foe or die.

Then take me ; but when (I charge you this)
You have come to the bloody field,
That the bell of God, to a cannon grown,
You will ne'er to the foeman yield.
By the love of the past,
Be that hour your last,

When the foe has reached this trust;
And make him a bed
Of patriot dead,
And let him sleep in this holy dust.

---

## THE TREE, THE SERPENT, AND THE STAR.

BY A. P. GRAY, OF SOUTH CAROLINA.

From the silver sands of a gleaming shore,
Where the wild sea-waves were breaking,
A lofty shoot from a twining root
Sprang forth as the dawn was waking;
And the crest, though fed by the sultry beam,
(And the shaft by the salt wave only,)
Spread green to the breeze of the curling seas,
And rose like a column lonely.
Then hail to the tree, the Palmetto tree,
Ensign of the noble, the brave, and the free.

As the sea-winds rustled the bladed crest,
And the sun to the noon rose higher,
A serpent came, with an eye of flame,
And coiled by the leafy pyre;
His ward he would keep by the lonely tree,
To guard it with constant devotion;

Oh, sharp was the fang, and the armèd clang,
That pierced through the roar of the ocean,
And guarded the tree, the Palmetto tree,
Ensign of the noble, the brave, and the free.

And the day wore down to the twilight close,
The breeze died away from the billow;
Yet the wakeful clang of the rattles rang
Anon from the serpent's pillow;
When I saw through the night a gleaming star
O'er the branching summit growing,
Till the foliage green and the serpent's sheen
In the golden light were glowing,
That hung o'er the tree, the Palmetto tree,
Ensign of the noble, the brave, and the free.

By the standard cleave every loyal son,
When the drums' long roll shall rattle;
Let the folds stream high to the victor's eye
Or sink in the shock of the battle.
Should triumph rest on the red field won,
With a victor's song let us hail it;
If the battle fail and the star grow pale,
Yet never in shame will we veil it,
But cherish the tree, the Palmetto tree,
Ensign of the noble, the brave, and the free.

## SOUTHERN WAR HYMN.

BY JOHN A. WAGENER, OF SOUTH CAROLINA.

Arise ! arise ! with arm of might,
  Sons of our sunny home !
Gird on the sword for the sacred fight,
  For the battle-hour hath come !
Arise ! for the felon foe draws nigh
  In battle's dread array ;
To the front, ye brave ! let the coward fly,
  'Tis the hero that bides the fray !

Strike hot and hard, my noble band,
  With the arm of fight and fire ;
Strike fast for God and Fatherland,
  For mother, and wife, and sire.
Though thunders roar and lightnings flash,
  Oh ! Southrons, never fear,
Ye shall turn the bolt with the sabre's clash,
  And the shaft with the steely spear.

Bright blooms shall wave o'er the hero's grave,
  While the craven finds no rest ;
Thrice cursed the traitor, the slave, the knave,
  While thrice is the hero blessed

To the front in the fight, ye Southrons, stand,
Brave spirits, with eagle eye,
And standing for God and for Fatherland,
Ye will gallantly do or die.

CHARLESTON COURIER.

---

## THE BATTLE RAINBOW.

BY JOHN R. THOMPSON, OF VIRGINIA.

The poem which follows was written just after the Seven Days of Battle, near Richmond, in 1862. It was suggested by the appearance of a rainbow, the evening before the grand trial of strength between the contending armies. This rainbow overspread the eastern sky, and exactly defined the position of the Confederate army, as seen from the Capitol at Richmond.

THE warm, weary day, was departing—the smile
Of the sunset gave token the tempest had ceased;
And the lightning yet fitfully gleamed for a while
On the cloud that sank sullen and dark in the east.

There our army—awaiting the terrible fight
Of the morrow—lay hopeful, and watching, and still;
Where their tents all the region had sprinkled with white,
From river to river, o'er meadow and hill.

While above them the fierce cannonade of the sky
Blazed and burst from the vapors that muffled the sun,
Their "counterfeit clamors" gave forth no reply;
And slept till the battle, the charge in each gun.

When lo! on the cloud, a miraculous thing!
  Broke in beauty the rainbow our host to enfold!
The centre o'erspread by its arch, and each wing
  Suffused with its azure and crimson and gold.

Blest omen of victory, symbol divine
  Of peace after tumult, repose after pain;
How sweet and how glowing with promise the sign,
  To eyes that should never behold it again!

For the fierce flame of war on the morrow flashed out,
  And its thunder-peals filled all the tremulous air:
Over slippery intrenchment and reddened redoubt,
  Rang the wild cheer of triumph, the cry of despair.

Then a long week of glory and agony came—
  Of mute supplication, and yearning, and dread;
When day unto day gave the record of fame,
  And night unto night gave the list of its dead.

We had triumphed—the foe had fled back to his ships—
  His standard in rags and his legions a wreck—
But alas! the stark faces and colorless lips
  Of our loved ones, gave triumph's rejoicing a check.

Not yet, oh not yet, as a sign of release,
  Had the Lord set in mercy his bow in the cloud;

Not yet had the Comforter whispered of peace
To the hearts that around us lay bleeding and bowed.

But the promise was given—the beautiful arc,
With its brilliant profusion of colors, that spanned
The sky on that exquisite eve, was the mark
Of the Infinite Love overarching the land :

And that Love, shining richly and full as the day,
Through the tear-drops that moisten each martyr's proud pall,
On the gloom of the past the bright bow shall display
Of Freedom, Peace, Victory, bent over all.

---

## STONEWALL JACKSON.

Mortally wounded—"*The Brigade must not know, sir.*"

"Who've ye got there ?"—"Only a dying brother,
Hurt in the front just now."
"Good boy ! he'll do. Somebody tell his mother
Where he was killed, and how."

"Whom have you there ?"—"A crippled courier, major,
Shot by mistake, we hear.
He was with Stonewall." "Cruel work they've made here
Quick with him to the rear !"

"Well, who comes next?"—"Doctor, speak low, speak low,
sir;
Don't let the men find out.
It's STONEWALL!" "God!" "The brigade must not know, sir,
While there's a foe about."

Whom have we *here*—shrouded in martial manner,
Crowned with a martyr's charm?
A grand dead hero, in a living banner,
Born of his heart and arm:

The heart whereon his cause hung—see how clingeth
That banner to his bier!
The arm wherewith his cause struck—hark! how ringeth
His trumpet in their rear!

What have we left? His glorious inspiration,
His prayers in council met.
Living, he laid the first stones of a nation;
And dead, he builds it yet.

---

## DIRGE FOR ASHBY.

BY MRS. M. J. PRESTON.

HEARD ye that thrilling word—
Accent of dread—
Fall, like a thunderbolt,
Bowing each head?

Over the battle dun,
Over each booming gun—
Ashby, our bravest one !
  Ashby is dead !

Saw ye the veterans—
  Hearts that had known
Never a quail of fear,
  Never a groan—
Sob, though the fight they win,
Tears their stern eyes within—
Ashby, our Paladin,
  Ashby is dead !

Dash, dash the tear away—
  Crush down the pain !
*Dulce et decus*, be
  Fittest refrain !
Why should the dreary pall,
Round *him*, be flung at all ?
Did not our hero fall
  Gallantly slain !

Catch the last words of cheer,
  Dropt from his tongue ;
Over the battle's din,
  Let them be rung !

"Follow *me!* follow *me!*"
Soldier, oh! could there be
Pæan or dirge for thee,
Loftier sung?

Bold as the lion's heart—
Dauntlessly brave—
Knightly as knightliest
Bayard might crave;
Sweet, with all Sydney's grace,
Tender as Hampden's face,
Who now shall fill the space,
Void by his grave?

'Tis not one broken heart,
Wild with dismay—
Crazed in her agony,
Weeps o'er his clay!
Ah! from a thousand eyes,
Flow the pure tears that rise—
Widowed Virginia lies
Stricken to-day!

Yet, charge as gallantly,
Ye, whom he led!
Jackson, the victor, still
Leads, at your head!

Heroes! be battle done
Bravelier, every one
Nerved by the thought alone—
  Ashby is dead!

---

## SACRIFICE.

I.

Another victim for the sacrifice!
  Oh! my own mother South,
  How terrible this wail above thy youth,
  Dying at the cannon's mouth,—
And for no crime—no vice—
No scheme of selfish greed—no avarice,
Or insolent ambition, seeking power;—
But that, with resolute soul and will sublime,
  They made their proud election to be free,—
To leave a grand inheritance to time,
  And to their sons and race, of liberty!

II.

Oh! widow'd woman, sitting in thy weeds,
  With thy young brood around thee, sad and lone—
Thy fancy sees thy hero where he bleeds,
  And still thou hear'st his moan!

Dying he calls on thee—again—again !
With blessing and fond memories. Be of cheer ;
He has not died—he did not bless—in vain :
For, in the eternal rounds of God, He squares
The account with sorrowing hearts ; and soothes the fears,
And leads the orphans home, and dries the widow's tears.

Charleston Mercury.

---

## SONNET.

### WRITTEN IN 1864.

What right to freedom when we are not free ?
When all the passions goad us into lust ;
When, for the worthless spoil we lick the dust,
And while one-half our people die, that we
May sit with peace and freedom 'neath our tree,
The other gloats for plunder and for spoil :
Bustles through daylight, vexes night with toil,
Cheats, swindles, lies and steals !—Shall such things be
Endowed with such grand boons as Liberty
Brings in her train of blessings ? Should we pray
That such as these should still maintain the sway—
These soulless, senseless, heartless enemies
Of all that's good and great, of all that's wise,
Worthy on earth, or in the Eternal Eyes !

Charleston Mercury.

## GRAVE OF A. SYDNEY JOHNSTON.

BY J. B. SYNNOTT.

THE Lone Star State secretes the clay
 Of him who led on Shiloh's field,
Where mourning wives will stop to pray,
 And maids a weeping tribute yield.

In after time, when spleen and strife
 Their madd'ning flame shall have expired,
The noble deeds that gemm'd this life
 By Age and Youth will be admired.

As o'er the stream the boatmen rove
 By Pittsburg Bend at early Spring,
They'll show with moist'ning eye the grave
 Where havoc spread her sable wing.

There, 'neath the budding foliage green,
 Ere Night evolved her dewy breath,
While Vict'ry smiled upon the scene,
 Our Chieftain met the blow of death.

Great men to come will bless the brave ;
 The soldier, bronzed in War's career,
Shall weave a chaplet o'er his grave,
 While Mem'ry drops the glist'ning tear.

Though envy wag her scorpion tongue,
  The march of Time shall find his fame ;
Where Bravery's loved and Glory's sung,
  There children's lips shall lisp his name.

---

## "NOT DOUBTFUL OF YOUR FATHERLAND.'

I.

Not doubtful of your fatherland,
  Or of the God who gave it ;
On, Southrons ! 'gainst the hireling band
  That struggle to enslave it ;
    Ring boldly out
    Your battle-shout,
Charge fiercely 'gainst these felon hordes :
    One hour of strife
    Is freedom's life,
And glory hangs upon your swords !

II.

A thousand mothers' matron eyes,
  Wives, sisters, daughters weeping,
Watch, where your virgin banner flies,
  To battle fiercely sweeping :
    Though science fails,
    The steel prevails,

When hands that wield, own hearts of oak:
These, though the wall
Of stone may fall,
Grow stronger with each hostile stroke.

III.

The faith that feels its cause as true,
The virtue to maintain it;
The soul to brave, the will to do,—
These seek the fight, and gain it!
The precious prize
Before your eyes,
The all that life conceives of charm,
Home, freedom, life,
Child, sister, wife,
All rest upon your soul and arm!

IV.

And what the foe, the felon race,
That seek your subjugation?
The scum of Europe, her disgrace,
The lepers of the nation.
And what the spoil
That tempts their toil,
The bait that goads them on to fight?
Lust, crime, and blood,
Each fiendish mood
That prompts and follows appetite.

V.

Shall such prevail, and shall you fail,
  Asserting cause so holy?
With souls of might, go, seek the fight,
  And crush these wretches lowly.
    On, with the cry,
    To do or die,
As did, in darker days, your sires,
    Nor stay the blow,
    Till every foe,
Down stricken, in your path, expires!

CHARLESTON MERCURY.

---

## ONLY A SOLDIER'S GRAVE.

BY S. A. JONES, OF ABERDEEN, MISSISSIPPI.

ONLY a soldier's grave! Pass by,
For soldiers, like other mortals, die.
Parents he had—they are far away;
No sister weeps o'er the soldier's clay;
No brother comes, with a tearful eye:
It's only a soldier's grave—pass by.

True, he was loving, and young, and brave,
Though no glowing epitaph honors his grave;
No proud recital of virtues known,
Of griefs endured, or of triumphs won;

No tablet of marble, or obelisk high ;—
Only a soldier's grave—pass by.

Yet bravely he wielded his sword in fight,
And he gave his life in the cause of right!
When his hope was high, and his youthful dream
As warm as the sunlight on yonder stream;
His heart unvexed by sorrow or sigh ;—
Yet, 'tis only a soldier's grave :—pass by.

Yet, should we mark it—the soldier's grave,
Some one may seek him in hope to save!
Some of the dear ones, far away,
Would bear him home to his native clay:
'Twere sad, indeed, should they wander nigh,
Find not the hillock, and pass him by.

---

## THE GUERRILLA MARTYRS.

I.

Ay, to the doom—the scaffold and the chain,—
To all your cruel tortures, bear them on,
Ye foul and coward Hangmen ;—but in vain!—
Ye cannot touch the glory they have won—
And win—thus yielding up the martyr's breath
For freedom!—Theirs is a triumphant death!—

A sacred pledge from Nature, that her womb
  Still keeps some sacred fires ;—that yet shall burst,
Even from the reeking ravage of their doom,
  As glorious—ay, more glorious—than the first !
Exult, shout, triumph ! Wretches, do your worst !
  'Tis for a season only ! There shall come
An hour when ye shall feel yourselves accurst ;
  When the dread vengeance of a century
Shall reap its harvest in a single day ;
  And ye shall howl in horror ;—and, to die,
Shall be escape and refuge ! Ye may slay ;—
  But to be cruel and brutal, does not make
Ye conquerors ; and the vulture yet shall prey
  On living hearts ; and vengeance fiercely slake
The unappeasable appetite ye wake,
  In the hot blood of victims, that have been,
Most eager, binding freemen to the stake,—
  Most greedy, in the orgies of this sin !

II.

Ye slaughter,—do ye triumph ? Ask your chains,
  Ye Sodom-hearted butchers !—turn your eyes,
Where reeks yon bloody scaffold ; and the pains,
  Ungroaned, of a true martyr, ere he dies,
Attest the damnéd folly of your crime,
  Now at its carnival ! His spirit flies,
Unscathed by all your fires, through every clime,
  Into the world's wide bosom. Thousands rise,

Prompt at its call, and principled to strike
The tyrants and the tyrannies alike !—
Voices, that doom ye, speak in all your deeds,
  And cry to heaven, arm earth, and kindle hell !
A host of freemen, where one martyr bleeds,
  Spring from his place of doom, and make his knell
The toscin, to arouse a myriad race,
T'avenge Humanity's wrong, and wipe off man's disgrace !

III.

We mourn not for our martyrs !—for they perish,
  As the good perish, for a deathless faith :
Their glorious memories men will fondly cherish,
  In terms and signs that shall ennoble death !
Their blood becomes a principle, to guide,
  Onward, forever onward, in proud flow,
Restless, resistless, as the ocean tide,
  The Spirit heaven yields freedom here below !
How should we mourn the martyrs, who arise,
Even from the stake and scaffold, to the skies ;—
And take their thrones, as stars ; and o'er the night,
  Shed a new glory ; and to other souls,
Shine out with blessed guidance, and true light,
  Which leads successive races to their goals !

CHARLESTON MERCURY.

## "LIBERA NOS, O DOMINE!"

BY JAMES BARRON HOPE.

WHAT! ye hold yourselves as freemen?
  Tyrants love just such as ye!
Go! abate your lofty manner!
Write upon the State's old banner,
    "*A furore Normanorum,*
    *Libera nos, O Domine!*"

Sink before the federal altar,
  Each one low, on bended knee,
Pray, with lips that sob and falter,
This prayer from the coward's psalter,—
    "*A furore Normanorum,*
    *Libera nos, O Domine!*"

But ye hold that quick repentance
  In the Northern mind will be;
This repentance comes no sooner
Than the robbers did, at Luna!
    "*A furore Normanorum,*
    *Libera nos, O Domine!*"

He repented *him*:—the Bishop
  Gave him absolution free;

Poured upon him sacred chrism
In the pomp of his baptism.
*"A furore Normanorum,*
*Libera nos, O Domine!"*

He repented ;—then he sickened !
Was he pining for the sea?
*In extremis* was he shriven,
The viaticum was given,
*"A furore Normanorum,*
*Libera nos, O Domine!"*

Then the old cathedral's choir
Took the plaintive minor key ;
With the Host upraised before him,
Down the marble aisles they bore him ;
*"A furore Normanorum,*
*Libera nos, O Domine!"*

While the bishop and the abbot—
All the monks of high degree,
Chanting praise to the Madonna,
Came to do him Christian honor !
*"A furore Normanorum,*
*Libera nos, O Domine!"*

Now the *miserere's* cadence,
Takes the voices of the sea ;

As the music-billows quiver,
See the dead freebooter shiver!
  "*A furore Normanorum,*
  *Libera nos, O Domine!*"

Is it that these intonations
 Thrill him thus from head to knee?
Lo, his cerements burst asunder!
'Tis a sight of fear and wonder!
  "*A furore Normanorum,*
  *Libera nos, O Domine!*"

Fierce, he stands before the bishop,
 Dark as shape of Destinie.
Hark! a shriek ascends, appalling,—
Down the prelate goes—dead—falling!
  "*A furore Normanorum,*
  *Libera nos, O Domine!*"

Hastings lives! He was but feigning!
 What! Repentant? Never he!
Down he smites the priests and friars,
And the city lights with fires!
  "*A furore Normanorum,*
  *Libera nos, O Domine!*"

Ah! the children and the maidens,
 'Tis in vain they strive to flee!

Where the white-haired priests lie bleeding,
Is no place for woman's pleading.
*"A furore Normanorum,*
*Libera nos, O Domine!"*

Louder swells the frightful tumult—
Pallid Death holds revelrie!
Dies the organ's mighty clamor,
By the horseman's iron hammer!
*"A furore Normanorum,*
*Libera nos, O Domine!"*

So they thought that he'd repented!
Had they nailed him to the tree,
He had not deserved their pity,
And they had not—lost their city.
*"A furore Normanorum,*
*Libera nos, O Domine!"*

For the moral in this story,
Which is plain as truth can be:
If we trust the North's relenting,
We shall shriek—too late repenting—
*"A furore Normanorum,*
*Libera nos, O Domine!"* *

* For this incident in the life of the sea-robber, Hastings, see Milman's History of Latin Christianity.

## THE KNELL SHALL SOUND ONCE MORE.

I KNOW that the knell shall sound once more,
  And the dirge be sung o'er a bloody grave;
And there shall be storm on the beaten shore,
  And there shall be strife on the stormy wave;
And we shall wail, with a mighty wail,
  And feel the keen sorrow through many years,
But shall not our banner at last prevail,
  And our eyes be dried of tears?

There's a bitter pledge for each fruitful tree,
  And the nation whose course is long to run,
Must make, though in anguish still it be,
  The tribute of many a noble son;
The roots of each mighty shaft must grow
  In the blood-red fountains of mighty hearts;
And to conquer the right from a bloody foe,
  Brings a pang as when soul and body parts!

But the blood and the pang are the need, alas!
  To strengthen the sovereign will that sways
The generations that rise, and pass
  To the full fruition that crowns their days!
'Tis still in the strife, they must grow to life:
  And sorrow shall strengthen the soul for care;
And the freedom sought must ever be bought
  By the best blood-offerings, held most dear.

Heroes, the noblest, shall still be first
  To mount the red altar of sacrifice;
Homes the most sacred shall fare the worst,
  Ere we conquer and win the precious prize!—
The struggle may last for a thousand years,
  And only with blood shall the field be bought;
But the sons shall inherit, through blood and tears,
  The birth-right for which their old fathers fought.

CHARLESTON MERCURY.

---

## GENDRON PALMER, OF THE HOLCOMBE LEGION

BY INA M. PORTER, OF ALABAMA.

HE sleeps upon Virginia's strand,
While comrades of the Legion stand
With arms reversed—a mournful band—
  Around his early bier!
His war-horse paws the shaking ground,
The volleys ring—they close around—
And on the white brow, laurel-bound,
  Falls many a soldier's tear.

Up, stricken mourners! look on high,
Loud anthems rend the echoing sky,

Re-born where heroes never die—
The warrior is at rest!
Gone is the weary, pain-traced frown;
Life's march is o'er, his arms cast down,
His plumes replaced by shining crown,
The red cross on his breast!

Though Gendron's arm is with the dust,
Let not his blood-stained weapon rust,
Bequeathed to one who'll bear the trust,
Where Southern banners fly!
Some brave, who followed where he led—
Aye, swear him o'er the martyred dead,
To avenge each drop of blood he shed,
Or, like him, bravely die!

He deemed a death for honor sweet.—
And thus he fell!—'Tis doubly meet,
Our flag should be his winding-sheet,
Proud banner of the free!
Oh, let his honored form be laid
Beneath the loved Palmetto's shade;
His praises sung by Southern maid,
While flows the broad Santee!

We come around his urn to twine
Sweet clusters of the jasmine vine,

Culled where our tropic sunbeams shine,
From skies deep-dyed and bright;
And, kneeling, vow no right to yield !—
On, brothers, on !—Fight ! win the field !
Or dead return on battered shield,
As martyrs for the right !

Where camp-fires light the reddened sod,
The grief-bowed Legion kneel to God,
In Palmer's name, and by his blood,
They swell the battle-cry ;
We'll sheathe no more our dripping steel,
'Till tyrants Southern vengeance feel,
And menial hordes as suppliants kneel,
Or, terror-stricken, fly !

---

## MUMFORD, THE MARTYR OF NEW ORLEANS.

BY INA M. PORTER, OF ALABAMA.

Where murdered Mumford lies,
Bewailed in bitter sighs,
Low-bowed beneath the flag he loved,
Martyrs of Liberty,
Defenders of the Free !
Come, humbly nigh,
And learn to die !

Ah, Freedom, on that day,
Turned fearfully away,
While pitying angels lingered near,
To gaze upon the sod,
Red with a martyr's blood ;
And woman's tear
Fell on his bier !

O God ! that he should die
Beneath a Southern sky !
Upon a felon's gallows swung,
Murdered by tyrant hand,—
While round a helpless band,
On Butler's name
Poured scorn and shame.

But hark ! loud pæans fly
From earth to vaulted sky,
He's crowned at Freedom's holy throne !
List ! sweet-voiced Israfel*
Tolls far the martyr's knell !
Shout, Southrons, high,
Our battle cry !

Come, all of Southern blood,
Come, kneel to Freedom's God !

* "The sweetest-voiced angel around the throne of God."—*Oriental Legend.*

Here at her crimsoned altar swear!
Accursed for evermore
The flag that Mumford tore,
And o'er his grave
Our colors wave!

---

## THE FOE AT THE GATES.—CHARLESTON.

BY J. DICKSON BRUNS, M. D.

Ring round her! children of her glorious skies,
  Whom she hath nursed to stature proud and great;
Catch one last glance from her imploring eyes,
  Then close your ranks and face the threat'ning fate.

Ring round her! with a wall of horrent steel
  Confront the foe, nor mercy ask nor give;
And in her hour of anguish let her feel
  That ye can die whom she has taught to live.

Ring round her! swear, by every lifted blade,
  To shield from wrong the mother who gave you birth;
That never villain hand on her be laid,
  Nor base foot desecrate her hallowed hearth.

See how she thrills all o'er with noble shame,
  As through deep sobs she draws the laboring breath,
Her generous brow and bosom all aflame
  At the bare thought of insult, worse than death.

And stained and rent her snowy garments are ;
  The big drops gather on her pallid face,
Gashed with great wounds by cowards who strove to mar
  The beauteous form that spurned their foul embrace.

And still she pleads, oh ! how she pleads, with prayers
  And bitter tears, to every loving child
To stand between her and the doom she fears,
  To keep her fame untarnished, undefiled !

Curst be the dastard who shall halt or doubt !
  And doubly damned who casts one look behind !
Ye who are men ! with unsheathed sword, and shout,
  Up with her banner ! give it to the wind.

Peal your wild slogan, echoing far and wide,
  Till every ringing avenue repeat
The gathering cry, and Ashley's angry tide
  Calls to the sea-waves beating round her feet.

Sons, to the rescue ! spurred and belted, come !
  Kneeling, with clasp'd hands, she invokes you now
By the sweet memories of your childhood's home,
  By every manly hope and filial vow,

To save her proud soul from that loathéd thrall
  Which yet her spirit cannot brook to name ;
Or, if her fate be near, and she must fall,
  Spare her—she sues—the agony and the shame.

From all her fanes let solemn bells be tolled,
  Heap with kind hands her costly funeral pyre,
And thus, with pæan sung and anthem rolled,
  Give her, unspotted, to the God of Fire.

Gather around her sacred ashes then,
  Sprinkle the cherished dust with crimson rain,
Die ! as becomes a race of free-born men,
  Who will not crouch to wear the bondman's chain.

So, dying, ye shall win a high renown,
  If not in life, at least by death, set free—
And send her fame, through endless ages down,
  The last grand holocaust of liberty.

## SAVANNAH FALLEN.

BY ALETHEA S. BURROUGHS, OF GEORGIA.

I.

Bowing her head to the dust of the earth,
 Smitten and stricken is she,
Light after light gone out from her hearth,
 Son after son from her knee.
Bowing her head to the dust at her feet,
 Weeping her beautiful slain,
Silence ! keep silenee, for aye in the street,
 See ! they are coming again.

II.

Coming again, oh ! glorious ones,
 Wrapped in the flag of the free ;
Queen of the South ! bright crowns for thy sons,
 Only the cypress for *thee!*
Laurel, and banner, and music, and drum,
 Marches, and requiems sweet ;
Silence ! keep silence ! alas, how they come,
 Oh ! how they move through the street !

III.

Slowly, ah ! mournfully, slowly they go,
 Bearing the young and the brave,

Fair as the summer, but white as the snow
  Bearing them down to the grave.
Some in the morning, and some in the noon,
  Some in the hey-day of life;
Bower nor blossom, nor summer nor June,
  Wooing them back to the strife.

IV.

Some in the billow, afar, oh! afar,
  Staining the waves with their blood;
One on the vessel's high deck, like a star,
  Sinking in glory's bright flood.*
Bowing her head to the dust of the earth,
  Humbled but honored is she,
Lighting the skies with the stars from her hearth,
  Who shall her comforter be?

V.

Bring her, oh! bring her the garments of woe,
  Sackcloth and ashes for aye;
Winds of the South! oh, a requiem blow,
  Sighing and sorrow to-day.
Sprinkle the showers from heaven's blue eyes
  Wide o'er the green summer lea,
Rachel is weeping, oh! Lord of the skies,
  *Thou* shalt her comforter be!

---

* Captain Thomas Pelot, C. S. N., killed at the capture of the "Water Witch."

## BULL RUN.—A PARODY.

I.

At Bull Run when the sun was low,
Each Southern face grew pale as snow,
While loud as jackdaws rose the crow
Of Yankees boasting terribly!

II.

But Bull Run saw another sight,
When at the deepening shades of night,
Towards Fairfax Court-House rose the flight
Of Yankees running rapidly.

III.

Then broke each corps with terror riven,
Then rushed the steeds from battle driven,
The men of battery Number Seven
Forsook their Red artillery!

IV.

Still on McDowell's farthest left,
The roar of cannon strikes one deaf,
Where furious Abe and fiery Jeff
Contend for death or victory.

V.

The panic thickens—off, ye brave!
Throw down your arms! your bacon save!
Waive, Washington, all scruples waive,
And fly, with all your chivalry!

---

## "STACK ARMS."

WRITTEN IN THE PRISON OF FORT DELAWARE, DEL., ON HEARING OF THE SURRENDER OF GENERAL LEE.

BY JOS. BLYTH ALSTON.

"Stack Arms!" I've gladly heard the cry
When, weary with the dusty tread
Of marching troops, as night drew nigh,
I sank upon my soldier bed,
And camly slept; the starry dome
Of heaven's blue arch my canopy,
And mingled with my dreams of home,
The thoughts of Peace and Liberty.

"Stack Arms!" I've heard it, when the shout
Exulting, rang along our line,
Of foes hurled back in bloody rout,
Captured, dispersed; its tones divine
Then came to mine enraptured ear.
Guerdon of duty nobly done,

And glistened on my cheek the tear
  Of grateful joy for victory won.

"Stack Arms!" In faltering accents, slow
  And sad, it creeps from tongue to tongue,
A broken, murmuring wail of woe,
  From manly hearts by anguish wrung.
Like victims of a midnight dream,
  We move, we know not how nor why,
For life and hope but phantoms seem,
  And it would be relief—to die!

---

## DOFFING THE GRAY.

BY LIEUTENANT FALLIGANT, OF SAVANNAH, GEO.

OFF with your gray suits, boys—
  Off with your rebel gear—
They smack too much of the cannons' peal,
The lightning flash of your deadly steel,
  The terror of your spear.

Their color is like the smoke
  That curled o'er your battle-line;
They call to mind the yell that woke
When the dastard columns before you broke,
  And their dead were your fatal sign.

Off with the starry wreath,
Ye who have led our van ;
To you 'twas the pledge of glorious death,
When we followed you over the gory heath,
Where we whipped them man to man.

Down with the cross of stars—
Too long hath it waved on high ;
'Tis covered all over with battle scars,
But its gleam the Northern banner mars—
'Tis time to lay it by.

Down with the vows we've made,
Down with each memory—
Down with the thoughts of our noble dead—
Down, down to the dust, where their forms are laid
And down with Liberty.

---

## IN THE LAND WHERE WE WERE DREAMING

BY D. B. LUCAS, ESQ., OF JEFFERSON.

Fair were our visions ! Oh, they were as grand
As ever floated out of Faerie land ;
Children were we in single faith,
But God-like children, whom, nor death,
Nor threat, nor danger drove from Honor's path,
In the land where we were dreaming.

Proud were our men, as pride of birth could render;
As violets, our women pure and tender;
  And when they spoke, their voice did thrill
  Until at eve, the whip-poor-will,
At morn the mocking-bird, were mute and still
  In the land where we were dreaming.

And we had graves that covered more of glory
Than ever tracked tradition's ancient story;
  And in our dream we wove the thread
  Of principles for which had bled
And suffered long our own immortal dead
  In the land where we were dreaming.

Though in our land we had both bond and free,
Both were content; and so God let them be;—
  'Till envy coveted our land
  And those fair fields our valor won:
But little recked we, for we still slept on,
  In the land where we were dreaming.

Our sleep grew troubled and our dreams grew wild—
Red meteors flashed across our heaven's field;
  Crimson the moon; between the Twins
  Barbed arrows fly, and then begins
Such strife as when disorder's Chaos reigns,
  In the land where we were dreaming.

Down from her sun-lit heights smiled Liberty
And waved her cap in sign of Victory—
  The world approved, and everywhere
  Except where growled the Russian bear,
The good, the brave, the just gave us their prayer
  In the land where we were dreaming.

We fancied that a Government was ours—
We challenged place among the world's great powers;
  We talked in sleep of Rank, Commission,
  Until so life-like grew our vision,
That he who dared to doubt but met derision
  In the land where we were dreaming.

We looked on high: a banner there was seen,
Whose field was blanched and spotless in its sheen—
  Chivalry's cross its Union bears,
  And vet'rans swearing by their scars
Vowed they would bear it through a hundred wars
  In the land where we were dreaming.

A hero came amongst us as we slept;
At first he lowly knelt—then rose and wept;
  Then gathering up a thousand spears
  He swept across the field of Mars;
Then bowed farewell and walked beyond the stars—
  In the land where we were dreaming.

We looked again : another figure still
Gave hope, and nerved each individual will—
  Full of grandeur, clothed with power,
  Self-poised, erect, he ruled the hour
With stern, majestic sway—of strength a tower
  In the land where we were dreaming.

As, while great Jove, in bronze, a warder God,
Gazed eastward from the Forum where he stood,
  Rome felt herself secure and free,
  So, "Richmond's safe," we said, while we
Beheld a bronzed Hero—God-like Lee,
  In the land where we were dreaming.

As wakes the soldier when the alarum calls—
As wakes the mother when the infant falls—
  As starts the traveller when around
  His sleeping couch the fire-bells sound—
So woke our nation with a single bound
  In the land where we were dreaming.

Woe ! woe is me ! the startled mother cried—
While we have slept our noble sons have died !
  Woe ! woe is me ! how strange and sad,
  That all our glorious vision's fled
And left us nothing real but the dead
  In the land where we were dreaming.

And are they really dead, our martyred slain?
No! dreamers! morn shall bid them rise again
  From every vale—from every height
  On which they *seemed* to die for right—
Their gallant spirits shall renew the fight
  In the land where we were dreaming.

---

## BALLAD—"YES, BUILD YOUR WALLS."

I.

Yes, build your walls of stone or sand,
  But know, when all is builded—then,
The proper breastworks of the land
  Are in a race of freeborn men!
The sons of sires, who knew, in life,
  That, of all virtues, manhood first,
Still nursing peace, yet arms for strife,
  And braves, for liberty, the worst!

II.

What grand examples have been ours!
  Oh! sons of Moultrie, Marion,—call
From mansions of the past, the powers,
  That plucked ye from the despot's thrall!
Do Sumter, Rutledge, Gadsden, live?
  Oh! for your City by the Sea,

They gladly gave, what men could give,
  Blood, life, and toil, and made it free!

III.

The grand inheritance, in trust
  For children of your loins, must know
No taint of shame, no loss by lust,
  Your own, or of the usurping foe!
Let not your sons, in future days,
  The children now that bear your name,
Exulting in a grandsire's praise,
  Droop o'er a father's grave in shame!

CHARLESTON MERCURY.

---

## THE LINES AROUND PETERSBURG.

BY SAMUEL DAVIS, OF NORTH CAROLINA.

"Such a sleep they sleep,
The men I loved!"
TENNYSON.

OH, silence, silence! now, when night is near,
  And I am left alone,
Thou art so strange, so sad reposing here—
  And all so changed hath grown,
Where all was once exuberant with life
Through day and night, in deep and deadly strife.

If I must weep, oh, tell me, is there not
Some plaintive story breathed into mine ear
By spirit-whispers from thy voiceless sphere,
  Haunting this awful spot?
To my sad soul, more mutely eloquent
Than words of fame on sculptured monument
Outspeaks yon crumbling parapet, where lies
The broken gun, the idly rusting ball,
Mute tokens of an ill-starred enterprise!
Rude altars reared for costly sacrifice!
Vast work of hero-hands left in thy fall!

Where are they now, that fearless brotherhood,
          Who marshalled here,
          That fearful year,
In pain and peril, yet undaunted stood,—
Though Death rode fiercest on the battle-storm
And earth lay strewn with many a glorious form?
Where are they now, who, when the strife was done,
With kindly greeting 'round the camp-fire met,—
And made an hour of mirth, from triumphs won,
Repay the day's stern toil, when the slow sun had set?

Where are they?—
Let the nameless grave declare,—
In strange unwonted hillocks—frequent seen!
Alas! who knows how much lies buried there!—
What worlds of love, and all that might have been!

The rest are scattered now, we know not where ;
And Life to each a new employment brings ;
But still they seem to gather round me here,
To whom these places were familiar things !
Wide sundered now, by mountain and by stream,
Once brothers—still a brotherhood they seem ;—
More firm united, since a common woe
Hath brought to common hopes their overthrow !

Brave souls and true ;—in toil and danger tried,—
I see them still as in those glorious years,
When strong, and battling bravely side by side,
All crowned their deeds with praise,—and some with tears
'Tis done ! the sword is sheathed ; the banner furled,
No sound where late the crashing missile whirled—
The dead alone possess the battle-plain ;
The living turn them to life's cares again.

Oh, Silence ! blessed dreams upon thee wait ;
Here Thought and Feeling ope their precious store,
And Memory, gathering from the spoils of Fate
Love's scattered treasures, brings them back once more !
So let me often dream,
As up the bright'ning stream
Of olden Time, thought gently leads me on,
Seeking those better days, lost, lost, alas ! and gone !

## ALL IS GONE.

FADETTE.—*Memphis Appeal.*

SISTER, hark! Atween the trees cometh naught but summer breeze?
All is gone—
Summer breezes come and go. Hope doth never wander so—
No, nor evermore doth Woe.

Sister, look! Adown the lane treadeth only April rain?
All is gone—
Through the tangled hedge-rows green glimmer thus the sunbeam's sheen,
Dropping from cloud-rifts between?

Sister, hark! the very air heavy on my heart doth bear—
All is gone!—
E'en the birds that chirped erewhile for the frowning sun to smile,
Hush at that drum near the stile.

Sister, pray!—it is the foe! On thy knees—aye, very low—
All is gone,
And the proud South on her knees to a mongrel race like these—
But the dead sleep 'neath the trees.

See—they come—their banners flare gayly in our gloomy air—
All is gone—
Flashed our Southern Cross all night—naught but a meteoric light
In a moment lost to sight?

Aye, so gay—the brave array—marching from no battle fray—
All is gone,—
Yet who vaunteth, of your host, maketh he but little boast
If he think on battles most.

On they wind, behind the wood. Dost remember once we stood—
All is gone—
All but memory, of those days—but we've stood here while the haze
Of the battle met the blaze

Of the sun adown yon hill. Charge on charge—I hear them still—
All is gone!—
Yet I hear the echoing crash—see the sabres gleam and flash—
See one gallant headlong dash.

One, amid the battle-wreck, restive plunged his charger black—
All is gone—
Whirrs the partridge there—didst see where he rode so recklessly?
Once he turned and waved to me.

"Ah," thou saidst, "the smoke is dark, scarce can I our banner mark"—
All is gone—
All but memory; yet I see, darksome howsoe'er it be, —
How to death—to death—rode he.

Not a star he proudly bore, but a sword all dripping gore—
All is gone—
Dashes on our little band like yon billow on the strand—
Like yon strand unmoved they stand.

For their serried ranks are strong: thousands upon thousands throng—
All is gone,
And the handful, true and brave, spent, like yonder dying wave,
Fall back slowly from that grave.

Low our banner drooped—and fell. Back he spurs, mid shot and shell—
All *was* gone,

But he waves it high—and then, on—we sweep them from
the glen—
But he ne'er rode back again.

Ah, I smiled to see him go. How my cheek with pride did
glow!
All is gone—
All, of pride or hope, for me—but that evening, hopefully
Stood I at the gate with thee,

Sister, when at twilight gray marched our soldiers back
this way—
All is gone—
In the woods rang many a cheer—how we smiled! I did
not fear
Till—at last was borne a bier

Sweetest sister, dost thou weep? Hush! he only fell
asleep—
All is gone—
And 'twere better he had died—free, whatever us betide—
Our galling chains untried.

We were leaning on the gate. Dost remember, it grew
late—
All is gone—
Yet I see the stars so pale—see the shadows down the
vale—
Hear the whip-poor-will's far wail,

As if all were in a dream. Through yon pines the moon did gleam—
All is gone—
On that banner-pall of death—on that red sword without sheath—
And—I knew who lay beneath.

Did I speak? I thought I said, let me look upon your dead—
All is gone—
Was I cold? I did not weep. Tears are spray from founts not deep—
My heart lies in frozen sleep

Sister, pray for me. Thine eyes gleam like God's own midnight skies—
All is gone—
Tuneless are my spirit's chords. I but look up, like the birds,
And trust Christ to say the words.

---

## BOWING HER HEAD.

Her head is bowed downwards; so pensive her air,
As she looks on the ground with her pale, solemn face,
It were hard to decide whether faith or despair,
Whether anguish or trust, in her heart holds a place.

Her hair was all gold in the sun's joyous light,
Her brow was as smooth as the soft, placid sea :
But the furrows of care came with shadows of night,
And the gold silvered pale when the light left the lea.

Her lips slightly parted, deep thought in her eye,
While sorrow cuts seams in her forehead so fair ;
Her bosom heaves gently, she stifles a sigh,
And just moistens her lid with the dews of a tear.

Why droops she thus earthward—why bends she ? Oh, see !
There are gyves on her limbs ! see her manacled hand !
She is loaded with chains ; but her spirit is free—
Free to love and to mourn for her desolate land.

Her jailer, though cunning, lacks wit to devise
How to fetter her thoughts, as her limbs he has done ;
The eagle that's snatched from his flight to the skies,
From the bars of his cage may still gaze at the sun.

No sound does she utter ; all voiceless her pains ;
The wounds of her spirit with pride she conceals ;
She is dumb to her shearers ; the clank of her chains
And the throbs of her heart only tell what she feels.

She looks sadly around her; now sombre the scene!
How thick the deep shadows that darken her view!
The black embers of homes where the earth was so green,
And the smokes of her wreck where the heavens shone blue.

Her daughters bereaved of all succor but God,
Her bravest sons perished—the light of her eyes;
But oppression's sharp heel does not cut 'neath the sod,
And she knows that the chains cannot bind in the skies.

She thinks of the vessel she aided to build,
Of all argosies richest that floated the seas;
Compacted so strong, framed by architects skilled,
Or to dare the wild storm, or to sail to the breeze.

The balmiest winds blowing soft where she steers,
The favor of heaven illuming her path—
She might sail as she pleased to the mild summer airs,
And avoid the dread regions of tempest and wrath.

But the crew quarrelled soon o'er the cargo she bore;
'Twas adjusted unfairly, the cavillers said;
And the anger of men marred the peace that of yore
Spread a broad path of glory and sunshine ahead.

There were seams in her planks—there were spots on her
flag—
So the fanatics said, as they seized on her helm ;
And from soft summer seas, turned her prow where the crag
And the wild breakers rose the good ship to o'erwhelm.

Then the South, though true love to the vessel she bore,
Since she first laid its keel in the days that were gone—
Saw it plunge madly on to the wild billows' roar,
And rush to destruction and ruin forlorn.

So she passed from the decks, in the faith of her heart
That justice and God her protectors would be ;
Not dashed like a frail, fragile spar, without chart,
In the fury and foam of the wild raging sea.

The life-boat that hung by the stout vessel's side
She seized, and embarked on the wide, trackless main,
In the faith that she'd reach, making virtue her guide,
The haven the mother-ship failed to attain

But the crew rose in wrath, and they swore by their might
They would sink the brave boat that did buffet the sea,
For daring to seek, by her honor and right,
A new port from the storms, a new home for the free.

So they crushed the brave boat; all forbearance they lost;
  They littered with ruins the ocean so wild—
Till the hulk of the parent ship, beaten and tossed,
  Drifted prone on the flood by the wreck of the child.

And the bold rower, loaded with fetters and chains,
  In the gloom of her heart sings the proud vessel's dirge;
Half forgets, in its wreck, all the pangs of her pains,
  As she sees its stout parts floating loose in the surge.

SAVANNAH BROADSIDE.

---

## THE CONFEDERATE FLAG.

BY ANNA PEYRE DINNIES, OF LOUISIANA.

TAKE that banner down, 'tis weary,
Round its staff 'tis drooping dreary,
  Furl it, hide it, let it rest;
For there's not a man to wave it—
For there's not a soul to lave it
In the blood that heroes gave it.
  Furl it, hide it, let it rest.

Take that banner down, 'tis tattered;
Broken is its staff, and shattered;
And the valiant hearts are scattered
  Over whom it floated high.

Oh ! 'tis hard for us to fold it—
Hard to think there's none to hold it—
Hard that those, who once unrolled it,
  Now must furl it with a sigh.

Furl that banner, furl it sadly ;
Once six millions hailed it gladly,
And three hundred thousand, madly,
  Swore it should forever wave—
Swore that foeman's sword should never
Hearts like theirs entwined dissever—
That their flag should float forever
  O'er their freedom or their grave !

Furl it, for the hands that grasped it,
And the hearts that fondly clasped it,
  Cold and dead are lying low ;
And that banner—it is trailing,
While around it sounds the wailing
  Of its people in their woe ;
For, though conquered, they adore it,
Love the cold, dead hands that bore it,
Weep for those who fell before it—
Oh ! how wildly they deplore it,
  Now to furl and fold it so !

Furl that banner ; true 'tis gory,
But 'tis wreathed around with glory,

And 'twill live in song and story,
  Though its folds are in the dust;
For its fame, on brightest pages—
Sung by poets, penned by sages—
Shall go sounding down to ages—
  Furl its folds though now we must.

Furl that banner—softly, slowly;
Furl it gently, it is holy,
  For it droops above the dead.
Touch it not, unfurl it never,
Let it droop there, furled forever,
  For its people's hopes are fled.

---

## ASHES OF GLORY.

BY A. J. REQUIER.

Fold up the gorgeous silken sun,
  By bleeding martyrs blest,
And heap the laurels it has won
  Above its place of rest.

No trumpet's note need harshly blare—
  No drum funereal roll—
Nor trailing sables drape the bier
  That frees a dauntless soul!

It lived with Lee, and decked his brow
  From Fate's empyreal Palm:
It sleeps the sleep of Jackson now—
  As spotless and as calm.

It was outnumbered—not outdone;
  And they shall shuddering tell,
Who struck the blow, its latest gun
  Flashed ruin as it fell.

Sleep, shrouded Ensign! not the breeze
  That smote the victor tar,
With death across the heaving seas
  Of fiery Trafalgar;

Not Arthur's knights, amid the gloom
  Their knightly deeds have starred;
Nor Gallic Henry's matchless plume,
  Nor peerless-born Bayard;

Not all that antique fables feign,
  And Orient dreams disgorge;
Nor yet, the Silver Cross of Spain,
  And Lion of St. George,

Can bid thee pale ! Proud emblem, still
  Thy crimson glory shines
Beyond the lengthened shades that fill
  Their proudest kingly lines.

Sleep ! in thine own historic night,—
  And be thy blazoned scroll,
*A warrior's Banner takes its flight,*
  *To greet the warrior's soul !*

THE END.

# The Romantic Tradition in American Literature

An Arno Press Collection

Alcott, A. Bronson, editor. **Conversations with Children on the Gospels.** Boston, 1836/1837. Two volumes in one.

Bartol, C[yrus] A. **Discourses on the Christian Spirit and Life.** 2nd edition. Boston, 1850.

Boker, George H[enry]. **Poems of the War.** Boston, 1864.

Brooks, Charles T. **Poems, Original and Translated.** Selected and edited by W. P. Andrews. Boston, 1885.

Brownell, Henry Howard. **War-Lyrics** and Other Poems. Boston, 1866.

Brownson, O[restes] A. **Essays and Reviews Chiefly on Theology, Politics, and Socialism.** New York, 1852.

Channing, [William] Ellery (The Younger). **Poems.** Boston, 1843.

Channing, [William] Ellery (The Younger). **Poems of Sixty-Five Years.** Edited by F. B. Sanborn. Philadelphia and Concord, 1902.

Chivers, Thomas Holley. **Eonchs of Ruby**: A Gift of Love. New York, 1851.

Chivers, Thomas Holley. **Virginalia**; or, Songs of My Summer Nights. (Reprinted from *Research Classics*, No. 2, 1942). Philadelphia, 1853.

Cooke, Philip Pendleton. **Froissart Ballads,** and Other Poems. Philadelphia, 1847.

Cranch, Christopher Pearse. **The Bird and the Bell,** with Other Poems. Boston, 1875.

[Dall], Caroline W. Healey, editor. **Margaret and Her Friends.** Boston, 1895.

[D'Arusmont], Frances Wright. **A Few Days in Athens.** Boston, 1850.

Everett, Edward. **Orations and Speeches,** on Various Occasions. Boston, 1836.

Holland, J[osiah] G[ilbert]. **The Marble Prophecy,** and Other Poems. New York, 1872.

Huntington, William Reed. **Sonnets and a Dream.** Jamaica, N. Y., 1899.

Jackson, Helen [Hunt]. **Poems.** Boston, 1892.

Miller, Joaquin (Cincinnatus Hiner Miller). **The Complete Poetical Works of Joaquin Miller.** San Francisco, 1897.

Parker, Theodore. **A Discourse of Matters Pertaining to Religion.** Boston, 1842.

Pinkney, Edward C. **Poems.** Baltimore, 1838.

Reed, Sampson. **Observations on the Growth of the Mind.** *Including,* **Genius** (Reprinted from *Aesthetic Papers,* Boston, 1849). 5th edition. Boston, 1859.

Sill, Edward Rowland. **The Poetical Works of Edward Rowland Sill.** Boston and New York, 1906.

Simms, William Gilmore. **Poems:** Descriptive, Dramatic, Legendary and Contemplative. New York, 1853. Two volumes in one.

Simms, William Gilmore, editor. **War Poetry of the South.** New York, 1866.

Stickney, Trumbull. **The Poems of Trumbull Stickney.** Boston and New York, 1905.

Timrod, Henry. **The Poems of Henry Timrod.** Edited by Paul H. Hayne. New York, 1873.

Trowbridge, John Townsend. **The Poetical Works of John Townsend Trowbridge.** Boston and New York, 1903.

Very, Jones. **Essays and Poems.** [Edited by R. W. Emerson]. Boston, 1839.

Very, Jones. **Poems and Essays.** Boston and New York, 1886.

White, Richard Grant, editor. **Poetry:** Lyrical, Narrative, and Satirical of the Civil War. New York, 1866.

Wilde, Richard Henry. **Hesperia:** A Poem. Edited by His Son (William Wilde). Boston, 1867.

Willis, Nathaniel Parker. **The Poems, Sacred, Passionate, and Humorous, of Nathaniel Parker Willis.** New York, 1868.